Cryptography: Principles and Practices

Cryptography: Principles and Practices

Edited by
Joey Holland

Larsen & Keller
www.larsen-keller.com

Cryptography: Principles and Practices
Edited by Joey Holland
ISBN: 978-1-63549-082-4 (Hardback)

© 2017 Larsen & Keller

 Larsen & Keller

Published by Larsen and Keller Education,
5 Penn Plaza,
19th Floor,
New York, NY 10001, USA

Cataloging-in-Publication Data

Cryptography : principles and practices / edited by Joey Holland.
    p. cm.
Includes bibliographical references and index.
ISBN 978-1-63549-082-4
   1. Cryptography. 2. Computer security.
3. Information technology--Security measures.
4. Data encryption (Computer science). 5. Ciphers.
I. Holland, Joey.
TK5102.94 .C79 2017
005.82--dc23

The publisher's policy is to use permanent paper from mills that operate a sustainable forestry policy. Furthermore, the publisher ensures that the text paper and cover boards used have met acceptable environmental accreditation standards.

Printed and bound in the United States of America.

For more information regarding Larsen and Keller Education and its products, please visit the publisher's website www.larsen-keller.com

Table of Contents

Permissions

Index

Preface

Cryptography is the interesting study of different methods to secure information and data communication. It concentrates on making and analyzing protocols which secure the information or message from outsiders or adversaries. It is the amalgamation of mathematics, electrical engineering and computer engineering. This book is compiled in such a manner, that it will provide in-depth knowledge about the theory and practice of cryptography. While understanding the long-term perspectives of the topics, the book makes an effort in highlighting their impact as a modern tool for the growth of the discipline. Coherent flow of topics, student-friendly language and extensive use of examples make this text an invaluable source of knowledge.

A foreword of all chapters of the book is provided below:

Chapter 1 - The practice of securing communication in the presence of third parties for the purpose of safety is known as cryptography. Some of the aspects, which are central to modern cryptography are data integrity, authentication and non-repudiation. Modern cryptography is at the junction of disciplines of mathematics, computer science and electrical engineering. This chapter will provide an integrated understanding of cryptography; **Chapter 2 -** The key concepts of cryptography are discussed in this chapter. Information security, information-theoretic security, cryptanalysis and strong cryptography are significant and important concepts of cryptography. This chapter elucidates the crucial concepts of cryptography; **Chapter 3 -** Cryptography is best understood in confluence with the major topics listed in the following chapter. The major types of cryptographic systems dealt within this chapter are symmetric key algorithm and public – key cryptography. The types and approaches of public key cryptography are ID based cryptography, RSA and elliptic curve cryptography; **Chapter 4 -** This chapter guides the reader on the technologies related to cryptography. It elaborately explains technologies such as the rotor machine, cryptographically secure pseudorandom number generator, disk encryption, onion routing and secure multi-party computation. The major components of cryptographic technology are discussed in this chapter; **Chapter 5 -** The process of encoding information in such a way that only the person authorized can read it is known as encryption. Other topics included in this chapter are key schedule, block size, avalanche effect, secure channels, etc. The topics discussed in the chapter are of great importance to broaden the existing knowledge on cryptography; **Chapter 6 -** The algorithm used for performing encryptions or decryptions in cryptography is known as a cipher. The major types of ciphers that this chapter elucidates are, among others, block cipher, product cipher, feistal cipher and substitution cipher. The topics discussed are of great importance to broaden the existing knowledge on ciphers; **Chapter 7 -** Key exchange, key size, key whitening and key agreement protocol are some of the topics illustrated in this chapter. It strategically encompasses and incorporates the major components and concepts of cryptography, contributing to the readers understanding on cryptography key; **Chapter 8 -** A word or string of characters used for security or to prove identity, which is to be kept a secret to secure confidential and sensitive information is called a password. This chapter elaborates on the applications of cryptography in today's times. Password-authenticated key agreement, trusted time stamping and digital signature are explained in detail for the reader's understanding; **Chapter 9 -** Cryptography in earlier times was referred to as encryption; it was an alteration of messages from a comprehensible to a non-comprehensible form. The earliest forms of secret writing needed a little more than writing implements, since literacy was still rare. With more literate opponents came the need for actual cryptography. The evolution of cryptography is of great importance to broaden the existing knowledge on this field.

At the end, I would like to thank all the people associated with this book devoting their precious time and providing their valuable contributions to this book. I would also like to express my gratitude to my fellow colleagues who encouraged me throughout the process.

Editor

Introduction to Cryptography

The practice of securing communication in the presence of third parties for the purpose of safety is known as cryptography. Some of the aspects, which are central to modern cryptography are data integrity, authentication and non-repudiation. Modern cryptography is at the junction of disciplines of mathematics, computer science and electrical engineering. This chapter will provide an integrated understanding of cryptography.

Cryptography or cryptology is the practice and study of techniques for secure communication in the presence of third parties called adversaries. More generally, cryptography is about constructing and analyzing protocols that prevent third parties or the public from reading private messages; various aspects in information security such as data confidentiality, data integrity, authentication, and non-repudiation are central to modern cryptography. Modern cryptography exists at the intersection of the disciplines of mathematics, computer science, and electrical engineering. Applications of cryptography include ATM cards, computer passwords, and electronic commerce.

German Lorenz cipher machine, used in World War II to encrypt very-high-level general staff messages

Cryptography prior to the modern age was effectively synonymous with *encryption*, the conversion of information from a readable state to apparent nonsense. The originator of an encrypted message (Alice) shared the decoding technique needed to recover the original information only with intended recipients (Bob), thereby precluding unwanted persons (Eve) from doing the same. The cryptography literature often uses Alice ("A") for the sender, Bob ("B") for the intended recipient, and Eve ("eavesdropper") for the adversary. Since the development of rotor cipher machines in World War I and the advent of computers in World War II, the methods used to carry out cryptology have become increasingly complex and its application more widespread.

Modern cryptography is heavily based on mathematical theory and computer science practice; cryptographic algorithms are designed around computational hardness assumptions, making such algorithms hard to break in practice by any adversary. It is theoretically possible to break such a system, but it is infeasible to do so by any known practical means. These schemes are therefore termed computationally secure; theoretical advances, e.g., improvements in integer factorization algorithms, and faster computing technology require these solutions to be continually adapted. There exist information-theoretically secure schemes that provably cannot be broken even with unlimited computing power—an example is the one-time pad—but these schemes are more difficult to implement than the best theoretically breakable but computationally secure mechanisms.

The growth of cryptographic technology has raised a number of legal issues in the information age. Cryptography's potential for use as a tool for espionage and sedition has led many governments to classify it as a weapon and to limit or even prohibit its use and export. In some jurisdictions where the use of cryptography is legal, laws permit investigators to compel the disclosure of encryption keys for documents relevant to an investigation. Cryptography also plays a major role in digital rights management and copyright infringement of digital media.

Terminology

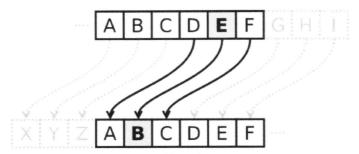

Alphabet shift ciphers are believed to have been used by Julius Caesar over 2,000 years ago. This is an example with k=3. In other words, the letters in the alphabet are shifted three in one direction to encrypt and three in the other direction to decrypt.

Until modern times, cryptography referred almost exclusively to *encryption*, which is the process of converting ordinary information (called plaintext) into unintelligible text (called ciphertext). Decryption is the reverse, in other words, moving from the unintelligible ciphertext back to plaintext. A *cipher* (or *cypher*) is a pair of algorithms that create the encryption and the reversing decryption. The detailed operation of a cipher is controlled both by the algorithm and in each instance by a "key". The key is a secret (ideally known only to the communicants), usually a short string of characters, which is needed to decrypt the ciphertext. Formally, a "cryptosystem" is the ordered list of elements of finite possible plaintexts, finite possible cyphertexts, finite possible keys, and the encryption and decryption algorithms which correspond to each key. Keys are important both formally and in actual practice, as ciphers without variable keys can be trivially broken with only the knowledge of the cipher used and are therefore useless (or even counter-productive) for most purposes. Historically, ciphers were often used directly for encryption or decryption without additional procedures such as authentication or integrity checks. There are two kinds of cryptosystems: symmetric and asymmetric. In symmetric systems the same key (the secret key) is used to encrypt and decrypt a message. Data manipulation in symmetric systems is faster than asymmetric systems as they generally use shorter key lengths. Asymmetric systems use a public key to encrypt a message and a private key to decrypt it. Use of asymmetric systems enhances the security of communication. Examples of asymmetric systems include RSA (Rivest-Shamir-Adleman), and ECC (Elliptic Curve Cryptography). Symmetric models include the commonly used AES (Advanced Encryption Standard) which replaced the older DES (Data Encryption Standard).

In colloquial use, the term "code" is often used to mean any method of encryption or concealment of meaning. However, in cryptography, *code* has a more specific meaning. It means the replacement of a unit of plaintext (i.e., a meaningful word or phrase) with a code word (for example, "wallaby" replaces "attack at dawn").

Cryptanalysis is the term used for the study of methods for obtaining the meaning of encrypted information without access to the key normally required to do so; i.e., it is the study of how to crack encryption algorithms or their implementations.

Some use the terms *cryptography* and *cryptology* interchangeably in English, while others (including US military practice generally) use *cryptography* to refer specifically to the use and practice of cryptographic techniques and *cryptology* to refer to the combined study of cryptography and cryptanalysis. English is more flexible than several other languages in which *cryptology* (done by cryptologists) is always used in the second sense above. RFC 2828 advises that steganography is sometimes included in cryptology.

The study of characteristics of languages that have some application in cryptography or cryptology (e.g. frequency data, letter combinations, universal patterns, etc.) is called cryptolinguistics.

History of Cryptography and Cryptanalysis

Before the modern era, cryptography was concerned solely with message confidentiality (i.e., encryption)—conversion of messages from a comprehensible form into an incomprehensible one and back again at the other end, rendering it unreadable by interceptors or eavesdroppers without secret knowledge (namely the key needed for decryption of that message). Encryption attempted to ensure secrecy in communications, such as those of spies, military leaders, and diplomats. In recent decades, the field has expanded beyond confidentiality concerns to include techniques for message integrity checking, sender/receiver identity authentication, digital signatures, interactive proofs and secure computation, among others.

Classic Cryptography

Reconstructed ancient Greek *scytale*, an early cipher device

The earliest forms of secret writing required little more than writing implements since most people could not read. More literacy, or literate opponents, required actual cryptography. The main classical cipher types are transposition ciphers, which rearrange the order of letters in a message (e.g., 'hello world' becomes 'ehlol owrdl' in a trivially simple rearrangement scheme), and substitution ciphers, which systematically replace letters or groups of letters with other letters or groups of letters (e.g., 'fly at once' becomes 'gmz bu podf' by replacing each letter with the one following it in the Latin alphabet). Simple versions of either have never offered much confidentiality from enterprising opponents. An early substitution cipher was the Caesar cipher, in which each letter in the plaintext was replaced by a letter some fixed number of positions further down the alphabet. Suetonius reports that Julius Caesar used it with a shift of three to communicate with his generals. Atbash is an example of an early Hebrew cipher. The earliest known use of cryptography is some carved ciphertext on stone in Egypt (ca 1900 BCE), but this may have been done for the amusement of literate observers rather than as a way of concealing information.

The Greeks of Classical times are said to have known of ciphers (e.g., the scytale transposition cipher claimed to have been used by the Spartan military). Steganography (i.e., hiding even the existence of a message so as to keep it confidential) was also first developed in ancient times. An early example, from Herodotus, was a message tattooed on a slave's shaved head and concealed under the regrown hair. More modern examples of steganography include the use of invisible ink, microdots, and digital watermarks to conceal information.

In India, the 2000-year-old Kamasutra of Vātsyāyana speaks of two different kinds of ciphers called Kautiliyam and Mulavediya. In the Kautiliyam, the cipher letter substitutions are based on phonetic relations, such as vowels becoming consonants. In the Mulavediya, the cipher alphabet consists of pairing letters and using the reciprocal ones.

First page of a book by Al-Kindi which discusses encryption of messages

Ciphertexts produced by a classical cipher (and some modern ciphers) will reveal statistical information about the plaintext, and that information can often be used to break the cipher. After the discovery of frequency analysis, perhaps by the Arab mathematician and polymath Al-Kindi (also known as *Alkindus*) in the 9th century, nearly all such ciphers could be broken by an informed attacker. Such classical ciphers still enjoy popularity today, though mostly as puzzles. Al-Kindi wrote a book on cryptography entitled *Risalah fi Istikhraj al-Mu'amma* (*Manuscript for the Deciphering Cryptographic Messages*), which described the first known use of frequency analysis cryptanalysis techniques.

16th-century book-shaped French cipher machine, with arms of Henri II of France

Language letter frequencies may offer little help for some extended historical encryption techniques such as homophonic cipher that tend to flatten the frequency distribution. For those ciphers, language letter group (or n-gram) frequencies may provide an attack.

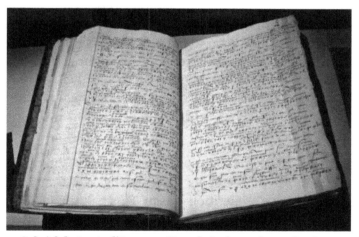

Enciphered letter from Gabriel de Luetz d'Aramon, French Ambassador to the Ottoman Empire, after 1546, with partial decipherment

Essentially all ciphers remained vulnerable to cryptanalysis using the frequency analysis technique until the development of the polyalphabetic cipher, most clearly by Leon Battista Alberti around the year 1467, though there is some indication that it was already known to Al-Kindi. Alberti's innovation was to use different ciphers (i.e., substitution alphabets) for various parts of a message (perhaps for each successive plaintext letter at the limit). He also invented what was probably the first automatic cipher device, a wheel which implemented a partial realization of his invention. In the polyalphabetic Vigenère cipher, encryption uses a *key word*, which controls letter substitution depending on which letter of the key word is used. In the mid-19th century Charles Babbage showed that the Vigenère cipher was vulnerable to Kasiski examination, but this was first published about ten years later by Friedrich Kasiski.

Although frequency analysis can be a powerful and general technique against many ciphers, encryption has still often been effective in practice, as many a would-be cryptanalyst was unaware of the technique. Breaking a message without using frequency analysis essentially required knowledge of the cipher used and perhaps of the key involved, thus making espionage, bribery, burglary, defection, etc., more attractive approaches to the cryptanalytically uninformed. It was finally explicitly recognized in the 19th century that secrecy of a cipher's algorithm is not a sensible nor practical safeguard of message security; in fact, it was further realized that any adequate cryptographic scheme (including ciphers) should remain secure even if the adversary fully understands the cipher algorithm itself. Security of the key used should alone be sufficient for a good cipher to maintain confidentiality under an attack. This fundamental principle was first explicitly stated in 1883 by Auguste Kerckhoffs and is generally called Kerckhoffs's Principle; alternatively and more bluntly, it was restated by Claude Shannon, the inventor of information theory and the fundamentals of theoretical cryptography, as *Shannon's Maxim*—'the enemy knows the system'.

Different physical devices and aids have been used to assist with ciphers. One of the earliest may have been the scytale of ancient Greece, a rod supposedly used by the Spartans as an aid for a transposition cipher. In medieval times, other aids were invented such as the cipher grille, which was also used for a kind of steganography. With the invention of polyalphabet-ic ciphers came more sophisticated aids such as Alberti's own cipher disk, Johannes Trithemius' tabula recta scheme, and Thomas Jefferson's multi cylinder (not publicly known, and reinvented independently by Bazeries around 1900). Many mechanical encryption/decryption devices were invented early in the 20th century, and several patented, among them rotor machines—famously including the Enigma machine used by the German government and military from the late 1920s and during World War II. The ciphers implemented by better quality examples of these machine designs brought about a substantial increase in cryptanalytic difficulty after WWI.

Computer Era

Cryptanalysis of the new mechanical devices proved to be both difficult and laborious. In the United Kingdom, cryptanalytic efforts at Bletchley Park during WWII spurred the development of more efficient means for carrying out repetitious tasks. This culminated in the development of the Colossus, the world's first fully electronic, digital, programmable computer, which assisted in the decryption of ciphers generated by the German Army's Lorenz SZ40/42 machine.

Just as the development of digital computers and electronics helped in cryptanalysis, it made possible much more complex ciphers. Furthermore, computers allowed for the encryption of any kind of data representable in any binary format, unlike classical ciphers which only encrypted written language texts; this was new and significant. Computer use has thus supplanted linguistic cryptography, both for cipher design and cryptanalysis. Many computer ciphers can be characterized by their operation on binary bit sequences (sometimes in groups or blocks), unlike classical and mechanical schemes, which generally manipulate traditional characters (i.e., letters and digits) directly. However, computers have also assisted cryptanalysis, which has compensated to some extent for increased cipher complexity. Nonetheless, good modern ciphers have stayed ahead of cryptanalysis; it is typically the case that use of a quality cipher is very efficient (i.e., fast and re-quiring few resources, such as memory or CPU capability), while breaking it requires an effort many orders of magnitude larger, and vastly larger than that required for any classical cipher, making cryptanalysis so inefficient and impractical as to be effectively impossible.

Extensive open academic research into cryptography is relatively recent; it began only in the mid-1970s. In recent times, IBM personnel designed the algorithm that became the Federal (i.e., US) Data Encryption Standard; Whitfield Diffie and Martin Hellman published their key agreement algorithm; and the RSA algorithm was published in Martin Gardner's *Scientific American* column. Since then, cryptography has become a widely used tool in communications, computer networks, and computer security generally. Some modern cryptographic techniques can only keep their keys secret if certain mathematical problems are intractable, such as the integer factorization or the discrete logarithm problems, so there are deep connections with abstract mathematics. There are very few cryptosystems that are proven to be unconditionally secure. The one-time pad is one. There are a few important ones that are proven secure under certain unproven assumptions. For example, the infeasibility of factoring extremely large integers is the basis for believing that RSA is secure, and some other systems, but even there, the proof is usually lost due to practical consider-ations. There are systems similar to RSA, such as one by Michael O. Rabin that is provably secure provided factoring $n = pq$ is impossible, but the more practical system RSA has never been proved secure in this sense. The discrete logarithm problem is the basis for believing some other crypto-systems are secure, and again, there are related, less practical systems that are provably secure relative to the discrete log problem.

As well as being aware of cryptographic history, cryptographic algorithm and system designers must also sensibly consider probable future developments while working on their designs. For instance, continuous improvements in computer processing power have increased the scope of brute-force attacks, so when specifying key lengths, the required key lengths are similarly advancing. The potential effects of quantum computing are already being considered by some cryptographic system designers; the announced imminence of small implementations of these machines may be making the need for this preemptive caution rather more than merely specu-lative.

Essentially, prior to the early 20th century, cryptography was chiefly concerned with linguis-tic and lexicographic patterns. Since then the emphasis has shifted, and cryptography now makes extensive use of mathematics, including aspects of information theory, computational complexity, statistics, combinatorics, abstract algebra, number theory, and finite mathematics generally. Cryptography is also a branch of engineering, but an unusual one since it deals with active, intelligent, and malevolent opposition; other kinds of engineering (e.g., civil or chemical engineering) need deal only with neutral natural forces. There is also active research examining the relationship between cryptographic problems and quantum physics.

Modern Cryptography

The modern field of cryptography can be divided into several areas of study.

Symmetric-key Cryptography

Symmetric-key cryptography refers to encryption methods in which both the sender and receiver share the same key (or, less commonly, in which their keys are different, but related in an easily computable way). This was the only kind of encryption publicly known until June 1976.

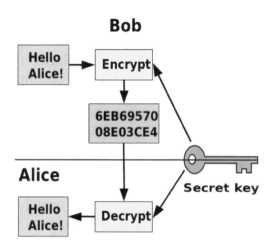

Symmetric-key cryptography, where a single key is used for encryption and decryption

Symmetric key ciphers are implemented as either block ciphers or stream ciphers. A block cipher enciphers input in blocks of plaintext as opposed to individual characters, the input form used by a stream cipher.

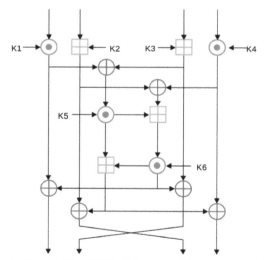

One round (out of 8.5) of the IDEA cipher, used in some versions of PGP for
high-speed encryption of, for instance, e-mail

The Data Encryption Standard (DES) and the Advanced Encryption Standard (AES) are block cipher designs that have been designated cryptography standards by the US government (though DES's designation was finally withdrawn after the AES was adopted). Despite its deprecation as an official standard, DES (especially its still-approved and much more secure triple-DES variant) remains quite popular; it is used across a wide range of applications, from ATM encryption to e-mail privacy and secure remote access. Many other block ciphers have been designed and released, with considerable variation in quality. Many have been thoroughly broken, such as FEAL.

Stream ciphers, in contrast to the 'block' type, create an arbitrarily long stream of key material, which is combined with the plaintext bit-by-bit or character-by-character, somewhat like the one-time pad. In a stream cipher, the output stream is created based on a hidden internal state that changes as the cipher operates. That internal state is initially set up using the secret key material. RC4 is a widely used stream cipher. Block ciphers can be used as stream ciphers.

Cryptographic hash functions are a third type of cryptographic algorithm. They take a message of any length as input, and output a short, fixed length hash, which can be used in (for example) a digital signature. For good hash functions, an attacker cannot find two messages that produce the same hash. MD4 is a long-used hash function that is now broken; MD5, a strengthened variant of MD4, is also widely used but broken in practice. The US National Security Agency developed the Secure Hash Algorithm series of MD5-like hash functions: SHA-0 was a flawed algorithm that the agency withdrew; SHA-1 is widely deployed and more secure than MD5, but cryptanalysts have identified attacks against it; the SHA-2 family improves on SHA-1, but it isn't yet widely deployed; and the US standards authority thought it "prudent" from a security perspective to develop a new standard to "significantly improve the robustness of NIST's overall hash algorithm toolkit." Thus, a hash function design competition was meant to select a new U.S. national standard, to be called SHA-3, by 2012. The competition ended on October 2, 2012 when the NIST announced that Keccak would be the new SHA-3 hash algorithm.

Message authentication codes (MACs) are much like cryptographic hash functions, except that a secret key can be used to authenticate the hash value upon receipt; this additional complication blocks an attack scheme against bare digest algorithms, and so has been thought worth the effort.

Public-key Cryptography

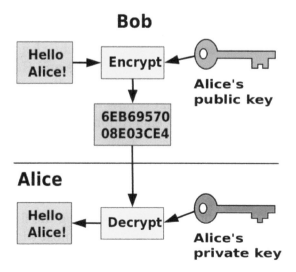

Public-key cryptography, where different keys are used for encryption and decryption

Symmetric-key cryptosystems use the same key for encryption and decryption of a message, though a message or group of messages may have a different key than others. A significant disadvantage of symmetric ciphers is the key management necessary to use them securely. Each distinct pair of communicating parties must, ideally, share a different key, and perhaps each ciphertext exchanged as well. The number of keys required increases as the square of the number of network members, which very quickly requires complex key management schemes to keep them all consistent and secret. The difficulty of securely establishing a secret key between two communicating parties, when a secure channel does not already exist between them, also presents a chicken-and-egg problem which is a considerable practical obstacle for cryptography users in the real world.

Whitfield Diffie and Martin Hellman, authors of the first published paper on public-key cryptography

In a groundbreaking 1976 paper, Whitfield Diffie and Martin Hellman proposed the notion of *public-key* (also, more generally, called *asymmetric key*) cryptography in which two different but mathematically related keys are used—a *public* key and a *private* key. A public key system is so constructed that calculation of one key (the 'private key') is computationally infeasible from the other (the 'public key'), even though they are necessarily related. Instead, both keys are generated secretly, as an interrelated pair. The historian David Kahn described public-key cryptography as "the most revolutionary new concept in the field since polyalphabetic substitution emerged in the Renaissance".

In public-key cryptosystems, the public key may be freely distributed, while its paired private key must remain secret. In a public-key encryption system, the *public key* is used for encryption, while the *private* or *secret key* is used for decryption. While Diffie and Hellman could not find such a system, they showed that public-key cryptography was indeed possible by presenting the Diffie–Hellman key exchange protocol, a solution that is now widely used in secure communications to allow two parties to secretly agree on a shared encryption key.

Diffie and Hellman's publication sparked widespread academic efforts in finding a practical public-key encryption system. This race was finally won in 1978 by Ronald Rivest, Adi Shamir, and Len Adleman, whose solution has since become known as the RSA algorithm.

The Diffie–Hellman and RSA algorithms, in addition to being the first publicly known examples of high quality public-key algorithms, have been among the most widely used. Others include the Cramer–Shoup cryptosystem, ElGamal encryption, and various elliptic curve techniques.

To much surprise, a document published in 1997 by the Government Communications Headquarters (GCHQ), a British intelligence organization, revealed that cryptographers at GCHQ had anticipated several academic developments. Reportedly, around 1970, James H. Ellis had conceived the principles of asymmetric key cryptography. In 1973, Clifford Cocks invented a solution that essentially resembles the RSA algorithm. And in 1974, Malcolm J. Williamson is claimed to have developed the Diffie–Hellman key exchange.

Padlock icon from the Firefox Web browser, which indicates that TLS, a public-key cryptography system, is in use.

Public-key cryptography can also be used for implementing digital signature schemes. A digital signature is reminiscent of an ordinary signature; they both have the characteristic of being easy for a user to produce, but difficult for anyone else to forge. Digital signatures can also be permanently tied to the content of the message being signed; they cannot then be 'moved' from one document to another, for any attempt will be detectable. In digital signature schemes, there are two algorithms: one for *signing*, in which a secret key is used to process the message (or a hash of the message, or both), and one for *verification,* in which the matching public key is used with the message to check the validity of the signature. RSA and DSA are two of the most popular digital signature schemes. Digital signatures are central to the operation of public key infrastructures and many network security schemes (e.g., SSL/TLS, many VPNs, etc.).

Public-key algorithms are most often based on the computational complexity of "hard" problems, often from number theory. For example, the hardness of RSA is related to the integer factorization problem, while Diffie–Hellman and DSA are related to the discrete logarithm problem. More recently, elliptic curve cryptography has developed, a system in which security is based on number theoretic problems involving elliptic curves. Because of the difficulty of the underlying problems, most public-key algorithms involve operations such as modular multiplication and exponentiation, which are much more computationally expensive than the techniques used in most block ciphers, especially with typical key sizes. As a result, public-key cryptosystems are commonly hybrid cryptosystems, in which a fast high-quality symmetric-key encryption algorithm is used for the message itself, while the relevant symmetric key is sent with the message, but encrypted using a public-key algorithm. Similarly, hybrid signature schemes are often used, in which a cryptographic hash function is computed, and only the resulting hash is digitally signed.

Cryptanalysis

The goal of cryptanalysis is to find some weakness or insecurity in a cryptographic scheme, thus permitting its subversion or evasion.

It is a common misconception that every encryption method can be broken. In connection with his WWII work at Bell Labs, Claude Shannon proved that the one-time pad cipher is unbreakable, provided the key material is truly random, never reused, kept secret from all possible attackers, and of equal or greater length than the message. Most ciphers, apart from the one-time pad, can be broken with enough computational effort by brute force attack, but the amount of effort needed may be exponentially dependent on the key size, as compared to the effort needed to make use of the cipher. In such cases, effective security could be achieved if it is proven that the effort required (i.e., "work factor", in Shannon's terms) is beyond the ability of any adversary. This means it must be shown that no efficient method (as opposed to the time-consuming brute force method) can be found to break the cipher. Since no such proof has been found to date, the one-time-pad remains the only theoretically unbreakable cipher.

Variants of the Enigma machine, used by Germany's military and civil authorities from the late 1920s through World War II, implemented a complex electro-mechanical polyalphabetic cipher. Breaking and reading of the Enigma cipher at Poland's Cipher Bureau, for 7 years before the war, and subsequent decryption at Bletchley Park, was important to Allied victory.

There are a wide variety of cryptanalytic attacks, and they can be classified in any of several ways. A common distinction turns on what Eve (an attacker) knows and what capabilities are available. In a ciphertext-only attack, Eve has access only to the ciphertext (good modern cryptosystems are usually effectively immune to ciphertext-only attacks). In a known-plaintext attack, Eve has access to a ciphertext and its corresponding plaintext (or to many such pairs). In a chosen-plaintext attack, Eve may choose a plaintext and learn its corresponding ciphertext (perhaps many times); an example is gardening, used by the British during WWII. In a chosen-ciphertext attack, Eve may be able to *choose* ciphertexts and learn their corresponding plaintexts. Finally in a man-in-the-middle attack Eve gets in between Alice (the sender) and Bob (the recipient), accesses and modifies the traffic and then forwards it to the recipient. Also important, often overwhelmingly so, are mistakes (generally in the design or use of one of the protocols involved.

Poznań monument (*center*) to Polish cryptologists whose breaking of Germany's Enigma machine ciphers, beginning in 1932, altered the course of World War II

Cryptanalysis of symmetric-key ciphers typically involves looking for attacks against the block ciphers or stream ciphers that are more efficient than any attack that could be against a perfect cipher. For example, a simple brute force attack against DES requires one known plaintext and 2^{55} decryptions, trying approximately half of the possible keys, to reach a point at which chances are better than even that the key sought will have been found. But this may not be enough assurance; a linear cryptanalysis attack against DES requires 2^{43} known plaintexts and approximately 2^{43} DES operations. This is a considerable improvement on brute force attacks.

Public-key algorithms are based on the computational difficulty of various problems. The most famous of these is integer factorization (e.g., the RSA algorithm is based on a problem related to integer factoring), but the discrete logarithm problem is also important. Much public-key cryptanalysis concerns numerical algorithms for solving these computational problems, or some of them, efficiently (i.e., in a practical time). For instance, the best known algorithms for solving the elliptic curve-based version of discrete logarithm are much more time-consuming than the best known algorithms for factoring, at least for problems of more or less equivalent size. Thus, other things being equal, to achieve an equivalent strength of attack resistance, factoring-based encryption techniques must use larger keys than elliptic curve techniques. For this reason, public-key cryptosystems based on elliptic curves have become popular since their invention in the mid-1990s.

While pure cryptanalysis uses weaknesses in the algorithms themselves, other attacks on cryptosystems are based on actual use of the algorithms in real devices, and are called *side-channel attacks*. If a cryptanalyst has access to, for example, the amount of time the device took to encrypt a number of plaintexts or report an error in a password or PIN character, he may be able to use a timing attack to break a cipher that is otherwise resistant to analysis. An attacker might also study the pattern and length of messages to derive valuable information; this is known as traffic analysis and can be quite useful to an alert adversary. Poor administration of a cryptosystem, such as permitting too short keys, will make any system vulnerable, regardless of other virtues. And, of course, social engineering, and other attacks against the personnel who work with cryptosystems or the messages they handle (e.g., bribery, extortion, blackmail, espionage, torture, ...) may be the most productive attacks of all.

Cryptographic Primitives

Much of the theoretical work in cryptography concerns cryptographic *primitives*—algorithms with basic cryptographic properties—and their relationship to other cryptographic problems. More complicated cryptographic tools are then built from these basic primitives. These primitives provide fundamental properties, which are used to develop more complex tools called *cryptosystems* or *cryptographic protocols*, which guarantee one or more high-level security properties. Note however, that the distinction between cryptographic *primitives* and cryptosystems, is quite arbitrary; for example, the RSA algorithm is sometimes considered a cryptosystem, and sometimes a primitive. Typical examples of cryptographic primitives include pseudorandom functions, one-way functions, etc.

Cryptosystems

One or more cryptographic primitives are often used to develop a more complex algorithm, called a cryptographic system, or *cryptosystem*. Cryptosystems (e.g., El-Gamal encryption) are designed to provide particular functionality (e.g., public key encryption) while guaranteeing certain security properties (e.g., chosen-plaintext attack (CPA) security in the random oracle model). Cryptosystems use the properties of the underlying cryptographic primitives to support the system's security properties. Of course, as the distinction between primitives and cryptosystems is somewhat arbitrary, a sophisticated cryptosystem can be derived from a combination of several more primitive cryptosystems. In many cases, the cryptosystem's structure involves back and forth communication among two or more parties in space (e.g., between the sender of a secure message and its receiver) or across time (e.g., cryptographically protected backup data). Such cryptosystems are sometimes called *cryptographic protocols*.

Some widely known cryptosystems include RSA encryption, Schnorr signature, El-Gamal encryption, PGP, etc. More complex cryptosystems include electronic cash systems, signcryption systems, etc. Some more 'theoretical' cryptosystems include interactive proof systems, (like zero-knowledge proofs), systems for secret sharing, etc.

Until recently, most security properties of most cryptosystems were demonstrated using empirical techniques or using ad hoc reasoning. Recently, there has been considerable effort to develop formal techniques for establishing the security of cryptosystems; this has been generally called *provable security*. The general idea of provable security is to give arguments about the computational difficulty needed to compromise some security aspect of the cryptosystem (i.e., to any adversary).

The study of how best to implement and integrate cryptography in software applications is itself a distinct field.

Legal Issues

Prohibitions

Cryptography has long been of interest to intelligence gathering and law enforcement agencies. Secret communications may be criminal or even treasonous. Because of its facilitation of privacy, and the diminution of privacy attendant on its prohibition, cryptography is also of considerable interest to civil rights supporters. Accordingly, there has been a history of controversial legal issues surrounding cryptography, especially since the advent of inexpensive computers has made widespread access to high quality cryptography possible.

In some countries, even the domestic use of cryptography is, or has been, restricted. Until 1999, France significantly restricted the use of cryptography domestically, though it has since relaxed many of these rules. In China and Iran, a license is still required to use cryptography. Many countries have tight restrictions on the use of cryptography. Among the more restrictive are laws in Belarus, Kazakhstan, Mongolia, Pakistan, Singapore, Tunisia, and Vietnam.

In the United States, cryptography is legal for domestic use, but there has been much conflict over legal issues related to cryptography. One particularly important issue has been the export of cryptography and cryptographic software and hardware. Probably because of the importance of cryptanalysis in World War II and an expectation that cryptography would continue to be important for national security, many Western governments have, at some point, strictly regulated export of cryptography. After World War II, it was illegal in the US to sell or distribute encryption technology overseas; in fact, encryption was designated as auxiliary military equipment and put on the United States Munitions List. Until the development of the personal computer, asymmetric key algorithms (i.e., public key techniques), and the Internet, this was not especially problematic. However, as the Internet grew and computers became more widely available, high-quality encryption techniques became well known around the globe.

Export Controls

In the 1990s, there were several challenges to US export regulation of cryptography. After the source code for Philip Zimmermann's Pretty Good Privacy (PGP) encryption program found its way onto the Internet in June 1991, a complaint by RSA Security (then called RSA Data Security, Inc.) resulted in a lengthy criminal investigation of Zimmermann by the US Customs Service and the FBI, though no charges were ever filed. Daniel J. Bernstein, then a graduate student at UC Berkeley, brought a lawsuit against the US government challenging some aspects of the restrictions based on free speech grounds. The 1995 case Bernstein v. United States ultimately resulted in a 1999 decision that printed source code for cryptographic algorithms and systems was protected as free speech by the United States Constitution.

In 1996, thirty-nine countries signed the Wassenaar Arrangement, an arms control treaty that deals with the export of arms and "dual-use" technologies such as cryptography. The treaty stipulated that the use of cryptography with short key-lengths (56-bit for symmetric encryption, 512-bit for RSA) would no longer be export-controlled. Cryptography exports from the US became less strictly regulated as a consequence of a major relaxation in 2000; there are no longer very many restrictions on key sizes in US-exported mass-market software. Since this relaxation in US export restrictions, and because most personal computers connected to the Internet include US-sourced web browsers such as Firefox or Internet Explorer, almost every Internet user worldwide has potential access to quality cryptography via their browsers (e.g., via Transport Layer Security). The Mozilla Thunderbird and Microsoft Outlook E-mail client programs similarly can transmit and receive emails via TLS, and can send and receive email encrypted with S/MIME. Many Internet users don't realize that their basic application software contains such extensive cryptosystems. These browsers and email programs are so ubiquitous that even governments whose intent is to regulate civilian use of cryptography generally don't find it practical to do much to control distribution or use of cryptography of this quality, so even when such laws are in force, actual enforcement is often effectively impossible.

NSA Involvement

Another contentious issue connected to cryptography in the United States is the influence of the National Security Agency on cipher development and policy. The NSA was involved with the design of DES during its development at IBM and its consideration by the National Bureau of Standards as a possible Federal Standard for cryptography. DES was designed to be resistant to differential cryptanalysis, a powerful and general cryptanalytic technique known to the NSA and IBM, that became publicly known only when it was rediscovered in the late 1980s. According to Steven Levy, IBM discovered differential cryptanalysis, but kept the technique secret at the NSA's request. The technique became publicly known only when Biham and Shamir re-discovered and announced it some years later. The entire affair illustrates the difficulty of determining what resources and knowledge an attacker might actually have.

NSA headquarters in Fort Meade, Maryland

Another instance of the NSA's involvement was the 1993 Clipper chip affair, an encryption microchip intended to be part of the Capstone cryptography-control initiative. Clipper was widely criticized by cryptographers for two reasons. The cipher algorithm (called Skipjack) was then classified (declassified in 1998, long after the Clipper initiative lapsed). The classified cipher caused concerns that the NSA had deliberately made the cipher weak in order to assist its intelligence efforts. The whole initiative was also criticized based on its violation of Kerckhoffs's Principle, as the scheme included a special escrow key held by the government for use by law enforcement, for example in wiretaps.

Digital Rights Management

Cryptography is central to digital rights management (DRM), a group of techniques for technologically controlling use of copyrighted material, being widely implemented and deployed at the behest of some copyright holders. In 1998, U.S. President Bill Clinton signed the Digital Millennium Copyright Act (DMCA), which criminalized all production, dissemination, and use of certain cryptanalytic techniques and technology (now known or later discovered); specifically, those that could be used to circumvent DRM technological schemes. This had a noticeable impact on the cryptography research community since an argument can be made that *any* cryptanalytic research violated, or might violate, the DMCA. Similar statutes have since been enacted in several countries and regions, including the implementation in the EU Copyright Directive. Similar restrictions are called for by treaties signed by World Intellectual Property Organization member-states.

The United States Department of Justice and FBI have not enforced the DMCA as rigorously as had been feared by some, but the law, nonetheless, remains a controversial one. Niels Ferguson, a well-respected cryptography researcher, has publicly stated that he will not release some of his research into an Intel security design for fear of prosecution under the DMCA. Both Alan Cox (longtime number 2 in Linux kernel development) and Edward Felten (and some of his students at Princeton) have encountered problems related to the Act. Dmitry Sklyarov was arrested during a visit to the US from Russia, and jailed for five months pending trial for alleged violations of the DMCA arising from work he had done in Russia, where the work was legal. In 2007, the cryptographic keys responsible for Blu-ray and HD DVD content scrambling were discovered and released onto the Internet. In both cases, the MPAA sent out numerous DMCA takedown notices, and there was a massive Internet backlash triggered by the perceived impact of such notices on fair use and free speech.

Forced Disclosure of Encryption Keys

In the United Kingdom, the Regulation of Investigatory Powers Act gives UK police the powers to force suspects to decrypt files or hand over passwords that protect encryption keys. Failure to comply is an offense in its own right, punishable on conviction by a two-year jail sentence or up to five years in cases involving national security. Successful prosecutions have occurred under the Act; the first, in 2009, resulted in a term of 13 months' imprisonment. Similar forced disclosure laws in Australia, Finland, France, and India compel individual suspects under investigation to hand over encryption keys or passwords during a criminal investigation.

In the United States, the federal criminal case of United States v. Fricosu addressed whether a search warrant can compel a person to reveal an encryption passphrase or password. The Electronic Frontier Foundation (EFF) argued that this is a violation of the protection from self-incrimination given by the Fifth Amendment. In 2012, the court ruled that under the All Writs Act, the defendant was required to produce an unencrypted hard drive for the court.

In many jurisdictions, the legal status of forced disclosure remains unclear.

The 2016 FBI–Apple encryption dispute concerns the ability of courts in the United States to compel manufacturers' assistance in unlocking cell phones whose contents are cryptographically protected.

As a potential counter-measure to forced disclosure some cryptographic software supports plausible deniability, where the encrypted data is indistinguishable from unused random data (for example such as that of a drive which has been securely wiped).

References

- Menezes, A. J.; van Oorschot, P. C.; Vanstone, S. A. Handbook of Applied Cryptography. ISBN 0-8493-8523-7. Archived from the original on 7 March 2005.

- Gannon, James (2001). Stealing Secrets, Telling Lies: How Spies and Codebreakers Helped Shape the Twentieth Century. Washington, D.C.: Brassey's. ISBN 1-57488-367-4.

- Shannon, Claude; Weaver, Warren (1963). The Mathematical Theory of Communication. University of Illinois Press. ISBN 0-252-72548-4.

- Levy, Steven (2001). Crypto: How the Code Rebels Beat the Government—Saving Privacy in the Digital Age. Penguin Books. p. 56. ISBN 0-14-024432-8. OCLC 244148644.

- Blaze, Matt; Diffie, Whitefield; Rivest, Ronald L.; Schneier, Bruce; Shimomura, Tsutomu; Thompson, Eric; Wiener, Michael (January 1996). "Minimal key lengths for symmetric ciphers to provide adequate commercial security". Fortify. Retrieved 26 March 2015.

- "FIPS PUB 197: The official Advanced Encryption Standard" (PDF). Computer Security Resource Center. National Institute of Standards and Technology. Retrieved 26 March 2015.

- "NIST Selects Winner of Secure Hash Algorithm (SHA-3) Competition". Tech Beat. National Institute of Standards and Technology. October 2, 2012. Retrieved 26 March 2015.

- Wayner, Peter (24 December 1997). "British Document Outlines Early Encryption Discovery". New York Times. Retrieved 26 March 2015.

- "Case Closed on Zimmermann PGP Investigation". IEEE Computer Society's Technical Committee on Security and Privacy. 14 February 1996. Retrieved 26 March 2015.

- "Bernstein v USDOJ". Electronic Privacy Information Center. United States Court of Appeals for the Ninth Circuit. 6 May 1999. Retrieved 26 March 2015.

- "DUAL-USE LIST - CATEGORY 5 – PART 2 – "INFORMATION SECURITY"" (DOC). Wassenaar Arrangement. Retrieved 26 March 2015.

- Coppersmith, D. (May 1994). "The Data Encryption Standard (DES) and its strength against attacks" (PDF). IBM Journal of Research and Development. 38 (3): 243–250. doi:10.1147/rd.383.0243. Retrieved 26 March 2015.

- Biham, E.; Shamir, A. (1991). "Differential cryptanalysis of DES-like cryptosystems" (PDF). Journal of Cryptology. Springer-Verlag. 4 (1): 3–72. doi:10.1007/bf00630563. Retrieved 26 March 2015.

- Ingold, John (January 4, 2012). "Password case reframes Fifth Amendment rights in context of digital world". The Denver Post. Retrieved 26 March 2015.

2

Key Concepts of Cryptography

The key concepts of cryptography are discussed in this chapter. Information security, information-theoretic security, cryptanalysis and strong cryptography are significant and important concepts of cryptography. This chapter elucidates the crucial concepts of cryptography.

Information Security

Information security, sometimes shortened to InfoSec, is the practice of defending information from unauthorized access, use, disclosure, disruption, modification, inspection, recording or destruction. It is a general term that can be used regardless of the form the data may take (e.g. electronic, physical).

Overview

IT Security

Sometimes referred to as computer security, information technology security is information security applied to technology (most often some form of computer system). It is worthwhile to note that a computer does not necessarily mean a home desktop. A computer is any device with a processor and some memory. Such devices can range from non-networked standalone devices as simple as calculators, to networked mobile computing devices such as smartphones and tablet computers. IT security specialists are almost always found in any major enterprise/establishment due to the nature and value of the data within larger businesses. They are responsible for keeping all of the technology within the company secure from malicious cyber attacks that often attempt to breach into critical private information or gain control of the internal systems.

Information Assurance

The act of providing trust of the information, that the Confidentiality, Integrity and Availability (CIA) of the information are not violated. E.g., ensuring that data is not lost when critical issues arise. These issues include, but are not limited to: natural disasters, computer/server malfunction or physical theft. Since most information is stored on computers in our modern era, information assurance is typically dealt with by IT security specialists. A common method of providing information assurance is to have an off-site backup of the data in case one of the mentioned issues arise.

Threats

Computer system threats come in many different forms. Some of the most common threats today are software attacks, theft of intellectual property, identity theft, theft of equipment or information, sabotage, and information extortion. Most people have experienced software attacks of some sort. Viruses, worms, phishing attacks, and Trojan horses are a few common examples of software attacks. The theft of intellectual property has also been an extensive issue for many businesses in the IT field. Intellectual property is the ownership of property usually consisting of some form of protection. Theft of software is probably the most common in IT businesses today. Identity theft is the attempt to act as someone else usually to obtain that person's personal information or to take advantage of their access to vital information. Theft of equipment or information is becoming more prevalent today due to the fact that most devices today are mobile. Cell phones are prone to theft and have also become far more desirable as the amount of data capacity increases. Sabotage usually consists of the destruction of an organization's website in an attempt to cause loss of confidence to its customers. Information extortion consists of theft of a company's property or information as an attempt to receive a payment in exchange for returning the information or property back to its owner. There are many ways to help protect yourself from some of these attacks but one of the most functional precautions is user carefulness.

Governments, military, corporations, financial institutions, hospitals and private businesses amass a great deal of confidential information about their employees, customers, products, research and financial status. Most of this information is now collected, processed and stored on electronic computers and transmitted across networks to other computers.

Should confidential information about a business' customers or finances or new product line fall into the hands of a competitor or a black hat hacker, a business and its customers could suffer widespread, irreparable financial loss, as well as damage to the company's reputation. Protecting confidential information is a business requirement and in many cases also an ethical and legal requirement. Hence a key concern for organizations today is to derive the optimal information security investment. The renowned Gordon-Loeb Model actually provides a powerful mathematical economic approach for addressing this critical concern.

For the individual, information security has a significant effect on privacy, which is viewed very differently in different cultures.

The field of information security has grown and evolved significantly in recent years. There are many ways of gaining entry into the field as a career. It offers many areas for specialization including securing network(s) and allied infrastructure, securing applications and databases, security testing, information systems auditing, business continuity planning and digital forensics.

History

Since the early days of communication, diplomats and military commanders understood that it was necessary to provide some mechanism to protect the confidentiality of correspondence and to have some means of detecting tampering. Julius Caesar is credited with the invention of the Caesar cipher c. 50 B.C., which was created in order to prevent his secret messages from being read should a message fall into the wrong hands, but for the most part protection was achieved through the application of procedural handling controls. Sensitive information was marked up to indicate that it should be protected and transported by trusted persons, guarded and stored in a secure environment or strong box. As postal services expanded, governments created official organizations to intercept, decipher, read and reseal letters (e.g. the UK Secret Office and Deciphering Branch in 1653).

In the mid-19th century more complex classification systems were developed to allow governments to manage their information according to the degree of sensitivity. The British Government codified this, to some extent, with the publication of the Official Secrets Act in 1889. By the time of the First World War, multi-tier classification systems were used to communicate information to and from various fronts, which encouraged greater use of code making and breaking sections in diplomatic and military headquarters. In the United Kingdom this led to the creation of the Government Code and Cypher School in 1919. Encoding became more sophisticated between the wars as machines were employed to scramble and unscramble information. The volume of information shared by the Allied countries during the Second World War necessitated formal alignment of classification systems and procedural controls. An arcane range of markings evolved to indicate who could handle documents (usually officers rather than men) and where they should be stored as increasingly complex safes and storage facilities were developed. Procedures evolved to ensure documents were destroyed properly and it was the failure to follow these procedures which led to some of the greatest intelligence coups of the war (e.g. U-570).

The end of the 20th century and early years of the 21st century saw rapid advancements in telecommunications, computing hardware and software, and data encryption. The availability of smaller, more powerful and less expensive computing equipment made electronic data processing within the reach of small business and the home user. These computers quickly became interconnected through the Internet.

The rapid growth and widespread use of electronic data processing and electronic business conducted through the Internet, along with numerous occurrences of international terrorism, fueled the need for better methods of protecting the computers and the information they store, process and transmit. The academic disciplines of computer security and information assurance emerged along with numerous professional organizations – all sharing the common goals of ensuring the security and reliability of information systems.

Definitions

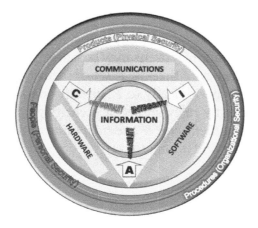

Information Security Attributes: or qualities, i.e., Confidentiality, Integrity and Availability (CIA).

Information Systems are composed in three main portions, hardware, software and communications with the purpose to help identify and apply information security industry standards, as mechanisms of protection and prevention, at three levels or layers: physical, personal and organizational. Essentially, procedures or policies are implemented to tell people (administrators, users and operators) how to use products to ensure information security within the organizations.

The definitions of InfoSec suggested in different sources are summarized below (adopted from).

1. "Preservation of confidentiality, integrity and availability of information. Note: In addition, other properties, such as authenticity, accountability, non-repudiation and reliability can also be involved." (ISO/IEC 27000:2009)

2. "The protection of information and information systems from unauthorized access, use, disclosure, disruption, modification, or destruction in order to provide confidentiality, integrity, and availability." (CNSS, 2010)

3. "Ensures that only authorized users (confidentiality) have access to accurate and complete information (integrity) when required (availability)." (ISACA, 2008)

4. "Information Security is the process of protecting the intellectual property of an organisation." (Pipkin, 2000)

5. "...information security is a risk management discipline, whose job is to manage the cost of information risk to the business." (McDermott and Geer, 2001)

6. "A well-informed sense of assurance that information risks and controls are in balance." (Anderson, J., 2003)

7. "Information security is the protection of information and minimises the risk of exposing information to unauthorised parties." (Venter and Eloff, 2003)

8. "Information Security is a multidisciplinary area of study and professional activity which is concerned with the development and implementation of security mechanisms of all available types (technical, organisational, human-oriented and legal) in order to keep information in all its locations (within and outside the organisation's perimeter) and, consequently, information systems, where information is created, processed, stored, transmitted and destroyed, free from threats.

Threats to information and information systems may be categorised and a corresponding security goal may be defined for each category of threats. A set of security goals, identified as a result of a threat analysis, should be revised periodically to ensure its adequacy and conformance with the evolving environment. The currently relevant set of security goals may include: *confidentiality, integrity, availability, privacy, authenticity & trustworthiness, non-repudiation, accountability and auditability.*" (Cherdantseva and Hilton, 2013)

Profession

Information security is a stable and growing profession. Information security professionals are very stable in their employment; more than 80 percent had no change in employer or employment in the past year, and the number of professionals is projected to continuously grow more than 11 percent annually from 2014 to 2019.

Basic Principles

Key Concepts

The CIA triad of confidentiality, integrity, and availability is at the heart of information security. (The members of the classic InfoSec triad — confidentiality, integrity and availability — are interchangeably referred to in the literature as security attributes, properties, security goals, fundamental aspects, information criteria, critical information characteristics and basic building blocks.) There is continuous debate about extending this classic trio. Other principles such as Accountability have sometimes been proposed for addition – it has been pointed out that issues such as non-repudiation do not fit well within the three core concepts.

In 1992 and revised in 2002, the OECD's *Guidelines for the Security of Information Systems and Networks* proposed the nine generally accepted principles: awareness, responsibility, response, ethics, democracy, risk assessment, security design and implementation, security management, and reassessment. Building upon those, in 2004 the NIST's *Engineering Principles for Information Technology Security* proposed 33 principles. From each of these derived guidelines and practices.

In 2002, Donn Parker proposed an alternative model for the classic CIA triad that he called the six atomic elements of information. The elements are confidentiality, possession, integrity, authenticity, availability, and utility. The merits of the Parkerian Hexad are a subject of debate amongst security professionals.

In 2011, The Open Group published the information security management standard O-ISM3. This standard proposed an operational definition of the key concepts of security, with elements called "security objectives", related to access control (9), availability (3), data quality (1), compliance and technical (4). This model is not currently widely adopted.

In 2013, based on a thorough analysis of Information Assurance and Security (IAS) literature, the IAS-octave was proposed as an extension of the CIA-triad. The IAS-octave includes Confidentiality, Integrity, Availability, Accountability, Auditability, Authenticity/Trustworthiness, Non-repudiation and Privacy. The completeness and accuracy of the IAS-octave was evaluated via a series of interviews with IAS academics and experts. The IAS-octave is one of the dimensions of a Reference Model of Information Assurance and Security (RMIAS), which summarizes the IAS knowledge in one all-encompassing model.

Confidentiality

In information security, confidentiality "is the property, that information is not made available or disclosed to unauthorized individuals, entities, or processes" (Except ISO27000).

Integrity

In information security, data integrity means maintaining and assuring the accuracy and completeness of data over its entire life-cycle. This means that data cannot be modified in an unauthorized or undetected manner. This is not the same thing as referential integrity in databases, although it can be viewed as a special case of consistency as understood in the classic ACID model of transaction processing. Information security systems typically provide message integrity in addition to data confidentiality.

Availability

For any information system to serve its purpose, the information must be available when it is needed. This means that the computing systems used to store and process the information, the security controls used to protect it, and the communication channels used to access it must be functioning correctly. High availability systems aim to remain available at all times, preventing service disruptions due to power outages, hardware failures, and system upgrades. Ensuring availability also involves preventing denial-of-service attacks, such as a flood of incoming messages to the target system essentially forcing it to shut down.

Non-repudiation

In law, non-repudiation implies one's intention to fulfill their obligations to a contract. It also implies that one party of a transaction cannot deny having received a transaction nor can the other party deny having sent a transaction. Note: This is also regarded as part of Integrity.

It is important to note that while technology such as cryptographic systems can assist in non-repudiation efforts, the concept is at its core a legal concept transcending the realm of technology. It is not, for instance, sufficient to show that the message matches a digital signature signed with the sender's private key, and thus only the sender could have sent the message and nobody else could have altered it in transit. The alleged sender could in return demonstrate that the digital signature algorithm is vulnerable or flawed, or allege or prove that his signing key has been compromised. The fault for these violations may or may not lie with the sender himself, and such assertions may or may not relieve the sender of liability, but the assertion would invalidate the claim that the signature necessarily proves authenticity and integrity and thus prevents repudiation.

Risk Management

The *Certified Information Systems Auditor (CISA) Review Manual 2006* provides the following definition of risk management: "Risk management is the process of identifying vulnerabilities and threats to the information resources used by an organization in achieving business objectives, and deciding what countermeasures, if any, to take in reducing risk to an acceptable level, based on the value of the information resource to the organization."

There are two things in this definition that may need some clarification. First, the *process* of risk management is an ongoing, iterative process. It must be repeated indefinitely. The business environment is constantly changing and new threats and vulnerabilities emerge every day. Second, the choice of countermeasures (controls) used to manage risks must strike a balance between productivity, cost, effectiveness of the countermeasure, and the value of the informational asset being protected.

Risk analysis and risk evaluation processes have their limitations since, when security incidents occur, they emerge in a context, and their rarity and even their uniqueness give rise to unpredictable threats. The analysis of these phenomena which are characterized by breakdowns, surprises and side-effects, requires a theoretical approach which is able to examine and interpret subjectively the detail of each incident.

Risk is the likelihood that something bad will happen that causes harm to an informational asset (or the loss of the asset). A vulnerability is a weakness that could be used to endanger or cause harm to an informational asset. A threat is anything (man-made or act of nature) that has the potential to cause harm.

The likelihood that a threat will use a vulnerability to cause harm creates a risk. When a threat does use a vulnerability to inflict harm, it has an impact. In the context of information security, the impact is a loss of availability, integrity, and confidentiality, and possibly other losses (lost income, loss of life, loss of real property). It should be pointed out that it is not possible to identify all risks, nor is it possible to eliminate all risk. The remaining risk is called "residual risk".

A risk assessment is carried out by a team of people who have knowledge of specific areas of the business. Membership of the team may vary over time as different parts of the business are assessed. The assessment may use a subjective qualitative analysis based on informed opinion, or where reliable dollar figures and historical information is available, the analysis may use quantitative analysis.

The research has shown that the most vulnerable point in most information systems is the human user, operator, designer, or other human. The ISO/IEC 27002:2005 Code of practice for information security management recommends the following be examined during a risk assessment:

- security policy,
- organization of information security,
- asset management,
- human resources security,
- physical and environmental security,
- communications and operations management,
- access control,
- information systems acquisition, development and maintenance,
- information security incident management,
- business continuity management, and
- regulatory compliance.

In broad terms, the risk management process consists of:

1. Identification of assets and estimating their value. Include: people, buildings, hardware, software, data (electronic, print, other), supplies.

2. Conduct a threat assessment. Include: Acts of nature, acts of war, accidents, malicious acts originating from inside or outside the organization.

3. Conduct a vulnerability assessment, and for each vulnerability, calculate the probability that it will be exploited. Evaluate policies, procedures, standards, training, physical security, quality control, technical security.

4. Calculate the impact that each threat would have on each asset. Use qualitative analysis or quantitative analysis.

5. Identify, select and implement appropriate controls. Provide a proportional response. Consider productivity, cost effectiveness, and value of the asset.

6. Evaluate the effectiveness of the control measures. Ensure the controls provide the required cost effective protection without discernible loss of productivity.

For any given risk, management can choose to accept the risk based upon the relative low value of the asset, the relative low frequency of occurrence, and the relative low impact on the business. Or, leadership may choose to mitigate the risk by selecting and implementing appropriate control measures to reduce the risk. In some cases, the risk can be transferred to another business by buying insurance or outsourcing to another business. The reality of some risks may be disputed. In such cases leadership may choose to deny the risk.

Controls

Selecting proper controls and implementing those will initially help an organization to bring down risk to acceptable levels. Control selection should follow and should be based on the risk assessment. Controls can vary in nature but fundamentally they are ways of protecting the confidentiality, integrity or availability of information. ISO/IEC 27001:2005 has defined 133 controls in different areas, but this is not exhaustive. Organizations can implement additional controls according to requirement of the organization. ISO 27001:2013 has cut down the number of controls to 113. From 08.11.2013 the technical standard of information security in place is: ABNT NBR ISO/IEC 27002:2013.

Administrative

Administrative controls (also called procedural controls) consist of approved written policies, procedures, standards and guidelines. Administrative controls form the framework for running the business and managing people. They inform people on how the business is to be run and how day-to-day operations are to be conducted. Laws and regulations created by government bodies are also a type of administrative control because they inform the business. Some industry sectors have policies, procedures, standards and guidelines that must be followed – the Payment Card Industry Data Security Standard (PCI DSS) required by Visa and MasterCard is such an example. Other examples of administrative controls include the corporate security policy, password policy, hiring policies, and disciplinary policies.

Administrative controls form the basis for the selection and implementation of logical and physical controls. Logical and physical controls are manifestations of administrative controls. Administrative controls are of paramount importance.

Logical

Logical controls (also called technical controls) use software and data to monitor and control access to information and computing systems. For example: passwords, network and host-based firewalls, network intrusion detection systems, access control lists, and data encryption are logical controls.

An important logical control that is frequently overlooked is the principle of least privilege. The principle of least privilege requires that an individual, program or system process is not granted any more access privileges than are necessary to perform the task. A blatant example of the failure to adhere to the principle of least privilege is logging into Windows as user Administrator to read email and surf the web. Violations of this principle can also occur when an individual collects additional access privileges over time. This happens when employees' job duties change, or they are promoted to a new position, or they transfer to another department. The access privileges required by their new duties are frequently added onto their already existing access privileges which may no longer be necessary or appropriate.

Physical

Physical controls monitor and control the environment of the work place and computing facilities. They also monitor and control access to and from such facilities. For example: doors, locks, heating and air conditioning, smoke and fire alarms, fire suppression systems, cameras, barricades, fencing, security guards, cable locks, etc. Separating the network and workplace into functional areas are also physical controls.

An important physical control that is frequently overlooked is the separation of duties. Separation of duties ensures that an individual can not complete a critical task by himself. For example: an employee who submits a request for reimbursement should not also be able to authorize payment or print the check. An applications programmer should not also be the server administrator or the database administrator – these roles and responsibilities must be separated from one another.

Defense in Depth

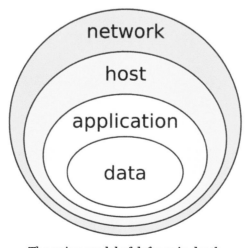

The onion model of defense in depth

Information security must protect information throughout the life span of the information, from the initial creation of the information on through to the final disposal of the information. The information must be protected while in motion and while at rest. During its lifetime, information may pass through many different information processing systems and through many different parts of information processing systems. There are many different ways the information and information systems can be threatened. To fully protect the information during its lifetime, each component of the information processing system must have its own protection mechanisms. The building up, layering on and overlapping of security measures is called defense in depth. In contrast to a metal chain, which is famously only as strong as its weakest link, the defense-in-depth aims at a structure where, should one defensive measure fail, other measures will continue to provide protection.

Recall the earlier discussion about administrative controls, logical controls, and physical controls. The three types of controls can be used to form the basis upon which to build a defense-in-depth strategy. With this approach, defense-in-depth can be conceptualized as three distinct layers or planes laid one on top of the other. Additional insight into defense-in- depth can be gained by thinking of it as forming the layers of an onion, with data at the core of the onion, people the next outer layer of the onion, and network security, host-based security and application security forming the outermost layers of the onion. Both perspectives are equally valid and each provides valuable insight into the implementation of a good defense-in-depth strategy.

Security Classification for Information

An important aspect of information security and risk management is recognizing the value of information and defining appropriate procedures and protection requirements for the information. Not all information is equal and so not all information requires the same degree of protection. This requires information to be assigned a security classification.

The first step in information classification is to identify a member of senior management as the owner of the particular information to be classified. Next, develop a classification policy. The policy should describe the different classification labels, define the criteria for information to be assigned a particular label, and list the required security controls for each classification.

Some factors that influence which classification information should be assigned include how much value that information has to the organization, how old the information is and whether or not the information has become obsolete. Laws and other regulatory requirements are also important considerations when classifying information.

The Business Model for Information Security enables security professionals to examine security from systems perspective, creating an environment where security can be managed holistically, allowing actual risks to be addressed.

The type of information security classification labels selected and used will depend on the nature of the organization, with examples being:

- In the business sector, labels such as: Public, Sensitive, Private, Confidential.

- In the government sector, labels such as: Unclassified, Unofficial, Protected, Confidential, Secret, Top Secret and their non-English equivalents.

- In cross-sectoral formations, the Traffic Light Protocol, which consists of: White, Green, Amber, and Red.

All employees in the organization, as well as business partners, must be trained on the classification schema and understand the required security controls and handling procedures for each classification. The classification of a particular information asset that has been assigned should be reviewed periodically to ensure the classification is still appropriate for the information and to ensure the security controls required by the classification are in place and are followed in their right procedures.

Access Control

Access to protected information must be restricted to people who are authorized to access the information. The computer programs, and in many cases the computers that process the information, must also be authorized. This requires that mechanisms be in place to control the access to protected information. The sophistication of the access control mechanisms should be in parity with the value of the information being protected – the more sensitive or valuable the information the stronger the control mechanisms need to be. The foundation on which access control mechanisms are built start with identification and authentication.

Access control is generally considered in three steps: Identification, Authentication, and Authorization.

Identification

Identification is an assertion of who someone is or what something is. If a person makes the statement "Hello, my name is John Doe" they are making a claim of who they are. However, their claim may or may not be true. Before John Doe can be granted access to protected information it will be necessary to verify that the person claiming to be John Doe really is John Doe. Typically the claim is in the form of a username. By entering that username you are claiming "I am the person the username belongs to".

Authentication

Authentication is the act of verifying a claim of identity. When John Doe goes into a bank to make a withdrawal, he tells the bank teller he is John Doe—a claim of identity. The bank teller asks to see a photo ID, so he hands the teller his driver's license. The bank teller checks the license to make sure it has John Doe printed on it and compares the photograph on the license against the person claiming to be John Doe. If the photo and name match the person, then the teller has authenticated that John Doe is who he claimed to be. Similarly by entering the correct password, the user is providing evidence that they are the person the username belongs to.

There are three different types of information that can be used for authentication:

- Something you know: things such as a PIN, a password, or your mother's maiden name.

- Something you have: a driver's license or a magnetic swipe card.

- Something you are: biometrics, including palm prints, fingerprints, voice prints and retina (eye) scans.

Strong authentication requires providing more than one type of authentication information (two-factor authentication). The username is the most common form of identification on computer systems today and the password is the most common form of authentication. Usernames and passwords have served their purpose but in our modern world they are no longer adequate. Usernames and passwords are slowly being replaced with more sophisticated authentication mechanisms.

Authorization

After a person, program or computer has successfully been identified and authenticated then it must be determined what informational resources they are permitted to access and what actions they will be allowed to perform (run, view, create, delete, or change). This is called authorization. Authorization to access information and other computing services begins with administrative policies and procedures. The policies prescribe what information and computing services can be accessed, by whom, and under what conditions. The access control mechanisms are then configured to enforce these policies. Different computing systems are equipped with different kinds of access control mechanisms—some may even offer a choice of different access control mechanisms. The access control mechanism a system offers will be based upon one of three approaches to access control or it may be derived from a combination of the three approaches.

The non-discretionary approach consolidates all access control under a centralized administration. The access to information and other resources is usually based on the individuals function (role) in the organization or the tasks the individual must perform. The discretionary approach gives the creator or owner of the information resource the ability to control access to those resources. In the Mandatory access control approach, access is granted or denied basing upon the security classification assigned to the information resource.

Examples of common access control mechanisms in use today include role-based access control available in many advanced database management systems—simple file permissions provided in the UNIX and Windows operating systems, Group Policy Objects provided in Windows network systems, Kerberos, RADIUS, TACACS, and the simple access lists used in many firewalls and routers.

To be effective, policies and other security controls must be enforceable and upheld. Effective policies ensure that people are held accountable for their actions. All failed and successful authentication attempts must be logged, and all access to information must leave some type of audit trail.

Also, need-to-know principle needs to be in effect when talking about access control. Need-to-know principle gives access rights to a person to perform their job functions. This principle is used in the government, when dealing with difference clearances. Even though two employees in different departments have a top-secret clearance, they must have a need-to-know in order for information to be exchanged. Within the need-to-know principle, network administrators grant the employee least amount privileges to prevent employees access and doing more than what they are supposed to. Need-to-know helps to enforce the confidentiality-integrity-availability (CIA) triad. Need-to-know directly impacts the confidential area of the triad.

Cryptography

Information security uses cryptography to transform usable information into a form that renders it unusable by anyone other than an authorized user; this process is called encryption. Information that has been encrypted (rendered unusable) can be transformed back into its original usable form by an authorized user, who possesses the cryptographic key, through the process of decryption. Cryptography is used in information security to protect information from unauthorized or accidental disclosure while the information is in transit (either electronically or physically) and while information is in storage.

Cryptography provides information security with other useful applications as well including improved authentication methods, message digests, digital signatures, non-repudiation, and encrypted network communications. Older less secure applications such as telnet and ftp are slowly being replaced with more secure applications such as ssh that use encrypted network communications. Wireless communications can be encrypted using protocols such as WPA/WPA2 or the older (and less secure) WEP. Wired communications (such as ITUT G.hn) are secured using AES for encryption and X.1035 for authentication and key exchange. Software applications such as GnuPG or PGP can be used to encrypt data files and Email.

Cryptography can introduce security problems when it is not implemented correctly. Cryptographic solutions need to be implemented using industry accepted solutions that have undergone rigorous peer review by independent experts in cryptography. The length and strength of the encryption key is also an important consideration. A key that is weak or too short will produce weak encryption. The keys used for encryption and decryption must be protected with the same degree of rigor as any other confidential information. They must be protected from unauthorized disclosure and destruction and they must be available when needed. Public key infrastructure (PKI) solutions address many of the problems that surround key management.

Process

The terms reasonable and prudent person, due care and due diligence have been used in the fields of Finance, Securities, and Law for many years. In recent years these terms have found their way into the fields of computing and information security. U.S.A. Federal Sentencing Guidelines now make it possible to hold corporate officers liable for failing to exercise due care and due diligence in the management of their information systems.

In the business world, stockholders, customers, business partners and governments have the expectation that corporate officers will run the business in accordance with accepted business practices and in compliance with laws and other regulatory requirements. This is often described as the "reasonable and prudent person" rule. A prudent person takes due care to ensure that everything necessary is done to operate the business by sound business principles and in a legal ethical manner. A prudent person is also diligent (mindful, attentive, and ongoing) in their due care of the business.

In the field of Information Security, Harris offers the following definitions of due care and due diligence:

"Due care are steps that are taken to show that a company has taken responsibility for the activities that take place within the corporation and has taken the necessary steps to help protect the company, its resources, and employees." And, [Due diligence are the] *"continual activities that make sure the protection mechanisms are continually maintained and operational."*

Attention should be made to two important points in these definitions. First, in due care, steps are taken to *show* - this means that the steps can be verified, measured, or even produce tangible artifacts. Second, in due diligence, there are continual activities - this means that people are actually doing things to monitor and maintain the protection mechanisms, and these activities are ongoing.

Security Governance

The Software Engineering Institute at Carnegie Mellon University, in a publication titled "Governing for Enterprise Security (GES)", defines characteristics of effective security governance. These include:

- An enterprise-wide issue
- Leaders are accountable
- Viewed as a business requirement
- Risk-based
- Roles, responsibilities, and segregation of duties defined
- Addressed and enforced in policy
- Adequate resources committed
- Staff aware and trained
- A development life cycle requirement
- Planned, managed, measurable, and measured
- Reviewed and audited

Incident Response Plans

1 to 3 paragraphs (non technical) that discuss:

- Selecting team members
- Define roles, responsibilities and lines of authority
- Define a security incident
- Define a reportable incident
- Training
- Detection
- Classification
- Escalation
- Containment

- Eradication

- Documentation

Change Management

Change management is a formal process for directing and controlling alterations to the information processing environment. This includes alterations to desktop computers, the network, servers and software. The objectives of change management are to reduce the risks posed by changes to the information processing environment and improve the stability and reliability of the processing environment as changes are made. It is not the objective of change management to prevent or hinder necessary changes from being implemented.

Any change to the information processing environment introduces an element of risk. Even apparently simple changes can have unexpected effects. One of Management's many responsibilities is the management of risk. Change management is a tool for managing the risks introduced by changes to the information processing environment. Part of the change management process ensures that changes are not implemented at inopportune times when they may disrupt critical business processes or interfere with other changes being implemented.

Not every change needs to be managed. Some kinds of changes are a part of the everyday routine of information processing and adhere to a predefined procedure, which reduces the overall level of risk to the processing environment. Creating a new user account or deploying a new desktop computer are examples of changes that do not generally require change management. However, relocating user file shares, or upgrading the Email server pose a much higher level of risk to the processing environment and are not a normal everyday activity. The critical first steps in change management are (a) defining change (and communicating that definition) and (b) defining the scope of the change system.

Change management is usually overseen by a Change Review Board composed of representatives from key business areas, security, networking, systems administrators, Database administration, applications development, desktop support and the help desk. The tasks of the Change Review Board can be facilitated with the use of automated work flow application. The responsibility of the Change Review Board is to ensure the organizations documented change management procedures are followed. The change management process is as follows:

- Requested: Anyone can request a change. The person making the change request may or may not be the same person that performs the analysis or implements the change. When a request for change is received, it may undergo a preliminary review to determine if the requested change is compatible with the organizations business model and practices, and to determine the amount of resources needed to implement the change.

- Approved: Management runs the business and controls the allocation of resources therefore, Management must approve requests for changes and assign a priority for every change. Management might choose to reject a change request if the change is not compatible with the business model, industry standards or best practices. Management might also choose to reject a change request if the change requires more resources than can be allocated for the change.

- Planned: Planning a change involves discovering the scope and impact of the proposed change; analyzing the complexity of the change; allocation of resources and, developing, testing and documenting both implementation and backout plans. Need to define the criteria on which a decision to back out will be made.

- Tested: Every change must be tested in a safe test environment, which closely reflects the actual production environment, before the change is applied to the production environment. The backout plan must also be tested.

- Scheduled: Part of the change review board's responsibility is to assist in the scheduling of changes by reviewing the proposed implementation date for potential conflicts with other scheduled changes or critical business activities.

- Communicated: Once a change has been scheduled it must be communicated. The communication is to give others the opportunity to remind the change review board about other changes or critical business activities that might have been overlooked when scheduling the change. The communication also serves to make the Help Desk and users aware that a change is about to occur. Another responsibility of the change review board is to ensure that scheduled changes have been properly communicated to those who will be affected by the change or otherwise have an interest in the change.

- Implemented: At the appointed date and time, the changes must be implemented. Part of the planning process was to develop an implementation plan, testing plan and, a back out plan. If the implementation of the change should fail or, the post implementation testing fails or, other "drop dead" criteria have been met, the back out plan should be implemented.

- Documented: All changes must be documented. The documentation includes the initial request for change, its approval, the priority assigned to it, the implementation, testing and back out plans, the results of the change review board critique, the date/time the change was implemented, who implemented it, and whether the change was implemented successfully, failed or postponed.

- Post change review: The change review board should hold a post implementation review of changes. It is particularly important to review failed and backed out changes. The review board should try to understand the problems that were encountered, and look for areas for improvement.

Change management procedures that are simple to follow and easy to use can greatly reduce the overall risks created when changes are made to the information processing environment. Good change management procedures improve the overall quality and success of changes as they are implemented. This is accomplished through planning, peer review, documentation and communication.

ISO/IEC 20000, The Visible OPS Handbook: Implementing ITIL in 4 Practical and Auditable Steps (Full book summary), and Information Technology Infrastructure Library all provide valuable guidance on implementing an efficient and effective change management program information security.

Business Continuity

Business continuity is the mechanism by which an organization continues to operate its critical business units, during planned or unplanned disruptions that affect normal business operations, by invoking planned and managed procedures.

Not only is business continuity simply about the business, but it is also an IT system and process. Today disasters or disruptions to business are a reality. Whether the disaster is natural or man-made, it affects normal life and so business. Therefore, planning is important.

The planning is merely getting better prepared to face it, knowing fully well that the best plans may fail. Planning helps to reduce cost of recovery, operational overheads and most importantly sail through some smaller ones effortlessly.

For businesses to create effective plans they need to focus upon the following key questions. Most of these are common knowledge, and anyone can do a BCP.

1. Should a disaster strike, what are the first few things that I should do? Should I call people to find if they are OK or call up the bank to figure out my money is safe? This is Emergency Response. Emergency Response services help take the first hit when the disaster strikes and if the disaster is serious enough the Emergency Response teams need to quickly get a Crisis Management team in place.

2. What parts of my business should I recover first? The one that brings me most money or the one where I spend the most, or the one that will ensure I shall be able to get sustained future growth? The identified sections are the critical business units. There is no magic bullet here, no one answer satisfies all. Businesses need to find answers that meet business requirements.

3. How soon should I target to recover my critical business units? In BCP technical jargon, this is called Recovery Time Objective, or RTO. This objective will define what costs the business will need to spend to recover from a disruption. For example, it is cheaper to re-cover a business in 1 day than in 1 hour.

4. What do I need to recover the business? IT, machinery, records...food, water, people...So many aspects to dwell upon. The cost factor becomes clearer now...Business leaders need to drive business continuity. Hold on. My IT manager spent $200000 last month and cre-ated a DRP (Disaster Recovery Plan), whatever happened to that? A DRP is about continu-ing an IT system, and is one of the sections of a comprehensive Business Continuity Plan. Look below for more on this.

5. And where do I recover my business from... Will the business center give me space to work, or would it be flooded by many people queuing up for the same reasons that I am.

6. But once I do recover from the disaster and work in reduced production capacity since my main operational sites are unavailable, how long can this go on. How long can I do without my original sites, systems, people? this defines the amount of business resilience a business may have.

7. Now that I know how to recover my business. How do I make sure my plan works? Most BCP pundits would recommend testing the plan at least once a year, reviewing it for adequacy and rewriting or updating the plans either annually or when businesses change.

Disaster Recovery Planning

While a business continuity plan (BCP) takes a broad approach to dealing with organizational-wide effects of a disaster, a disaster recovery plan (DRP), which is a subset of the business continuity plan, is instead focused on taking the necessary steps to resume normal business operations as quickly as possible. A disaster recovery plan is executed immediately after the disaster occurs and details what steps are to be taken in order to recover critical information technology infrastructure. Disaster recovery planning includes establishing a planning group, performing risk assessment, establishing priorities, developing recovery strategies, preparing inventories and documentation of the plan, developing verification criteria and procedure, and lastly implementing the plan.

Laws and Regulations

Privacy International 2007 privacy ranking
green: Protections and safeguards
red: Endemic surveillance societies

Below is a partial listing of European, United Kingdom, Canadian and US governmental laws and regulations that have, or will have, a significant effect on data processing and information security. Important industry sector regulations have also been included when they have a significant impact on information security.

- UK Data Protection Act 1998 makes new provisions for the regulation of the processing of information relating to individuals, including the obtaining, holding, use or disclosure of such information. The European Union Data Protection Directive (EUDPD) requires that all EU member must adopt national regulations to standardize the protection of data privacy for citizens throughout the EU.

- The Computer Misuse Act 1990 is an Act of the UK Parliament making computer crime (e.g. hacking) a criminal offence. The Act has become a model upon which several other countries including Canada and the Republic of Ireland have drawn inspiration when subsequently drafting their own information security laws.

- EU Data Retention laws requires Internet service providers and phone companies to keep data on every electronic message sent and phone call made for between six months and two years.

- The Family Educational Rights and Privacy Act (FERPA) (20 U.S.C. § 1232 g; 34 CFR Part 99) is a US Federal law that protects the privacy of student education records. The law applies to all schools that receive funds under an applicable program of the U.S. Department of Education. Generally, schools must have written permission from the parent or eligible student in order to release any information from a student's education record.

- Federal Financial Institutions Examination Council's (FFIEC) security guidelines for auditors specifies requirements for online banking security.

- Health Insurance Portability and Accountability Act (HIPAA) of 1996 requires the adoption of national standards for electronic health care transactions and national identifiers for providers, health insurance plans, and employers. And, it requires health care providers, insurance providers and employers to safeguard the security and privacy of health data.

- Gramm–Leach–Bliley Act of 1999 (GLBA), also known as the Financial Services Modernization Act of 1999, protects the privacy and security of private financial information that financial institutions collect, hold, and process.

- Sarbanes–Oxley Act of 2002 (SOX). Section 404 of the act requires publicly traded companies to assess the effectiveness of their internal controls for financial reporting in annual reports they submit at the end of each fiscal year. Chief information officers are responsible for the security, accuracy and the reliability of the systems that manage and report the financial data. The act also requires publicly traded companies to engage independent auditors who must attest to, and report on, the validity of their assessments.

- Payment Card Industry Data Security Standard (PCI DSS) establishes comprehensive requirements for enhancing payment account data security. It was developed by the founding payment brands of the PCI Security Standards Council, including American Express, Discover Financial Services, JCB, MasterCard Worldwide and Visa International, to help facilitate the broad adoption of consistent data security measures on a global basis. The PCI DSS is a multifaceted security standard that includes requirements for security management, policies, procedures, network architecture, software design and other critical protective measures.

- State security breach notification laws (California and many others) require businesses, nonprofits, and state institutions to notify consumers when unencrypted "personal information" may have been compromised, lost, or stolen.

- Personal Information Protection and Electronics Document Act (PIPEDA) – An Act to support and promote electronic commerce by protecting personal information that is collected, used or disclosed in certain circumstances, by providing for the use of electronic means to communicate or record information or transactions and by amending the Canada Evidence Act, the Statutory Instruments Act and the Statute Revision Act.

- Hellenic Authority for Communication Security and Privacy (ADAE) (Law 165/2011) - The Greek Law establishes and describes the minimum Information Security controls that should be deployed by every company which provides electronic communication networks and/or services in Greece in order to protect customers' Confidentiality. These include both managerial and technical controls (i.e. log records should be stored for two years).

- Hellenic Authority for Communication Security and Privacy (ADAE) (Law 205/2013)- The latest Greek Law published by ADAE concentrates around the protection of the Integrity and Availability of the services and data offered by the Greek Telecommunication Companies.The new Law forces Telcos and associated companies to build, deploy and test appropriate Business Continuity Plans and redundant infrastructures.

Information Security Culture

Employee's behavior has a big impact to information security in organizations. Cultural concept can help different segments of the organization to concern about the information security within the organization."Exploring the Relationship between Organizational Culture and Information Security Culture" provides the following definition of information security culture: "ISC is the totality of patterns of behavior in an organization that contribute to the protection of information of all kinds."

Information security culture needs to be improved continuously. In "Information Security Culture from Analysis to Change", authors commented, "It's a never ending process, a cycle of evaluation and change or maintenance." To manage the information security culture, five steps should be taken: Pre-evaluation, strategic planning, operative planning, implementation, and post-evaluation.

- Pre-Evaluation: to identify the awareness of information security within employees and to analysis current security policy.

- Strategic Planning: to come up a better awareness-program, we need to set clear targets. Clustering people is helpful to achieve it.

- Operative Planning: we can set a good security culture based on internal communication, management-buy-in, and security awareness and training program.

- Implementation: four stages should be used to implement the information security culture. They are commitment of the management, communication with organizational members, courses for all organizational members, and commitment of the employees.

Sources of Standards

International Organization for Standardization (ISO) is a consortium of national standards institutes from 157 countries, coordinated through a secretariat in Geneva, Switzerland. ISO is the world's largest developer of standards. ISO 15443: "Information technology - Security techniques - A framework for IT security assurance", ISO/IEC 27002: "Information technology - Security techniques - Code of practice for information security management", ISO-20000: "Information technology - Service management", and ISO/IEC 27001: "Information technology - Security techniques - Information security management systems - Requirements" are of particular interest to information security professionals.

The US National Institute of Standards and Technology (NIST) is a non-regulatory federal agency within the U.S. Department of Commerce. The NIST Computer Security Division develops standards, metrics, tests and validation programs as well as publishes standards and guidelines to increase secure IT planning, implementation, management and operation. NIST is also the custodian of the US Federal Information Processing Standard publications (FIPS).

The Internet Society is a professional membership society with more than 100 organizations and over 20,000 individual members in over 180 countries. It provides leadership in addressing issues that confront the future of the Internet, and is the organization home for the groups responsible for Internet infrastructure standards, including the Internet Engineering Task Force (IETF) and the Internet Architecture Board (IAB). The ISOC hosts the Requests for Comments (RFCs) which includes the Official Internet Protocol Standards and the RFC-2196 Site Security Handbook.

The Information Security Forum is a global nonprofit organization of several hundred leading organizations in financial services, manufacturing, telecommunications, consumer goods, government, and other areas. It undertakes research into information security practices and offers advice in its biannual Standard of Good Practice and more detailed advisories for members.

The Institute of Information Security Professionals (IISP) is an independent, non-profit body governed by its members, with the principal objective of advancing the professionalism of information security practitioners and thereby the professionalism of the industry as a whole. The Institute developed the IISP Skills Framework©. This framework describes the range of competencies expected of Information Security and Information Assurance Professionals in the effective performance of their roles. It was developed through collaboration between both private and public sector organisations and world-renowned academics and security leaders.

The German Federal Office for Information Security (in German *Bundesamt für Sicherheit in der Informationstechnik (BSI)*) BSI-Standards 100-1 to 100-4 are a set of recommendations including "methods, processes, procedures, approaches and measures relating to information security". The BSI-Standard 100-2 *IT-Grundschutz Methodology* describes how an information security management can be implemented and operated. The Standard includes a very specific guide, the IT Baseline Protection Catalogs (also known as IT-Grundschutz Catalogs). Before 2005 the catalogs were formerly known as "IT Baseline Protection Manual". The Catalogs are a collection of documents useful for detecting and combating security-relevant weak points in the IT environment (IT cluster). The collection encompasses as of September 2013 over 4.400 pages with the introduction and catalogs. The IT-Grundschutz approach is aligned with to the ISO/IEC 2700x family.

At the European Telecommunications Standards Institute a catalog of Information security indicators have been standardized by the Industrial Specification Group (ISG) ISI.

Scholars Working in the Field

- Adam Back
- Annie Anton
- Brian LaMacchia
- Bruce Schneier
- Cynthia Dwork
- Dawn Song
- Deborah Estrin

- Gene Spafford

- Ian Goldberg

- Lawrence A. Gordon

- Martin P. Loeb

- Monica S. Lam

- Joan Feigenbaum

- L Jean Camp

- Lance Cottrell

- Lorrie Cranor

- Khalil Sehnaoui

- Paul C. van Oorschot

- Peter Gutmann

- Peter Landrock

- Ross J. Anderson

- Stefan Brands

Information-theoretic Security

A cryptosystem is information-theoretically secure if its security derives purely from information theory. That is, it cannot be broken even when the adversary has unlimited computing power. The adversary simply does not have enough information to break the encryption, so these cryptosystems are considered cryptanalytically unbreakable.

An encryption protocol that has information-theoretic security does not depend for its effectiveness on unproven assumptions about computational hardness, and such an algorithm is not vulnerable to future developments in computer power such as quantum computing. An example of an information-theoretically secure cryptosystem is the one-time pad. The concept of information-theoretically secure communication was introduced in 1949 by American mathematician Claude Shannon, the inventor of information theory, who used it to prove that the one-time pad system was secure. Information-theoretically secure cryptosystems have been used for the most sensitive governmental communications, such as diplomatic cables and high-level military communications, because of the great efforts enemy governments expend toward breaking them.

An interesting special case is perfect security: an encryption algorithm is perfectly secure if a ciphertext produced using it provides no information about the plaintext without knowledge of the key. If E is a perfectly secure encryption function, for any fixed message m there must exist for each ciphertext c at least one key k such that $c = E_k(m)$. It has been proved that any cipher with the perfect secrecy property must use keys with effectively the same requirements as one-time pad keys.

It is common for a cryptosystem to leak some information but nevertheless maintain its security properties even against an adversary that has unlimited computational resources. Such a cryptosystem would have information theoretic but not perfect security. The exact definition of security would depend on the cryptosystem in question.

There are a variety of cryptographic tasks for which information-theoretic security is a meaningful and useful requirement. A few of these are:

1. Secret sharing schemes such as Shamir's are information-theoretically secure (and also perfectly secure) in that less than the requisite number of shares of the secret provide no information about the secret.

2. More generally, secure multiparty computation protocols often, but not always, have information-theoretic security.

3. Private information retrieval with multiple databases can be achieved with information-theoretic privacy for the user's query.

4. Reductions between cryptographic primitives or tasks can often be achieved information-theoretically. Such reductions are important from a theoretical perspective, because they establish that primitive Π can be realized if primitive Π' can be realized.

5. Symmetric encryption can be constructed under an information-theoretic notion of security called entropic security, which assumes that the adversary knows almost nothing about the message being sent. The goal here is to hide *all functions* of the plaintext rather than all information about it.

6. Quantum cryptography is largely part of information-theoretic cryptography.

Conventional secrecy entails encrypting messages. Beyond this, some scenarios require *covert communication*, a stronger type of secrecy which also hides the fact that communication is happening at all.

Physical Layer Encryption

A weaker notion of security defined by Aaron D. Wyner established a now flourishing area of research known as physical layer encryption. This exploits the physical wireless channel for its security by communications, signal processing, and coding techniques. The security is provable, unbreakable, and quantifiable (in bits/second/hertz).

Wyner's initial physical layer encryption work in the 1970s posed the Alice – Bob – Eve problem in which Alice wants to send a message to Bob without Eve decoding it. It was shown that if the channel from Alice to Bob is statistically better than the channel from Alice to Eve, secure communication is possible. This is intuitive, but Wyner measured the secrecy in information theoretic terms defining secrecy capacity, which essentially is the rate at which Alice can transmit secret information to Bob. Shortly after, Imre Csiszár and Körner showed that secret communication was possible even when Eve had a statistically better channel to Alice than did Bob. More recent theoretical results are concerned with determining the secrecy capacity and optimal power allocation in broadcast fading channels. There are caveats, as many capacities are not computable unless the assumption is made that Alice knows the channel to Eve. If this were known, Alice could simply place a null in Eve's direction. Secrecy capacity for MIMO and multiple colluding eavesdroppers is more recent and ongoing work, and these results still make the non-useful assumption about eavesdropper channel state information knowledge.

Still other work is less theoretical and attempts to compare implementable schemes. One physical layer encryption scheme is to broadcast artificial noise in all directions except that of Bob's channel, basically jamming Eve. One paper by Negi and Goel details the implementation, and Khisti and Wornell computed the secrecy capacity when only statistics about Eve's channel are known.

Parallel to this work in the information theory community is work in the antenna community that has been termed near-field direct antenna modulation or directional modulation. It was shown that by using a parasitic array, the transmitted modulation in different directions could be controlled independently. Secrecy could be realized by making the modulations in undesired directions difficult to decode. Directional modulation data transmission was experimentally demonstrated using a phased array. Others have demonstrated directional modulation with switched arrays and phase-conjugating lenses.

This type of directional modulation is really a subset of Negi and Goel's additive artificial noise encryption scheme. Another scheme using pattern-reconfigurable transmit antennas for Alice called reconfigurable multiplicative noise (RMN) complements additive artificial noise. The two work well together in channel simulations in which nothing is assumed known to Alice or Bob about the eavesdroppers.

Unconditional Security

Information-theoretic security is often used interchangeably with unconditional security. However, the latter term can also refer to systems that don't rely on unproven computational hardness assumptions. Today these systems are essentially the same as those that are information-theoretically secure. Nevertheless, it does not always have to be that way. One day RSA might be proved secure (it relies on the assertion that factoring large numbers is hard), thus becoming unconditionally secure, but it will never be information-theoretically secure (because even though no efficient algorithms for factoring large primes may exist, in principle it can still be done given unlimited computational power).

Steganography

Steganography is the practice of concealing a file, message, image, or video within another file, message, image, or video.

The first recorded use of the term was in 1499 by Johannes Trithemius in his *Steganographia*, a treatise on cryptography and steganography, disguised as a book on magic. Generally, the hidden messages appear to be (or be part of) something else: images, articles, shopping lists, or some other *cover text*. For example, the hidden message may be in invisible ink between the visible lines of a private letter. Some implementations of steganography that lack a shared secret are forms of security through obscurity, whereas key-dependent steganographic schemes adhere to Kerckhoffs's principle.

The advantage of steganography over cryptography alone is that the intended secret message does not attract attention to itself as an object of scrutiny. Plainly visible encrypted messages—no matter how unbreakable—arouse interest, and may in themselves be incriminating in countries where encryption is illegal. Thus, whereas cryptography is the practice of protecting the contents of a message alone, steganography is concerned with concealing the fact that a secret message is being sent, as well as concealing the contents of the message.

Steganography includes the concealment of information within computer files. In digital steganography, electronic communications may include steganographic coding inside of a transport layer, such as a document file, image file, program or protocol. Media files are ideal for steganographic transmission because of their large size. For example, a sender might start with an innocuous image file and adjust the color of every 100th pixel to correspond to a letter in the alphabet, a change so subtle that someone not specifically looking for it is unlikely to notice it.

History

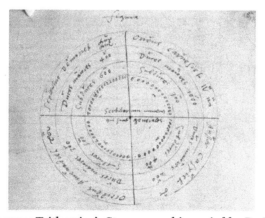

A chart from Johannes Trithemius's Steganographia copied by Dr John Dee in 1591

The first recorded uses of steganography can be traced back to 440 BC when Herodotus mentions two examples in his *Histories*. Histiaeus sent a message to his vassal, Aristagoras, by shaving the head of his most trusted servant, "marking" the message onto his scalp, then sending him on his way once his hair had regrown, with the instruction, "When thou art come to Miletus, bid Aristagoras shave thy head, and look thereon." And Demaratus, who sent a warning about a forthcoming attack to Greece by writing it directly on the wooden backing of a wax tablet before applying its beeswax surface. Wax tablets were in common use then as reusable writing surfaces, sometimes used for shorthand.

In his work *Polygraphiae* Johannes Trithemius developed his so-called "Ave-Maria-Cipher" that can hide information in a Latin praise of God. "*Auctor Sapientissimus Conseruans Angelica Deferat Nobis Charitas Potentissimi Creatoris*" for example contains the concealed word *VICIPEDIA* .It is also known as "short writing".

Techniques

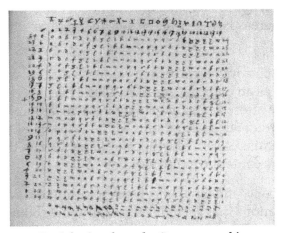

Deciphering the code. *Steganographia*

Physical

Steganography has been widely used, including in recent historical times and the present day. Known examples include:

- Hidden messages within wax tablet—in ancient Greece, people wrote messages on wood and covered it with wax that bore an innocent covering message.

- Hidden messages on messenger's body—also used in ancient Greece. Herodotus tells the story of a message tattooed on the shaved head of a slave of Histiaeus, hidden by the hair that afterwards grew over it, and exposed by shaving the head. The message allegedly carried a warning to Greece about Persian invasion plans. This method has obvious drawbacks, such as delayed transmission while waiting for the slave's hair to grow, and restrictions on the number and size of messages that can be encoded on one person's scalp.

- During World War II, the French Resistance sent some messages written on the backs of couriers in invisible ink.

- Hidden messages on paper written in secret inks, under other messages or on the blank parts of other messages

- Messages written in Morse code on yarn and then knitted into a piece of clothing worn by a courier.

- Messages written on envelopes in the area covered by postage stamps.

- In the early days of the printing press, it was common to mix different typefaces on a printed page due to the printer not having enough copies of some letters in one typeface. Because of this, a message could be hidden using two (or more) different typefaces, such as normal or italic.

- During and after World War II, espionage agents used photographically produced microdots to send information back and forth. Microdots were typically minute (less than the size of the period produced by a typewriter). World War II microdots were embedded in the paper and covered with an adhesive, such as collodion. This was reflective, and thus detectable by viewing against glancing light. Alternative techniques included inserting microdots into slits cut into the edge of post cards.

- During WWII, Velvalee Dickinson, a spy for Japan in New York City, sent information to accommodation addresses in neutral South America. She was a dealer in dolls, and her letters discussed the quantity and type of doll to ship. The stegotext was the doll orders, while the concealed "plaintext" was itself encoded and gave information about ship movements, etc. Her case became somewhat famous and she became known as the Doll Woman.

- Jeremiah Denton repeatedly blinked his eyes in Morse Code during the 1966 televised press conference that he was forced into as an American POW by his North Vietnamese captors, spelling out "T-O-R-T-U-R-E". This confirmed for the first time to the U.S. Military (naval intelligence) and Americans that the North Vietnamese were torturing American POWs.

- Cold War counter-propaganda. In 1968, crew members of the USS *Pueblo* intelligence ship held as prisoners by North Korea, communicated in sign language during staged photo opportunities, informing the United States they were not defectors, but captives of the North Koreans. In other photos presented to the US, crew members gave "the finger" to the unsuspecting North Koreans, in an attempt to discredit photos that showed them smiling and comfortable.

Digital Messages

Image of a tree with a steganographically hidden image. The hidden image is revealed by removing all but the two least significant bits of each color component and a subsequent normalization. The hidden image is shown below.

Image of a cat extracted from the tree image above.

Modern steganography entered the world in 1985 with the advent of personal computers being applied to classical steganography problems. Development following that was very slow, but has since taken off, going by the large number of steganography software available:

- Concealing messages within the lowest bits of noisy images or sound files.

- Concealing data within encrypted data or within random data. The message to conceal is encrypted, then used to overwrite part of a much larger block of encrypted data or a block of random data (an unbreakable cipher like the one-time pad generates ciphertexts that look perfectly random without the private key).

- Chaffing and winnowing.

- Mimic functions convert one file to have the statistical profile of another. This can thwart statistical methods that help brute-force attacks identify the right solution in a cipher-text-only attack.

- Concealed messages in tampered executable files, exploiting redundancy in the targeted instruction set.

- Pictures embedded in video material (optionally played at slower or faster speed).

- Injecting imperceptible delays to packets sent over the network from the keyboard. Delays in keypresses in some applications (telnet or remote desktop software) can mean a delay in packets, and the delays in the packets can be used to encode data.

- Changing the order of elements in a set.

- Content-Aware Steganography hides information in the semantics a human user assigns to a datagram. These systems offer security against a nonhuman adversary/warden.

- Blog-Steganography. Messages are fractionalized and the (encrypted) pieces are added as comments of orphaned web-logs (or pin boards on social network platforms). In this case the selection of blogs is the symmetric key that sender and recipient are using; the carrier of the hidden message is the whole blogosphere.

- Modifying the echo of a sound file (Echo Steganography).

- Steganography for audio signals.

- Image bit-plane complexity segmentation steganography

- Including data in ignored sections of a file, such as after the logical end of the carrier file.

Digital Text

- Making text the same color as the background in word processor documents, e-mails, and forum posts.

- Using Unicode characters that look like the standard ASCII character set. On most systems, there is no visual difference from ordinary text. Some systems may display the fonts differently, and the extra information would then be easily spotted, of course.

- Using hidden (control) characters, and redundant use of markup (e.g., empty bold, underline or italics) to embed information within HTML, which is visible by examining the document source. HTML pages can contain code for extra blank spaces and tabs at the end of lines, and colours, fonts and sizes, which are not visible when displayed.

- Using non-printing Unicode characters Zero-Width Joiner (ZWJ) and Zero-Width Non-Joiner (ZWNJ). These characters are used for joining and disjoining letters in Arabic and Persian, but can be used in Roman alphabets for hiding information because they have no meaning in Roman alphabets: because they are "zero-width" they are not displayed. ZWJ and ZWNJ can represent "1" and "0".

Social Steganography

In communities with social or government taboos or censorship, people use cultural steganography—hiding messages in idiom, pop culture references, and other messages they share publicly and assume are monitored. This relies on social context to make the underlying messages visible only to certain readers. Examples include:

- Hiding a message in the title and context of a shared video or image

- Misspelling names or words that are popular in the media in a given week, to suggest an alternate meaning

- Hiding a Picture which can be traced by using Paint or any other Drawing tool.

Network

All information hiding techniques that may be used to exchange steganograms in telecommunication networks can be classified under the general term of network steganography. This nomenclature was originally introduced by Krzysztof Szczypiorski in 2003. Contrary to typical steganographic methods that use digital media (images, audio and video files) to hide data, network steganography uses communication protocols' control elements and their intrinsic functionality. As a result, such methods are harder to detect and eliminate.

Typical network steganography methods involve modification of the properties of a single network protocol. Such modification can be applied to the PDU (Protocol Data Unit), to the time relations between the exchanged PDUs, or both (hybrid methods).

Moreover, it is feasible to utilize the relation between two or more different network protocols to enable secret communication. These applications fall under the term inter-protocol steganography.

Network steganography covers a broad spectrum of techniques, which include, among others:

- Steganophony — the concealment of messages in Voice-over-IP conversations, e.g. the employment of delayed or corrupted packets that would normally be ignored by the receiver (this method is called LACK — Lost Audio Packets Steganography), or, alternatively, hiding information in unused header fields.

- WLAN Steganography – transmission of steganograms in Wireless Local Area Networks. A practical example of WLAN Steganography is the HICCUPS system (Hidden Communication System for Corrupted Networks)

Printed

Digital steganography output may be in the form of printed documents. A message, the *plaintext*, may be first encrypted by traditional means, producing a *ciphertext*. Then, an innocuous *covertext* is modified in some way so as to contain the ciphertext, resulting in the *stegotext*. For example, the letter size, spacing, typeface, or other characteristics of a covertext can be manipulated to carry the hidden message. Only a recipient who knows the technique used can recover the message and then decrypt it. Francis Bacon developed Bacon's cipher as such a technique.

The ciphertext produced by most digital steganography methods, however, is not printable. Traditional digital methods rely on perturbing noise in the channel file to hide the message, as such, the channel file must be transmitted to the recipient with no additional noise from the transmission. Printing introduces much noise in the ciphertext, generally rendering the message unrecoverable. There are techniques that address this limitation, one notable example is ASCII Art Steganography.

Although no classic steganography, some types of modern color laser printers integrate the model, serial number and timestamps on each printout for traceability reasons using a dot-matrix code made of small, yellow dots not recognizable by the bare eye.

Using Puzzles

The art of concealing data in a puzzle can take advantage of the degrees of freedom in stating the puzzle, using the starting information to encode a key within the puzzle / puzzle image.

For instance, steganography using sudoku puzzles has as many keys as there are possible solutions of a sudoku puzzle, which is 6.71×10^{21}. This is equivalent to around 70 bits, making it much stronger than the DES method, which uses a 56 bit key.

Additional Terminology

Discussions of steganography generally use terminology analogous to (and consistent with) conventional radio and communications technology. However, some terms show up in software specifically, and are easily confused. These are most relevant to digital steganographic systems.

The *payload* is the data covertly communicated. The *carrier* is the signal, stream, or data file that hides the payload—which differs from the *channel* (which typically means the type of input, such as a JPEG image). The resulting signal, stream, or data file with the encoded payload is sometimes called the *package*, *stego file*, or *covert message*. The percentage of bytes, samples, or other signal elements modified to encode the payload is called the *encoding density*, and is typically expressed as a number between 0 and 1.

In a set of files, those files considered likely to contain a payload are *suspects*. A *suspect* identified through some type of statistical analysis might be referred to as a *candidate*.

Countermeasures and Detection

Detecting physical steganography requires careful physical examination—including the use of magnification, developer chemicals and ultraviolet light. It is a time-consuming process with obvious resource implications, even in countries that employ large numbers of people to spy on their fellow nationals. However, it is feasible to screen mail of certain suspected individuals or institutions, such as prisons or prisoner-of-war (POW) camps.

During World War II, prisoner of war camps gave prisoners specially treated paper that would reveal invisible ink. An article in the 24 June 1948 issue of *Paper Trade Journal* by the Technical Director of the United States Government Printing Office, Morris S. Kantrowitz, describes, in general terms, the development of this paper. They used three prototype papers named *Sensicoat*, *Anilith*, and *Coatalith*. These were for the manufacture of post cards and stationery provided to German prisoners of war in the US and Canada. If POWs tried to write a hidden message, the special paper rendered it visible. The U.S. granted at least two patents related to this technology—one to Kantrowitz, U.S. Patent 2,515,232, "Water-Detecting paper and Water-Detecting Coating Composition Therefor," patented 18 July 1950, and an earlier one, "Moisture-Sensitive Paper and the Manufacture Thereof", U.S. Patent 2,445,586, patented 20 July 1948. A similar strategy is to issue prisoners with writing paper ruled with a water-soluble ink that runs in contact with water-based invisible ink.

In computing, steganographically encoded package detection is called steganalysis. The simplest method to detect modified files, however, is to compare them to known originals. For example, to detect information being moved through the graphics on a website, an analyst can maintain known clean-copies of these materials and compare them against the current contents of the site. The differences, assuming the carrier is the same, comprise the payload. In general, using extremely high compression rates makes steganography difficult, but not impossible. Compression errors provide a hiding place for data, but high compression reduces the amount of data available to hold the payload, raising the encoding density, which facilitates easier detection (in extreme cases, even by casual observation).

Applications

Use in Modern Printers

Some modern computer printers use steganography, including HP and Xerox brand color laser printers. These printers add tiny yellow dots to each page. The barely-visible dots contain encoded printer serial numbers and date and time stamps.

Example from Modern Practice

The larger the cover message (in binary data, the number of bits) relative to the hidden message, the easier it is to hide the latter. For this reason, digital pictures (which contain large amounts of data) are used to hide messages on the Internet and on other communication media. It is not clear how common this actually is. For example: a 24-bit bitmap uses 8 bits to represent each of the three color values (red, green, and blue) at each pixel. The blue alone has 2^8 different levels of blue intensity. The difference between 11111111 and 11111110 in the value for blue intensity is likely to be undetectable by the human eye. Therefore, the least significant bit can be used more or less undetectably for something else other than color information. If this is repeated for the green and the red elements of each pixel as well, it is possible to encode one letter of ASCII text for every three pixels.

Stated somewhat more formally, the objective for making steganographic encoding difficult to detect is to ensure that the changes to the carrier (the original signal) due to the injection of the payload (the signal to covertly embed) are visually (and ideally, statistically) negligible; that is to say, the changes are indistinguishable from the noise floor of the carrier. Any medium can be a carrier, but media with a large amount of redundant or compressible information are better suited.

From an information theoretical point of view, this means that the channel must have more capacity than the "surface" signal requires; that is, there must be redundancy. For a digital image, this may be noise from the imaging element; for digital audio, it may be noise from recording techniques or amplification equipment. In general, electronics that digitize an analog signal suffer from several noise sources such as thermal noise, flicker noise, and shot noise. This noise provides enough variation in the captured digital information that it can be exploited as a noise cover for hidden data. In addition, lossy compression schemes (such as JPEG) always introduce some error into the decompressed data; it is possible to exploit this for steganographic use as well.

Steganography can be used for digital watermarking, where a message (being simply an identifier) is hidden in an image so that its source can be tracked or verified (for example, Coded Anti-Piracy), or even just to identify an image (as in the EURion constellation).

Alleged use by Intelligence Services

In 2010, the Federal Bureau of Investigation alleged that the Russian foreign intelligence service uses customized steganography software for embedding encrypted text messages inside image files for certain communications with "illegal agents" (agents under non-diplomatic cover) stationed abroad.

Distributed Steganography

There are distributed steganography methods, including methodologies that distribute the payload through multiple carrier files in diverse locations to make detection more difficult. For example, U.S. Patent 8,527,779 by cryptographer William Easttom (Chuck Easttom).

Online Challenge

The puzzles presented by Cicada 3301 incorporates steganography with cryptography and other solving techniques since 2012.

Cryptanalysis

Cryptanalysis (from the Greek *kryptós*, "hidden", and *analýein*, "to loosen" or "to untie") is the study of analyzing information systems in order to study the hidden aspects of the systems. Cryptanalysis is used to breach cryptographic security systems and gain access to the contents of encrypted messages, even if the cryptographic key is unknown.

Close-up of the rotors in a Fialka cipher machine

In addition to mathematical analysis of cryptographic algorithms, cryptanalysis includes the study of side-channel attacks that do not target weaknesses in the cryptographic algorithms themselves, but instead exploit weaknesses in their implementation.

Even though the goal has been the same, the methods and techniques of cryptanalysis have changed drastically through the history of cryptography, adapting to increasing cryptographic complexity, ranging from the pen-and-paper methods of the past, through machines like the British Bombes and Colossus computers at Bletchley Park in World War II, to the mathematically advanced computerized schemes of the present. Methods for breaking modern cryptosystems often involve solving carefully constructed problems in pure mathematics, the best-known being integer factorization.

Overview

Given some encrypted data (*"ciphertext"*), the goal of the *cryptanalyst* is to gain as much information as possible about the original, unencrypted data (*"plaintext"*).

Amount of Information Available to the Attacker

Attacks can be classified based on what type of information the attacker has available. As a basic starting point it is normally assumed that, for the purposes of analysis, the general algorithm is known; this is Shannon's Maxim "the enemy knows the system"—in its turn, equivalent to Kerckhoffs' principle. This is a reasonable assumption in practice — throughout history, there are countless examples of secret algorithms falling into wider knowledge, variously through espionage, betrayal and reverse engineering. (And on occasion, ciphers have been reconstructed through pure deduction; for example, the German Lorenz cipher and the Japanese Purple code, and a variety of classical schemes):

- *Ciphertext-only*: the cryptanalyst has access only to a collection of ciphertexts or codetexts.

- *Known-plaintext*: the attacker has a set of ciphertexts to which he knows the corresponding plaintext.

- *Chosen-plaintext* (*chosen-ciphertext*): the attacker can obtain the ciphertexts (plaintexts) corresponding to an arbitrary set of plaintexts (ciphertexts) of his own choosing.

- *Adaptive chosen-plaintext*: like a chosen-plaintext attack, except the attacker can choose subsequent plaintexts based on information learned from previous encryptions. Similarly *Adaptive chosen ciphertext attack*.

- *Related-key attack*: Like a chosen-plaintext attack, except the attacker can obtain ciphertexts encrypted under two different keys. The keys are unknown, but the relationship between them is known; for example, two keys that differ in the one bit.

Computational Resources Required

Attacks can also be characterised by the resources they require. Those resources include:

- Time — the number of *computation steps* (e.g., test encryptions) which must be performed.

- Memory — the amount of *storage* required to perform the attack.

- Data — the quantity and type of *plaintexts and ciphertexts* required for a particular approach.

It's sometimes difficult to predict these quantities precisely, especially when the attack isn't practical to actually implement for testing. But academic cryptanalysts tend to provide at least the estimated *order of magnitude* of their attacks' difficulty, saying, for example, "SHA-1 collisions now 2^{52}."

Bruce Schneier notes that even computationally impractical attacks can be considered breaks: "Breaking a cipher simply means finding a weakness in the cipher that can be exploited with a complexity less than brute force. Never mind that brute-force might require 2^{128} encryptions; an attack requiring 2^{110} encryptions would be considered a break...simply put, a break can just be a certificational weakness: evidence that the cipher does not perform as advertised."

Partial Breaks

The results of cryptanalysis can also vary in usefulness. For example, cryptographer Lars Knudsen (1998) classified various types of attack on block ciphers according to the amount and quality of secret information that was discovered:

- *Total break* — the attacker deduces the secret key.

- *Global deduction* — the attacker discovers a functionally equivalent algorithm for encryption and decryption, but without learning the key.

- *Instance (local) deduction* — the attacker discovers additional plaintexts (or ciphertexts) not previously known.

- *Information deduction* — the attacker gains some Shannon information about plaintexts (or ciphertexts) not previously known.

- *Distinguishing algorithm* — the attacker can distinguish the cipher from a random permutation.

Academic attacks are often against weakened versions of a cryptosystem, such as a block cipher or hash function with some rounds removed. Many, but not all, attacks become exponentially more difficult to execute as rounds are added to a cryptosystem, so it's possible for the full cryptosystem to be strong even though reduced-round variants are weak. Nonetheless, partial breaks that come close to breaking the original cryptosystem may mean that a full break will follow; the successful attacks on DES, MD5, and SHA-1 were all preceded by attacks on weakened versions.

In academic cryptography, a *weakness* or a *break* in a scheme is usually defined quite conservatively: it might require impractical amounts of time, memory, or known plaintexts. It also might require the attacker be able to do things many real-world attackers can't: for example, the attacker may need to choose particular plaintexts to be encrypted or even to ask for plaintexts to be encrypted using several keys related to the secret key. Furthermore, it might only reveal a small amount of information, enough to prove the cryptosystem imperfect but too little to be useful to real-world attackers. Finally, an attack might only apply to a weakened version of cryptographic tools, like a reduced-round block cipher, as a step towards breaking of the full system.

History

TELEGRAM RECEIVED.

FROM 2nd from London # 5747.

"We intend to begin on the first of February unrestricted submarine warfare. We shall endeavor in spite of this to keep the United States of America neutral. In the event of this not succeeding, we make Mexico a proposal of alliance on the following basis: make war together, make peace together, generous financial support and an understanding on our part that Mexico is to reconquer the lost territory in Texas, New Mexico, and Arizona. The settlement in detail is left to you. You will inform the President of the above most secretly as soon as the outbreak of war with the United States of America is certain and add the suggestion that he should, on his own initiative, invite Japan to immediate adherence and at the same time mediate between Japan and ourselves. Please call the President's attention to the fact that the ruthless employment of our submarines now offers the prospect of compelling England in a few months to make peace." Signed, ZIMMERMANN.

The decrypted Zimmermann Telegram.

Cryptanalysis has coevolved together with cryptography, and the contest can be traced through the history of cryptography—new ciphers being designed to replace old broken designs, and new cryptanalytic techniques invented to crack the improved schemes. In practice, they are viewed as two sides of the same coin: in order to create secure cryptography, you have to design against possible cryptanalysis.

Successful cryptanalysis has undoubtedly influenced history; the ability to read the presumed-secret thoughts and plans of others can be a decisive advantage. For example, in England in 1587, Mary, Queen of Scots was tried and executed for treason as a result of her involvement in three plots to assassinate Elizabeth I of England. The plans came to light after her coded correspondence with fellow conspirators was deciphered by Thomas Phelippes.

In World War I, the breaking of the Zimmermann Telegram was instrumental in bringing the United States into the war. In World War II, the Allies benefitted enormously from their joint success cryptanalysis of the German ciphers — including the Enigma machine and the Lorenz cipher — and Japanese ciphers, particularly 'Purple' and JN-25. 'Ultra' intelligence has been credited with everything between shortening the end of the European war by up to two years, to determining the eventual result. The war in the Pacific was similarly helped by 'Magic' intelligence.

Governments have long recognized the potential benefits of cryptanalysis for intelligence, both military and diplomatic, and established dedicated organizations devoted to breaking the codes and ciphers of other nations, for example, GCHQ and the NSA, organizations which are still very active today. In 2004, it was reported that the United States had broken Iranian ciphers. (It is unknown, however, whether this was pure cryptanalysis, or whether other factors were involved:).

Classical Ciphers

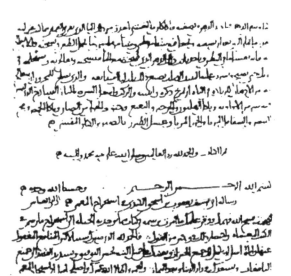

First page of Al-Kindi's 9th century *Manuscript on Deciphering Cryptographic Messages*

Although the actual word *"cryptanalysis"* is relatively recent (it was coined by William Friedman in 1920), methods for breaking codes and ciphers are much older. The first known recorded explanation of cryptanalysis was given by 9th-century Arabian polymath, Al-Kindi (also known as "Alkindus" in Europe), in *A Manuscript on Deciphering Cryptographic Messages*. This treatise includes a description of the method of frequency analysis (Ibrahim Al-Kadi, 1992- ref-3). Italian scholar Giambattista della Porta was author of a seminal work on cryptanalysis *"De Furtivis Literarum Notis"*.

Frequency analysis is the basic tool for breaking most classical ciphers. In natural languages, certain letters of the alphabet appear more frequently than others; in English, "E" is likely to be the most common letter in any sample of plaintext. Similarly, the digraph "TH" is the most likely pair of letters in English, and so on. Frequency analysis relies on a cipher failing to hide these statistics. For example, in a simple substitution cipher (where each letter is simply replaced with another), the most frequent letter in the ciphertext would be a likely candidate for "E". Frequency analysis of such a cipher is therefore relatively easy, provided that the ciphertext is long enough to give a reasonably representative count of the letters of the alphabet that it contains.

In Europe during the 15th and 16th centuries, the idea of a polyalphabetic substitution cipher was developed, among others by the French diplomat Blaise de Vigenère (1523–96). For some three centuries, the Vigenère cipher, which uses a repeating key to select different encryption alphabets in rotation, was considered to be completely secure (*le chiffre indéchiffrable*—"the indecipherable cipher"). Nevertheless, Charles Babbage (1791–1871) and later, independently, Friedrich Kasiski (1805–81) succeeded in breaking this cipher. During World War I, inventors in several countries developed rotor cipher machines such as Arthur Scherbius' Enigma, in an attempt to minimise the repetition that had been exploited to break the Vigenère system.

Ciphers from World War I and World War II

Cryptanalysis of enemy messages played a significant part in the Allied victory in World War II. F. W. Winterbotham, quoted the western Supreme Allied Commander, Dwight D. Eisenhower, at the war's end as describing Ultra intelligence as having been "decisive" to Allied victory. Sir Harry Hinsley, official historian of British Intelligence in World War II, made a similar assessment about Ultra, saying that it shortened the war "by not less than two years and probably by four years"; moreover, he said that in the absence of Ultra, it is uncertain how the war would have ended.

In practice, frequency analysis relies as much on linguistic knowledge as it does on statistics, but as ciphers became more complex, mathematics became more important in cryptanalysis. This change was particularly evident before and during World War II, where efforts to crack Axis ciphers required new levels of mathematical sophistication. Moreover, automation was first applied to cryptanalysis in that era with the Polish Bomba device, the British Bombe, the use of punched card equipment, and in the Colossus computers — the first electronic digital computers to be controlled by a program.

Indicator

With reciprocal machine ciphers such as the Lorenz cipher and the Enigma machine used by Nazi Germany during World War II, each message had its own key. Usually, the transmitting operator informed the receiving operator of this message key by transmitting some plaintext and/or ciphertext before the enciphered message. This is termed the *indicator*, as it indicates to the receiving operator how to set his machine to decipher the message.

Poorly designed and implemented indicator systems allowed first the Poles and then the British at Bletchley Park to break the Enigma cipher system. Similar poor indicator systems allowed the British to identify *depths* that led to the diagnosis of the Lorenz SZ40/42 cipher system, and the comprehensive breaking of its messages without the cryptanalysts seeing the cipher machine.

Depth

Sending two or more messages with the same key is an insecure process. To a cryptanalyst the messages are then said to be *"in depth."* This may be detected by the messages having the same *indicator* by which the sending operator informs the receiving operator about the key generator initial settings for the message.

Generally, the cryptanalyst may benefit from lining up identical enciphering operations among a set of messages. For example, the Vernam cipher enciphers by bit-for-bit combining plaintext with a long key using the "exclusive or" operator, which is also known as "modulo-2 addition" (symbolized by $\oplus$):

> Plaintext $\oplus$ Key = Ciphertext

Deciphering combines the same key bits with the ciphertext to reconstruct the plaintext:

> Ciphertext $\oplus$ Key = Plaintext

(In modulo-2 arithmetic, addition is the same as subtraction.) When two such ciphertexts are aligned in depth, combining them eliminates the common key, leaving just a combination of the two plaintexts:

> Ciphertext1 $\oplus$ Ciphertext2 = Plaintext1 $\oplus$ Plaintext2

The individual plaintexts can then be worked out linguistically by trying *probable words* (or phrases), also known as *"cribs,"* at various locations; a correct guess, when combined with the merged plaintext stream, produces intelligible text from the other plaintext component:

> (Plaintext1 $\oplus$ Plaintext2) $\oplus$ Plaintext1 = Plaintext2

The recovered fragment of the second plaintext can often be extended in one or both directions, and the extra characters can be combined with the merged plaintext stream to extend the first plaintext. Working back and forth between the two plaintexts, using the intelligibility criterion to check guesses, the analyst may recover much or all of the original plaintexts. (With only two plaintexts in depth, the analyst may not know which one corresponds to which ciphertext, but in practice this is not a large problem.) When a recovered plaintext is then combined with its ciphertext, the key is revealed:

> Plaintext1 $\oplus$ Ciphertext1 = Key

Knowledge of a key of course allows the analyst to read other messages encrypted with the same key, and knowledge of a set of related keys may allow cryptanalysts to diagnose the system used for constructing them.

Development of Modern Cryptography

Even though computation was used to great effect in Cryptanalysis of the Lorenz cipher and other systems during World War II, it also made possible new methods of cryptography orders of magnitude more complex than ever before. Taken as a whole, modern cryptography has become much more impervious to cryptanalysis than the pen-and-paper systems of the past, and now seems to have the upper hand against pure cryptanalysis. The historian David Kahn notes:

The Bombe replicated the action of several Enigma machines wired together. Each of the rapidly rotating drums, pictured above in a Bletchley Park museum mockup, simulated the action of an Enigma rotor.

Many are the cryptosystems offered by the hundreds of commercial vendors today that cannot be broken by any known methods of cryptanalysis. Indeed, in such systems even a chosen plaintext attack, in which a selected plaintext is matched against its ciphertext, cannot yield the key that unlock[s] other messages. In a sense, then, cryptanalysis is dead. But that is not the end of the story. Cryptanalysis may be dead, but there is - to mix my metaphors - more than one way to skin a cat.

Kahn goes on to mention increased opportunities for interception, bugging, side channel attacks, and quantum computers as replacements for the traditional means of cryptanalysis. In 2010, former NSA technical director Brian Snow said that both academic and government cryptographers are "moving very slowly forward in a mature field."

However, any postmortems for cryptanalysis may be premature. While the effectiveness of cryptanalytic methods employed by intelligence agencies remains unknown, many serious attacks against both academic and practical cryptographic primitives have been published in the modern era of computer cryptography:

- The block cipher Madryga, proposed in 1984 but not widely used, was found to be susceptible to ciphertext-only attacks in 1998.

- FEAL-4, proposed as a replacement for the DES standard encryption algorithm but not widely used, was demolished by a spate of attacks from the academic community, many of which are entirely practical.

- The A5/1, A5/2, CMEA, and DECT systems used in mobile and wireless phone technology can all be broken in hours, minutes or even in real-time using widely available computing equipment.

- Brute-force keyspace search has broken some real-world ciphers and applications, including single-DES, 40-bit "export-strength" cryptography, and the DVD Content Scrambling System.

- In 2001, Wired Equivalent Privacy (WEP), a protocol used to secure Wi-Fi wireless networks, was shown to be breakable in practice because of a weakness in the RC4 cipher and aspects of the WEP design that made related-key attacks practical. WEP was later replaced by Wi-Fi Protected Access.

- In 2008, researchers conducted a proof-of-concept break of SSL using weaknesses in the MD5 hash function and certificate issuer practices that made it possible to exploit collision attacks on hash functions. The certificate issuers involved changed their practices to prevent the attack from being repeated.

Thus, while the best modern ciphers may be far more resistant to cryptanalysis than the Enigma, cryptanalysis and the broader field of information security remain quite active.

Symmetric Ciphers

- Boomerang attack
- Brute force attack
- Davies' attack
- Differential cryptanalysis
- Impossible differential cryptanalysis
- Improbable differential cryptanalysis
- Integral cryptanalysis
- Linear cryptanalysis
- Meet-in-the-middle attack
- Mod-n cryptanalysis
- Related-key attack
- Sandwich attack
- Slide attack
- XSL attack

Asymmetric Ciphers

Asymmetric cryptography (or public key cryptography) is cryptography that relies on using two (mathematically related) keys; one private, and one public. Such ciphers invariably rely on "hard" mathematical problems as the basis of their security, so an obvious point of attack is to develop methods for solving the problem. The security of two-key cryptography depends on mathematical questions in a way that single-key cryptography generally does not, and conversely links cryptanalysis to wider mathematical research in a new way.

Asymmetric schemes are designed around the (conjectured) difficulty of solving various mathematical problems. If an improved algorithm can be found to solve the problem, then the system is weakened. For example, the security of the Diffie-Hellman key exchange scheme depends on the difficulty of calculating the discrete logarithm. In 1983, Don Coppersmith found a faster way to find discrete logarithms (in certain groups), and thereby requiring cryptographers to use larger groups (or different types of groups). RSA's security depends (in part) upon the difficulty of integer factorization — a breakthrough in factoring would impact the security of RSA.

In 1980, one could factor a difficult 50-digit number at an expense of 10^{12} elementary computer operations. By 1984 the state of the art in factoring algorithms had advanced to a point where a 75-digit number could be factored in 10^{12} operations. Advances in computing technology also meant that the operations could be performed much faster, too. Moore's law predicts that computer speeds will continue to increase. Factoring techniques may continue to do so as well, but will most likely depend on mathematical insight and creativity, neither of which has ever been successfully predictable. 150-digit numbers of the kind once used in RSA have been factored. The effort was greater than above, but was not unreasonable on fast modern computers. By the start of the 21st century, 150-digit numbers were no longer considered a large enough key size for RSA. Numbers with several hundred digits were still considered too hard to factor in 2005, though methods will probably continue to improve over time, requiring key size to keep pace or other methods such as elliptic curve cryptography to be used.

Another distinguishing feature of asymmetric schemes is that, unlike attacks on symmetric cryptosystems, any cryptanalysis has the opportunity to make use of knowledge gained from the public key.

Attacking Cryptographic Hash Systems

- Birthday attack
- Rainbow table

Side-channel Attacks

- Black-bag cryptanalysis
- Man-in-the-middle attack
- Power analysis
- Replay attack
- Rubber-hose cryptanalysis
- Timing analysis

Quantum Computing Applications for Cryptanalysis

Quantum computers, which are still in the early phases of research, have potential use in cryptanalysis. For example, Shor's Algorithm could factor large numbers in polynomial time, in effect breaking some commonly used forms of public-key encryption.

By using Grover's algorithm on a quantum computer, brute-force key search can be made quadratically faster. However, this could be countered by doubling the key length.

Shared Secret

In cryptography, a shared secret is a piece of data, known only to the parties involved, in a secure communication. The shared secret can be a password, a passphrase, a big number or an array of randomly chosen bytes.

The shared secret is either shared beforehand between the communicating parties, in which case it can also be called a pre-shared key, or it is created at the start of the communication session by using a key-agreement protocol, for instance using public-key cryptography such as Diffie-Hellman or using symmetric-key cryptography such as Kerberos.

The shared secret can be used for authentication (for instance when logging into a remote system) using methods such as challenge-response or it can be fed to a key derivation function to produce one or more keys to use for encryption and/or MACing of messages.

To make unique session and message keys the shared secret is usually combined with an initialization vector (IV). An example of this is the derived unique key per transaction method.

It is also often used as an authentication measure in APIs.

Strong Cryptography

Strong cryptography or cryptographically strong are general terms applied to cryptographic systems or components that are considered highly resistant to cryptanalysis.

Demonstrating the resistance of any cryptographic scheme to attack is a complex matter, requiring extensive testing and reviews, preferably in a public forum. Good algorithms and protocols are required, and good system design and implementation is needed as well. For instance, the operating system on which the crypto software runs should be as carefully secured as possible. Users may handle passwords insecurely, or trust 'service' personnel overly much, or simply misuse the software. "Strong" thus is an imprecise term and may not apply in particular situations.

Background

The use of computers changed the process of cryptanalysis, famously with Bletchley Park's Colossus. But just as the development of digital computers and electronics helped in cryptanalysis, it also made possible much more complex ciphers. It is typically the case that use of a quality cipher is very efficient, while breaking it requires an effort many orders of magnitude larger - making cryptanalysis so inefficient and impractical as to be effectively impossible.

Since the publication of Data Encryption Standard, the Diffie-Hellman and RSA algorithm in the 1970s, cryptography has had deep connections with abstract mathematics and become a widely used tool in communications, computer networks, and computer security generally.

Cryptographically Strong Algorithms

This term "cryptographically strong" is often used to describe an encryption algorithm, and implies, in comparison to some other algorithm (which is thus cryptographically weak), greater resistance to attack. But it can also be used to describe hashing and unique identifier and filename creation algorithms. NET runtime library function Path.GetRandomFileName. In this usage, the term means "difficult to guess".

An encryption algorithm is intended to be unbreakable (in which case it is as strong as it can ever be), but might be breakable (in which case it is as weak as it can ever be) so there is not, in principle, a continuum of strength as the idiom would seem to imply: Algorithm A is stronger than Algorithm B which is stronger than Algorithm C, and so on. The situation is made more complex, and less subsumable into a single strength metric, by the fact that there are many types of cryptanalytic attack and that any given algorithm is likely to force the attacker to do more work to break it when using one attack than another.

There is only one known unbreakable cryptographic system, the one-time pad, this is not generally possible to use because of the difficulties involved in exchanging one-time pads without their being compromised. So any encryption algorithm can be compared to the perfect algorithm, the one-time pad.

The usual sense in which this term is (loosely) used, is in reference to a particular attack, brute force key search — especially in explanations for newcomers to the field. Indeed, with this attack (always assuming keys to have been randomly chosen), there is a continuum of resistance depending on the length of the key used. But even so there are two major problems: many algorithms allow use of different length keys at different times, and any algorithm can forgo use of the full key length possible. Thus, Blowfish and RC5 are block cipher algorithms whose design specifically allowed for several key lengths, and who cannot therefore be said to have any particular strength with respect to brute force key search. Furthermore, US export regulations restrict key length for exportable crypto products and in several cases in the 1980s and 1990s (e.g., famously in the case of Lotus Notes' export approval) only partial keys were used, decreasing 'strength' against brute force attack for those (export) versions. More or less the same thing happened outside the US as well, as for example in the case of more than one of the crypto algorithms in the GSM cellular telephone standard.

The term is commonly used to convey that some algorithm is suitable for some task in cryptography or information security, but also resists cryptanalysis and has no, or fewer, security weaknesses. Tasks are varied, and might include:

- generating randomness

- encrypting data

- providing a method to ensure data integrity

Cryptographically strong would seem to mean that the described method has some kind of maturity, perhaps even approved for use against different kinds of systematic attacks in theory and/or practice. Indeed, that the method may resist those attacks long enough to protect the information carried (and what stands behind the information) for a useful length of time. But due to the complexity and subtlety of the field, neither is almost ever the case. Since such assurances are not actually available in real practice, sleight of hand in language which implies that they are will generally be misleading.

There will always be uncertainty as advances (e.g., in cryptanalytic theory or merely affordable computer capacity) may reduce the effort needed to successfully use some attack method against an algorithm.

In addition, actual use of cryptographic algorithms requires their encapsulation in a cryptosystem, and doing so often introduces vulnerabilities which are not due to faults in an algorithm. For example, essentially all algorithms require random choice of keys, and any cryptosystem which does not provide such keys will be subject to attack regardless of any attack resistant qualities of the encryption algorithm(s) used.

Legal Issues

Since use of strong cryptography makes the job of intelligence agencies more difficult, many countries have enacted law or regulation restricting or simply banning the non-official use of strong crypto. For instance, the United States has defined cryptographic products as munitions since World War II and has prohibited export of cryptography beyond a certain 'strength' (measured in part by key size), and Russia banned its use by private individuals in 1995. It is not clear if the Russian ban is still in effect. France had quite strict regulations in this field, but has relaxed them in recent years.

Examples

- PGP is generally considered an example of strong cryptography, with versions running under most popular operating systems and on various hardware platforms. The open source standard for PGP operations is OpenPGP, and GnuPG is an implementation of that standard from the FSF.

- The AES algorithm is considered strong after being selected in a lengthy selection process that was open and involved numerous tests.

Examples that are not considered cryptographically strong include:

- The DES, whose 56-bit keys allow attacks via exhaustive search.

- Wired Equivalent Privacy which is subject to a number of attacks due to flaws in its design.

- The Clipper Chip, a failed initiative of the U.S. government that included key escrow provisions, allowing the government to gain access to the keys.

- Almost all classical ciphers.

The latest version of TLS protocol (version 1.2), used to secure Internet transactions, is generally considered strong. Several vulnerabilities exist in previous versions, including demonstrated attacks such as POODLE. Worse, some cipher-suites are deliberately weakened to use a 40-bit effective key to allow export under pre-1996 U.S. regulations.

References

- Kiountouzis, E.A.; Kokolakis, S.A. Information systems security: facing the information society of the 21st century. London: Chapman & Hall, Ltd. ISBN 0-412-78120-4.

- Shon Harris (2003). All-in-one CISSP Certification Exam Guide (2nd ed.). Emeryville, California: McGraw-Hill/Osborne. ISBN 0-07-222966-7.

- Harris, Shon (2008). All-in-one CISSP Certification Exam Guide (4th ed.). New York, NY: McGraw-Hill. ISBN 978-0-07-149786-2.

- Schmeh, Klaus (2003). Cryptography and public key infrastructure on the Internet. John Wiley & Sons. p. 45. ISBN 978-0-470-84745-9.

- Wyner, A. D. (October 1975). "The Wire-Tap Channel" (PDF). Bell System Technical Journal. AT&T Corporation. 54 (8): 1355–1387. doi:10.1002/j.1538-7305.1975.tb02040.x. Retrieved 2013-04-11.

- Boritz, J. Efrim. "IS Practitioners' Views on Core Concepts of Information Integrity". International Journal of Accounting Information Systems. Elsevier. Retrieved 12 August 2011.

- Krzysztof Szczypiorski (4 November 2003). "Steganography in TCP/IP Networks. State of the Art and a Proposal of a New System - HICCUPS" (PDF). Institute of Telecommunications Seminar. Retrieved 17 June 2010.

- Patrick Philippe Meier (5 June 2009). "Steganography 2.0: Digital Resistance against Repressive Regimes". irevolution.wordpress.com. Retrieved 17 June 2010.

- Steven J. Murdoch & Stephen Lewis (2005). "Embedding Covert Channels into TCP/IP" (PDF). Information Hiding Workshop. Retrieved 16 June 2010.

- Kamran Ahsan & Deepa Kundur (December 2002). "Practical Data Hiding in TCP/IP" (PDF). ACM Wksp. Multimedia Security. Retrieved 16 June 2010.

- Kundur D. & Ahsan K. (April 2003). "Practical Internet Steganography: Data Hiding in IP" (PDF). Texas Wksp. Security of Information Systems. Retrieved 16 June 2010.

- Wojciech Mazurczyk & Krzysztof Szczypiorski (November 2008). "Steganography of VoIP Streams" (PDF). Lecture Notes in Computer Science (LNCS) 5332, Springer-Verlag Berlin Heidelberg, Proc. of The 3rd International Symposium on Information Security (IS'08), Monterrey, Mexico. Retrieved 16 June 2010.

- Józef Lubacz; Wojciech Mazurczyk; Krzysztof Szczypiorski (February 2010). "Vice Over IP: The VoIP Steganography Threat". IEEE Spectrum. Retrieved 11 February 2010.

3

Types of Cryptographic Systems

Cryptography is best understood in confluence with the major topics listed in the following chapter. The major types of cryptographic systems dealt within this chapter are symmetric key algorithm and public – key cryptography. The types and approaches of public key cryptography are ID based cryptography, RSA and elliptic curve cryptography.

Symmetric-key Algorithm

Symmetric-key algorithms are algorithms for cryptography that use the same cryptographic keys for both encryption of plaintext and decryption of ciphertext. The keys may be identical or there may be a simple transformation to go between the two keys. The keys, in practice, represent a shared secret between two or more parties that can be used to maintain a private information link. This requirement that both parties have access to the secret key is one of the main drawbacks of symmetric key encryption, in comparison to public-key encryption (also known as asymmetric key encryption).

Types of Symmetric-key Algorithms

Symmetric-key encryption can use either stream ciphers or block ciphers.

- Stream ciphers encrypt the digits (typically bytes) of a message one at a time.

- Block ciphers take a number of bits and encrypt them as a single unit, padding the plaintext so that it is a multiple of the block size. Blocks of 64 bits was commonly used. The Advanced Encryption Standard (AES) algorithm approved by NIST in December 2001, and the GCM block cipher mode of operation use 128-bit blocks.

Implementations

Examples of popular symmetric algorithms include Twofish, Serpent, AES (Rijndael), Blowfish, CAST5, Grasshopper, RC4, 3DES, Skipjack, Safer+/++ (Bluetooth), and IDEA.

Cryptographic Primitives based on Symmetric Ciphers

Symmetric ciphers are commonly used to achieve other cryptographic primitives than just encryption.

Encrypting a message does not guarantee that this message is not changed while encrypted. Hence often a message authentication code is added to a ciphertext to ensure that changes to the ciphertext will be noted by the receiver. Message authentication codes can be constructed from symmetric ciphers (e.g. CBC-MAC).

However, symmetric ciphers cannot be used for non-repudiation purposes except by involving additional parties.

Another application is to build hash functions from block ciphers.

Construction of Symmetric Ciphers

Many modern block ciphers are based on a construction proposed by Horst Feistel. Feistel's construction makes it possible to build invertible functions from other functions that are themselves not invertible.

Security of Symmetric Ciphers

Symmetric ciphers have historically been susceptible to known-plaintext attacks, chosen-plaintext attacks, differential cryptanalysis and linear cryptanalysis. Careful construction of the functions for each round can greatly reduce the chances of a successful attack.

Key Generation

When used with asymmetric ciphers for key transfer, pseudorandom key generators are nearly always used to generate the symmetric cipher session keys. However, lack of randomness in those generators or in their initialization vectors is disastrous and has led to cryptanalytic breaks in the past. Therefore, it is essential that an implementation uses a source of high entropy for its initialization.

Reciprocal Cipher

A reciprocal cipher is a cipher where, just as one enters the plaintext into the cryptography system to get the ciphertext, one could enter the ciphertext into the same place in the system to get the plaintext. A reciprocal cipher is also sometimes referred as self-reciprocal cipher. Examples of reciprocal ciphers include:

- Beaufort cipher
- Enigma machine
- ROT13
- XOR cipher
- Vatsyayana cipher

Public-key Cryptography

Public-key cryptography, or asymmetric cryptography, is any cryptographic system that uses pairs of keys: *public keys* that may be disseminated widely paired with *private keys* which are known only to the owner. There are two functions that can be achieved: using a public key to authenticate that a message originated with a holder of the paired private key; or encrypting a message with a public key to ensure that only the holder of the paired private key can decrypt it.

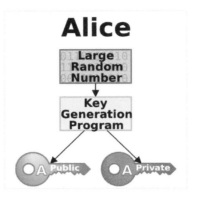

An unpredictable (typically large and random) number is used to begin generation of an acceptable pair of keys suitable for use by an asymmetric key algorithm.

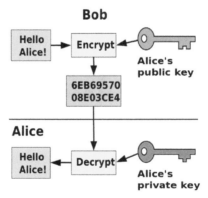

In an asymmetric key encryption scheme, anyone can encrypt messages using the public key, but only the holder of the paired private key can decrypt. Security depends on the secrecy of the private key.

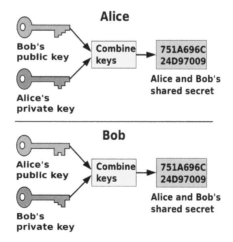

In the Diffie–Hellman key exchange scheme, each party generates a public/private key pair and distributes the public key. After obtaining an authentic copy of each other's public keys, Alice and Bob can compute a shared secret offline. The shared secret can be used, for instance, as the key for a symmetric cipher.

In a public-key encryption system, any person can encrypt a message using the public key of the receiver, but such a message can be decrypted only with the receiver's private key. For this to work it must be computationally easy for a user to generate a public and private key-pair to be used for encryption and decryption. The strength of a public-key cryptography system relies on the degree of difficulty (computational impracticality) for a properly generated private key to be determined from its corresponding public key. Security then depends only on keeping the private key private, and the public key may be published without compromising security.

Public-key cryptography systems often rely on cryptographic algorithms based on mathematical problems that currently admit no efficient solution—particularly those inherent in certain integer factorization, discrete logarithm, and elliptic curve relationships. Public key algorithms, unlike symmetric key algorithms, do *not* require a secure channel for the initial exchange of one (or more) secret keys between the parties.

Because of the computational complexity of asymmetric encryption, it is usually used only for small blocks of data, typically the transfer of a symmetric encryption key (e.g. a session key). This symmetric key is then used to encrypt the rest of the potentially long message sequence. The symmetric encryption/decryption is based on simpler algorithms and is much faster.

Message authentication involves hashing the message to produce a "digest," and encrypting the digest with the private key to produce a digital signature. Thereafter anyone can verify this signature by:

1. computing the hash of the message

2. decrypting the signature with the signer's public key

3. comparing the computed digest with the decrypted digest

Equality between the digests confirms the message is unmodified since it was signed, and that the signer, and no one else, intentionally performed the signature operation — presuming the signer's private key has remained secret. The security of such procedure depends on a hash algorithm of such quality that it is computationally impossible to alter or find a substitute message that produces the same digest - but studies have shown that even with the MD5 and SHA-1 algorithms, producing an altered or substitute message is not impossible. The current hashing standard for encryption is SHA-2. The message itself can also be used in place of the digest.

Public-key algorithms are fundamental security ingredients in cryptosystems, applications and protocols. They underpin various Internet standards, such as Transport Layer Security (TLS), S/MIME, PGP, and GPG. Some public key algorithms provide key distribution and secrecy (e.g., Diffie–Hellman key exchange), some provide digital signatures (e.g., Digital Signature Algorithm), and some provide both (e.g., RSA).

Public-key cryptography finds application in, among others, the information technology security discipline, information security. Information security (IS) is concerned with all aspects of protecting electronic information assets against security threats. Public-key cryptography is used as a method of assuring the confidentiality, authenticity and non-repudiability of electronic communications and data storage.

Description

Two of the best-known uses of public-key cryptography are:

- *Public-key encryption*, in which a message is encrypted with a recipient's public key. The message cannot be decrypted by anyone who does not possess the matching private key, who is thus presumed to be the owner of that key and the person associated with the public key. This is used in an attempt to ensure confidentiality.

- *Digital signatures*, in which a message is signed with the sender's private key and can be verified by anyone who has access to the sender's public key. This verification proves that the sender had access to the private key, and therefore is likely to be the person associated with the public key. This also ensures that the message has not been tampered with, as any manipulation of the message will result in changes to the encoded message digest, which otherwise remains unchanged between the sender and receiver.

An analogy to public-key encryption is that of a locked mail box with a mail slot. The mail slot is exposed and accessible to the public – its location (the street address) is, in essence, the public key. Anyone knowing the street address can go to the door and drop a written message through the slot. However, only the person who possesses the key can open the mailbox and read the message.

An analogy for digital signatures is the sealing of an envelope with a personal wax seal. The message can be opened by anyone, but the presence of the unique seal authenticates the sender.

A central problem with the use of public-key cryptography is confidence/proof that a particular public key is authentic, in that it is correct and belongs to the person or entity claimed, and has not been tampered with or replaced by a malicious third party. The usual approach to this problem is to use a public-key infrastructure (PKI), in which one or more third parties – known as certificate authorities – certify ownership of key pairs. PGP, in addition to being a certificate authority structure, has used a scheme generally called the "web of trust", which decentralizes such authentication of public keys by a central mechanism, and substitutes individual endorsements of the link between user and public key. To date, no fully satisfactory solution to the "public key authentication problem" has been found.

History

During the early history of cryptography, two parties would rely upon a key that they would exchange by means of a secure, but non-cryptographic, method such as a face-to-face meeting or a trusted courier. This key, which both parties kept absolutely secret, could then be used to exchange encrypted messages. A number of significant practical difficulties arise with this approach to distributing keys.

In the 1874 book *The Principles of Science* by William Stanley Jevons, he wrote:

"Can the reader say what two numbers multiplied together will produce the number 8616460799? I think it unlikely that anyone but myself will ever know." -William Stanley Jevons

Here he described the relationship of one-way functions to cryptography, and went on to discuss specifically the factorization problem used to create a trapdoor function. In July 1996, mathematician Solomon W. Golomb said: "Jevons anticipated a key feature of the RSA Algorithm for public key cryptography, although he certainly did not invent the concept of public key cryptography." (In 1869, Jevons had also invented a computing machine he called a "Logic Piano".)

Classified Discovery

In 1970, James H. Ellis, a British cryptographer at the UK Government Communications Head-quarters (GCHQ), conceived of the possibility of "non-secret encryption", (now called public-key cryptography), but could see no way to implement it. In 1973, his colleague Clifford Cocks implemented what has become known as the RSA encryption algorithm, giving a practical method of "non-secret encryption", and in 1974, another GCHQ mathematician and cryptographer, Malcolm J. Williamson, developed what is now known as Diffie–Hellman key exchange. The scheme was also passed to the NSA. With a military focus, and low computing power, the power of public-key cryptography was unrealised in both organisations:

I judged it most important for military use .... if you can share your key rapidly and electronically, you have a major advantage over your opponent. Only at the end of the evolution from Berners-Lee designing an open internet architecture for CERN, its adaptation and adoption for the Arpanet ... did public key cryptography realise its full potential. -Ralph Benjamin

Their discovery did not become public knowledge for 27 years, until the research was declassified by the British government in 1997.

Public Discovery

In 1976, an asymmetric-key cryptosystem was published by Whitfield Diffie and Martin Hellman who, influenced by Ralph Merkle's work on public-key distribution, disclosed a method of public-key agreement. This method of key exchange, which uses exponentiation in a finite field, came to be known as Diffie–Hellman key exchange. This was the first published practical method for establishing a shared secret-key over an authenticated (but not confidential) communications channel without using a prior shared secret. Merkle's "public-key-agreement technique" became known as Merkle's Puzzles, and was invented in 1974 and published in 1978.

In 1977, a generalization of Cocks' scheme was independently invented by Ron Rivest, Adi Shamir and Leonard Adleman, all then at MIT. The latter authors published their work in 1978, and the algorithm came to be known as RSA, from their initials. RSA uses exponentiation modulo a product of two very large primes, to encrypt and decrypt, performing both public key encryption and public key digital signature. Its security is connected to the extreme difficulty of factoring large integers, a problem for which there is no known efficient general technique. In 1979, Michael O. Rabin published a related cryptosystem that is probably secure as long as the factorization of the public key remains difficult – it remains an assumption that RSA also enjoys this security.

Since the 1970s, a large number and variety of encryption, digital signature, key agreement, and other techniques have been developed in the field of public-key cryptography. The ElGamal cryptosystem, invented by Taher ElGamal relies on the similar and related high level of difficulty of the discrete logarithm problem, as does the closely related DSA, which was developed at the US National Security Agency (NSA) and published by NIST as a proposed standard.

The introduction of elliptic curve cryptography by Neal Koblitz and Victor Miller, independently and simultaneously in the mid-1980s, has yielded new public-key algorithms based on the discrete logarithm problem. Although mathematically more complex, elliptic curves provide smaller key sizes and faster operations for approximately equivalent estimated security.

Typical use

Public-key cryptography is often used to secure electronic communication over an open networked environment such as the Internet, without relying on a hidden or covert channel, even for key exchange. Open networked environments are susceptible to a variety of communication security problems, such as man-in-the-middle attacks and spoofs. Communication security typically includes requirements that the communication must not be readable during transit (preserving confidentiality), the communication must not be modified during transit (preserving the integrity of the communication), the communication must originate from an identified party (sender authenticity), and the recipient must not be able to repudiate or deny receiving the communication. Combining public-key cryptography with an Enveloped Public Key Encryption (EPKE) method, allows for the secure sending of a communication over an open networked environment.

The distinguishing technique used in public-key cryptography is the use of asymmetric key algorithms, where a key used by one party to perform encryption is not the same as the key used by another in decryption. Each user has a pair of cryptographic keys – a public encryption key and a private decryption key. For example, a key pair used for digital signatures consists of a private signing key and a public verification key. The public key may be widely distributed, while the private key is known only to its proprietor. The keys are related mathematically, but the parameters are chosen so that calculating the private key from the public key is unfeasible.

In contrast, symmetric-key algorithms – variations of which have been used for thousands of years – use a *single* secret key, which must be shared and kept private by both the sender (for encryption) and the receiver (for decryption). To use a symmetric encryption scheme, the sender and receiver must securely share a key in advance.

Because symmetric key algorithms are nearly always much less computationally intensive than asymmetric ones, it is common to exchange a key using a key-exchange algorithm, then transmit data using that key and a symmetric key algorithm. PGP and the SSL/TLS family of schemes use this procedure, and are thus called *hybrid cryptosystems*.

Security

Some encryption schemes can be proven secure on the basis of the presumed difficulty of a mathematical problem, such as factoring the product of two large primes or computing discrete logarithms. Note that "secure" here has a precise mathematical meaning, and there are multiple different (meaningful) definitions of what it means for an encryption scheme to be "secure". The "right" definition depends on the context in which the scheme will be deployed.

The most obvious application of a public key encryption system is confidentiality – a message that a sender encrypts using the recipient's public key can be decrypted only by the recipient's paired private key. This assumes, of course, that no flaw is discovered in the basic algorithm used.

Another application in public-key cryptography is the digital signature. Digital signature schemes can be used for sender authentication and non-repudiation. The sender computes a digital signature for the message to be sent, then sends the signature (together with the message) to the intended receiver. Digital signature schemes have the property that signatures can be computed only with the knowledge of the correct private key. To verify that a message has been signed by a user and has not been modified, the receiver needs to know only the corresponding public key. In some cases (e.g., RSA), a single algorithm can be used to both encrypt and create digital signatures. In other cases (e.g., DSA), each algorithm can only be used for one specific purpose.

To achieve both authentication and confidentiality, the sender should include the recipient's name in the message, sign it using his private key, and then encrypt both the message and the signature using the recipient's public key.

These characteristics can be used to construct many other (sometimes surprising) cryptographic protocols and applications, such as digital cash, password-authenticated key agreement, multi-party key agreement, time-stamping services, non-repudiation protocols, etc.

Practical Considerations

Enveloped Public Key Encryption

Enveloped Public Key Encryption (EPKE) is the method of applying public-key cryptography and ensuring that an electronic communication is transmitted confidentially, has the contents of the communication protected against being modified (communication integrity) and cannot be denied from having been sent (non-repudiation). This is often the method used when securing communication on an open networked environment such by making use of the Transport Layer Security (TLS) or Secure Sockets Layer (SSL) protocols.

EPKE consists of a two-stage process that includes both Public Key Encryption (PKE) and a digital signature. Both Public Key Encryption and digital signatures make up the foundation of Enveloped Public Key Encryption (these two processes are described in full in their own sections).

For EPKE to work effectively, it is required that:

- Every participant in the communication has their own unique pair of keys. The first key that is required is a public key and the second key that is required is a private key.

- Each person's own private and public keys must be mathematically related where the private key is used to decrypt a communication sent using a public key and vice versa. Some well-known asymmetric encryption algorithms are based on the RSA cryptosystem.

- The private key must be kept absolutely private by the owner, though the public key can be published in a public directory such as with a certification authority.

To send a message using EPKE, the sender of the message first signs the message using their own private key, this ensures non-repudiation of the message. The sender then encrypts their digitally signed message using the receiver's public key thus applying a digital envelope to the message. This step ensures confidentiality during the transmission of the message. The receiver of the message then uses their private key to decrypt the message thus removing the digital envelope and then uses the sender's public key to decrypt the sender's digital signature. At this point, if the message has been unaltered during transmission, the message will be clear to the receiver.

Due to the computationally complex nature of RSA-based asymmetric encryption algorithms, the time taken to encrypt large documents or files to be transmitted can be relatively long. To speed up the process of transmission, instead of applying the sender's digital signature to the large documents or files, the sender can rather hash the documents or files using a cryptographic hash function and then digitally sign the generated hash value, therefore enforcing non-repudiation. Hashing is a much faster computation to complete as opposed to using an RSA-based digital signature algorithm alone. The sender would then sign the newly generated hash value and encrypt the original documents or files with the receiver's public key. The transmission would then take place securely and with confidentiality and non-repudiation still intact. The receiver would then verify the signature and decrypt the encrypted documents or files with their private key.

Note: The sender and receiver do not usually carry out the process mentioned above manually though, but rather rely on sophisticated software to automatically complete the EPKE process.

Public Key Encryption

The goal of Public Key Encryption (PKE) is to ensure that the communication being sent is kept confidential during transit.

To send a message using PKE, the sender of the message uses the public key of the receiver to encrypt the contents of the message. The encrypted message is then transmitted electronically to the receiver and the receiver can then use their own matching private key to decrypt the message.

The encryption process of using the receivers public key is useful for preserving the confidentiality of the message as only the receiver has the matching private key to decrypt the message. Therefore, the sender of the message cannot decrypt the message once it has been encrypted using the receivers public key. However, PKE does not address the problem of non-repudiation, as the message could have been sent by anyone that has access to the receivers public key.

Digital Signatures

The goal of a digital signature scheme is to ensure that the sender of the communication that is being sent is known to the receiver and that the sender of the message cannot repudiate a message that they sent. Therefore, the purpose of digital signatures is to ensure the non-repudiation of the message being sent. This is useful in a practical setting where a sender wishes to make an electronic purchase of shares and the receiver wants to be able to prove who requested the purchase. Digital signatures do not provide confidentiality for the message being sent.

The message is signed using the sender's private signing key. The digitally signed message is then sent to the receiver, who can then use the sender's public key to verify the signature.

Certification Authority

In order for Enveloped Public Key Encryption to be as secure as possible, there needs to be a "gatekeeper" of public and private keys, or else anyone could create key pairs and masquerade as the intended sender of a communication, proposing them as the keys of the intended sender. This digital key "gatekeeper" is known as a certification authority. A certification authority is a trusted third party that can issue public and private keys, thus certifying public keys. It also works as a depository to store key chain and enforce the trust factor.

Postal Analogies

An analogy that can be used to understand the advantages of an asymmetric system is to imagine two people, Alice and Bob, who are sending a secret message through the public mail. In this example, Alice wants to send a secret message to Bob, and expects a secret reply from Bob.

With a symmetric key system, Alice first puts the secret message in a box, and locks the box using a padlock to which she has a key. She then sends the box to Bob through regular mail. When Bob receives the box, he uses an identical copy of Alice's key (which he has somehow obtained previously, maybe by a face-to-face meeting) to open the box, and reads the message. Bob can then use the same padlock to send his secret reply.

In an asymmetric key system, Bob and Alice have separate padlocks. First, Alice asks Bob to send his open padlock to her through regular mail, keeping his key to himself. When Alice receives it she uses it to lock a box containing her message, and sends the locked box to Bob. Bob can then unlock the box with his key and read the message from Alice. To reply, Bob must similarly get Alice's open padlock to lock the box before sending it back to her.

The critical advantage in an asymmetric key system is that Bob and Alice never need to send a copy of their keys to each other. This prevents a third party – perhaps, in this example, a corrupt postal worker who opens unlocked boxes – from copying a key while it is in transit, allowing the third party to spy on all future messages sent between Alice and Bob. So, in the public key scenario, Alice and Bob need not trust the postal service as much. In addition, if Bob were careless and allowed someone else to copy *his* key, Alice's messages to *Bob* would be compromised, but Alice's messages to *other people* would remain secret, since the other people would be providing different padlocks for Alice to use.

Another kind of asymmetric key system, called a three-pass protocol, requires neither party to even touch the other party's padlock (or key to get access); Bob and Alice have separate padlocks. First, Alice puts the secret message in a box, and locks the box using a padlock to which only she has a key. She then sends the box to Bob through regular mail. When Bob receives the box, he adds his own padlock to the box, and sends it back to Alice. When Alice receives the box with the two padlocks, she removes her padlock and sends it back to Bob. When Bob receives the box with only his padlock on it, Bob can then unlock the box with his key and read the message from Alice. Note that, in this scheme, the order of decryption is NOT the same as the order of encryption – this is only possible if commutative ciphers are used. A commutative cipher is one in which the order of encryption and decryption is interchangeable, just as the order of multiplication is interchangeable (i.e., $A*B*C = A*C*B = C*B*A$). This method is secure for certain choices of commutative ciphers, but insecure for others (e.g., a simple XOR). For example, let $E_1()$ and $E_2()$ be two encryption functions, and let "M" be the message so that if Alice encrypts it using $E_1()$ and sends $E_1(M)$ to Bob. Bob then again encrypts the message as $E_2(E_1(M))$ and sends it to Alice. Now, Alice decrypts $E_2(E_1(M))$ using $E_1()$. Alice will now get $E_2(M)$, meaning when she sends this again to Bob, he will be able to decrypt the message using $E_2()$ and get "M". Although none of the keys were ever exchanged, the message "M" may well be a key (e.g., Alice's Public key). This three-pass protocol is typically used during key exchange.

Actual Algorithms: Two Linked Keys

Not all asymmetric key algorithms operate in this way. In the most common, Alice and Bob each own *two* keys, one for encryption and one for decryption. In a secure asymmetric key encryption scheme, the private key should not be deducible from the public key. This makes possible public-key encryption, since an encryption key can be published without compromising the security of messages encrypted with that key.

In other schemes, either key can be used to encrypt the message. When Bob encrypts a message with his private key, only his public key will successfully decrypt it, authenticating Bob's authorship of the message. In the alternative, when a message is encrypted with the public key, only the private key can decrypt it. In this arrangement, Alice and Bob can exchange secret messages with no prior secret agreement, each using the other's public key to encrypt, and each using his own to decrypt.

Weaknesses

Among symmetric key encryption algorithms, only the one-time pad can be proven to be secure against any adversary – no matter how much computing power is available. However, there is no public-key scheme with this property, since all public-key schemes are susceptible to a "brute-force key search attack". Such attacks are impractical if the amount of computation needed to succeed – termed the "work factor" by Claude Shannon – is out of reach of all potential attackers. In many cases, the work factor can be increased by simply choosing a longer key. But other algorithms may have much lower work factors, making resistance to a brute-force attack irrelevant. Some special and specific algorithms have been developed to aid in attacking some public key encryption algorithms – both RSA and ElGamal encryption have known attacks that are much faster than the brute-force approach. These factors have changed dramatically in recent decades, both with the decreasing cost of computing power and with new mathematical discoveries.

Aside from the resistance to attack of a particular key pair, the security of the certification hierarchy must be considered when deploying public key systems. Some certificate authority – usually a purpose-built program running on a server computer – vouches for the identities assigned to specific private keys by producing a digital certificate. Public key digital certificates are typically valid for several years at a time, so the associated private keys must be held securely over that time. When a private key used for certificate creation higher in the PKI server hierarchy is compromised, or accidentally disclosed, then a "man-in-the-middle attack" is possible, making any subordinate certificate wholly insecure.

Major weaknesses have been found for several formerly promising asymmetric key algorithms. The 'knapsack packing' algorithm was found to be insecure after the development of a new attack. Recently, some attacks based on careful measurements of the exact amount of time it takes known hardware to encrypt plain text have been used to simplify the search for likely decryption keys. Thus, mere use of asymmetric key algorithms does not ensure security. A great deal of active research is currently underway to both discover, and to protect against, new attack algorithms.

Another potential security vulnerability in using asymmetric keys is the possibility of a "man-in-the-middle" attack, in which the communication of public keys is intercepted by a third party (the "man in the middle") and then modified to provide different public keys instead. Encrypted messages and responses must also be intercepted, decrypted, and re-encrypted by the attacker using the correct public keys for different communication segments, in all instances, so as to avoid suspicion. This attack may seem to be difficult to implement in practice, but it is not impossible when using insecure media (e.g., public networks, such as the Internet or wireless forms of communications) – for example, a malicious staff member at Alice or Bob's Internet Service Provider (ISP) might find it quite easy to carry out. In the earlier postal analogy, Alice would have to have a way to make sure that the lock on the returned packet really belongs to Bob before she removes her lock and sends the packet back. Otherwise, the lock could have been put on the packet by a corrupt postal worker pretending to be Bob, so as to fool Alice.

One approach to prevent such attacks involves the use of a certificate authority, a trusted third party responsible for verifying the identity of a user of the system. This authority issues a tamper-resistant, non-spoofable digital certificate for the participants. Such certificates are signed data blocks stating that this public key belongs to that person, company, or other entity. This approach also has its weaknesses – for example, the certificate authority issuing the certificate must be trusted to have properly checked the identity of the key-holder, must ensure the correctness of the public key when it issues a certificate, must be secure from computer piracy, and must have made arrangements with all participants to check all their certificates before protected communications can begin. Web browsers, for instance, are supplied with a long list of "self-signed identity certificates" from PKI providers – these are used to check the *bona fides* of the certificate authority and then, in a second step, the certificates of potential communicators. An attacker who could subvert any single one of those certificate authorities into issuing a certificate for a bogus public key could then mount a "man-in-the-middle" attack as easily as if the certificate scheme were not used at all. In an alternate scenario rarely discussed, an attacker who penetrated an authority's servers and obtained its store of certificates and keys (public and private) would be able to spoof, masquerade, decrypt, and forge transactions without limit.

Despite its theoretical and potential problems, this approach is widely used. Examples include SSL and its successor, TLS, which are commonly used to provide security for web browser transactions (for example, to securely send credit card details to an online store).

Computational Cost

The public key algorithms known thus far are relatively computationally costly compared with most symmetric key algorithms of apparently equivalent security. The difference factor is the use of typically quite large keys. This has important implications for their practical use. Most are used in hybrid cryptosystems for reasons of efficiency – in such a cryptosystem, a shared secret key ("session key") is generated by one party, and this much briefer session key is then encrypted by each recipient's public key. Each recipient then uses his own private key to decrypt the session key.

Once all parties have obtained the session key, they can use a much faster symmetric algorithm to encrypt and decrypt messages. In many of these schemes, the session key is unique to each message exchange, being pseudo-randomly chosen for each message.

Associating Public Keys with Identities

The binding between a public key and its "owner" must be correct, or else the algorithm may function perfectly and yet be entirely insecure in practice. As with most cryptography applications, the protocols used to establish and verify this binding are critically important. Associating a public key with its owner is typically done by protocols implementing a public key infrastructure – these allow the validity of the association to be formally verified by reference to a trusted third party in the form of either a hierarchical certificate authority (e.g., X.509), a local trust model (e.g., SPKI), or a web of trust scheme, like that originally built into PGP and GPG, and still to some extent usable with them. Whatever the cryptographic assurance of the protocols themselves, the association between a public key and its owner is ultimately a matter of subjective judgment on the part of the trusted third party, since the key is a mathematical entity, while the owner – and the connection between owner and key – are not. For this reason, the formalism of a public key infrastructure must provide for explicit statements of the policy followed when making this judgment. For example, the complex and never fully implemented X.509 standard allows a certificate authority to identify its policy by means of an object identifier, which functions as an index into a catalog of registered policies. Policies may exist for many different purposes, ranging from anonymity to military classifications.

Relation to Real World Events

A public key will be known to a large and, in practice, unknown set of users. All events requiring revocation or replacement of a public key can take a long time to take full effect with all who must be informed (i.e., all those users who possess that key). For this reason, systems that must react to events in real time (e.g., safety-critical systems or national security systems) should not use public-key encryption without taking great care. There are four issues of interest:

Privilege of Key Revocation

A malicious (or erroneous) revocation of some (or all) of the keys in the system is likely, or in the second case, certain, to cause a complete failure of the system. If public keys can be revoked individually, this is a possibility. However, there are design approaches that can reduce the practical chance of this occurring. For example, by means of certificates, we can create what is called a "compound principal" – one such principal could be "Alice and Bob have Revoke Authority". Now, only Alice and Bob (in concert) can revoke a key, and neither Alice nor Bob can revoke keys alone. However, revoking a key now requires both Alice *and* Bob to be available, and this creates a problem of reliability. In concrete terms, from a security point of view, there is now a "single point of failure" in the public key revocation system. A successful Denial of Service attack against either Alice or Bob (or both) will block a required revocation. In fact, any partition of authority between Alice and Bob will have this effect, regardless of how it comes about.

Because the principle allowing revocation authority for keys is very powerful, the mechanisms used to control it should involve both as many participants as possible (to guard against malicious attacks of this type), while at the same time as few as possible (to ensure that a key can be revoked without dangerous delay). Public key certificates that include an expiration date are unsatisfactory in that the expiration date may not correspond with a real-world revocation but at least such certificates need not all be tracked down system-wide, nor must all users be in constant contact with the system at all times.

Distribution of a New Key

After a key has been revoked, or when a new user is added to a system, a new key must be distributed in some predetermined manner. Assume that Carol's key has been revoked (e.g., by exceeding its expiration date, or because of a compromise of Carol's matching private key). Until a new key has been distributed, Carol is effectively "out of contact". No one will be able to send her messages without violating system protocols (i.e., without a valid public key, no one can encrypt messages to her), and messages from her cannot be signed, for the same reason. Or, in other words, the "part of the system" controlled by Carol is, in essence, unavailable. Security requirements have been ranked higher than system availability in such designs.

One could leave the power to create (and certify) keys (as well as to revoke them) in the hands of each user – the original PGP design did so – but this raises problems of user understanding and operation. For security reasons, this approach has considerable difficulties – if nothing else, some users will be forgetful, or inattentive, or confused. On the one hand, a message revoking a public key certificate should be spread as fast as possible, while on the other hand, parts of the system might be rendered inoperable *before* a new key can be installed. The time window can be reduced to zero by always issuing the new key together with the certificate that revokes the old one, but this requires co-location of authority to both revoke keys and generate new keys.

It is most likely a system-wide failure if the (possibly combined) principal that issues new keys fails by issuing keys improperly. This is an instance of a "common mutual exclusion" – a design can make the reliability of a system high, but only at the cost of system availability (and *vice versa*).

Spreading the Revocation

Notification of a key certificate revocation must be spread to all those who might potentially hold it, and as rapidly as possible.

There are but two means of spreading information (i.e., a key revocation) in a distributed system: either the information is "pushed" to users from a central point (or points), or else it is "pulled" from a central point(or points) by the end users.

Pushing the information is the simplest solution, in that a message is sent to all participants. However, there is no way of knowing whether all participants will actually *receive* the message. If the number of participants is large, and some of their physical or network distances are great, then the probability of complete success (which is, in ideal circumstances, required for system security) will be rather low. In a partly updated state, the system is particularly vulnerable to "denial of service" attacks as security has been breached, and a vulnerability window will continue to exist as long as some users have not "gotten the word". Put another way, pushing certificate revocation messages is neither easy to secure, nor very reliable.

The alternative to pushing is pulling. In the extreme, all certificates contain all the keys needed to verify that the public key of interest (i.e., the one belonging to the user to whom one wishes to send a message, or whose signature is to be checked) is still valid. In this case, at least some use of the system will be blocked if a user cannot reach the verification service (i.e., one of the systems that can establish the current validity of another user's key). Again, such a system design can be made as reliable as one wishes, at the cost of lowering security – the more servers to check for the possibility of a key revocation, the longer the window of vulnerability.

Another trade-off is to use a somewhat less reliable, but more secure, verification service, but to include an expiration date for each of the verification sources. How long this "timeout" should be is a decision that requires a trade-off between availability and security that will have to be decided in advance, at the time of system design.

Recovery from a Leaked Key

Assume that the principal authorized to revoke a key has decided that a certain key must be revoked. In most cases, this happens after the fact – for instance, it becomes known that at some time in the past an event occurred that endangered a private key. Let us denote the time at which it is decided that the compromise occurred as T.

Such a compromise has two implications. First, messages encrypted with the matching public key (now or in the past) can no longer be assumed to be secret. One solution to avoid this problem is to use a protocol that has perfect forward secrecy. Second, signatures made with the *no-longer-trusted-to-be-actually-private key* after time T can no longer be assumed to be authentic without additional information (i.e., who, where, when, etc.) about the events leading up to the digital signature. These will not always be available, and so all such digital signatures will be less than credible. A solution to reduce the impact of leaking a private key of a signature scheme is to use timestamps.

Loss of secrecy and/or authenticity, even for a single user, has system-wide security implications, and a strategy for recovery must thus be established. Such a strategy will determine who has authority to, and under what conditions one must, revoke a public key certificate. One must also decide how to spread the revocation, and ideally, how to deal with all messages signed with the key since time T (which will rarely be known precisely). Messages sent to that user (which require the proper – now compromised – private key to decrypt) must be considered compromised as well, no matter when they were sent.

Examples

Examples of well-regarded asymmetric key techniques for varied purposes include:

- Diffie–Hellman key exchange protocol
- DSS (Digital Signature Standard), which incorporates the Digital Signature Algorithm
- ElGamal
- Various elliptic curve techniques
- Various password-authenticated key agreement techniques

- Paillier cryptosystem

- RSA encryption algorithm (PKCS#1)

- Cramer–Shoup cryptosystem

- YAK authenticated key agreement protocol

Examples of asymmetric key algorithms not widely adopted include:

- NTRUEncrypt cryptosystem

- McEliece cryptosystem

Examples of notable – yet insecure – asymmetric key algorithms include:

- Merkle–Hellman knapsack cryptosystem

Examples of protocols using asymmetric key algorithms include:

- S/MIME

- GPG, an implementation of OpenPGP

- Internet Key Exchange

- PGP

- ZRTP, a secure VoIP protocol

- Secure Socket Layer, now codified as the IETF standard Transport Layer Security (TLS)

- SILC

- SSH

- Bitcoin

- Off-the-Record Messaging

Types and Approaches of Public Key Cryptography

ID-based Cryptography

ID-based encryption, or identity-based encryption (IBE), is an important primitive of ID-based cryptography. As such it is a type of public-key encryption in which the public key of a user is some unique information about the identity of the user (e.g. a user's email address). This means that a sender who has access to the public parameters of the system can encrypt a message using e.g. the text-value of the receiver's name or email address as a key. The receiver obtains its decryption key from a central authority, which needs to be trusted as it generates secret keys for every user.

ID-based encryption was proposed by Adi Shamir in 1984. He was however only able to give an instantiation of identity-based signatures. Identity-based encryption remained an open problem for many years. The pairing-based Boneh–Franklin scheme and Cocks's encryption scheme based on quadratic residues both solved the IBE problem in 2001.

Usage

Identity-based systems allow any party to generate a public key from a known identity value such as an ASCII string. A trusted third party, called the Private Key Generator (PKG), generates the corresponding private keys. To operate, the PKG first publishes a master public key, and retains the corresponding master private key (referred to as *master key*). Given the master public key, any party can compute a public key corresponding to the identity *ID* by combining the master public key with the identity value. To obtain a corresponding private key, the party authorized to use the identity *ID* contacts the PKG, which uses the master private key to generate the private key for identity *ID*.

As a result, parties may encrypt messages (or verify signatures) with no prior distribution of keys between individual participants. This is extremely useful in cases where pre-distribution of authenticated keys is inconvenient or infeasible due to technical restraints. However, to decrypt or sign messages, the authorized user must obtain the appropriate private key from the PKG. A caveat of this approach is that the PKG must be highly trusted, as it is capable of generating any user's private key and may therefore decrypt (or sign) messages without authorization. Because any user's private key can be generated through the use of the third party's secret, this system has inherent key escrow. A number of variant systems have been proposed which remove the escrow including certificate-based encryption, secure key issuing cryptography and certificateless cryptography.

The steps involved are depicted in this diagram:

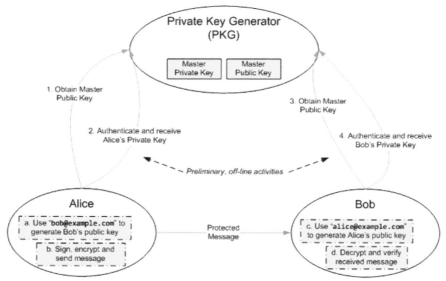

ID Based Encryption: Offline and Online Steps

Protocol Framework

Dan Boneh and Matthew K. Franklin defined a set of four algorithms that form a complete IBE system:

- Setup: This algorithm is run by the PKG one time for creating the whole IBE environment. The master key is kept secret and used to derive users' private keys, while the system parameters are made public. It accepts a security parameter k (i.e. binary length of key material) and outputs:

1. A set $\mathcal{P}$ of system parameters, including the message space and ciphertext space $\mathcal{M}$ and $\mathcal{C}$,

2. a master key K_m.

- Extract: This algorithm is run by the PKG when a user requests his private key. Note that the verification of the authenticity of the requestor and the secure transport of d are problems with which IBE protocols do not try to deal. It takes as input $\mathcal{P}$, K_m and an identifier $ID \in \{0,1\}^*$ and returns the private key d for user ID.

- Encrypt: Takes $\mathcal{P}$, a message $m \in \mathcal{M}$ and $ID \in \{0,1\}^*$ and outputs the encryption $c \in \mathcal{C}$.

- Decrypt: Accepts d, $\mathcal{P}$ and $c \in \mathcal{C}$ and returns $m \in \mathcal{M}$.

Correctness Constraint

In order for the whole system to work, one has to postulate that:

$$\forall m \in \mathcal{M}, ID \in \{0,1\}^* : Decrypt\left(Extract\left(\mathcal{P}, K_m, ID\right), \mathcal{P}, Encrypt\left(\mathcal{P}, m, ID\right)\right) = m$$

Encryption Schemes

The most efficient identity-based encryption schemes are currently based on bilinear pairings on elliptic curves, such as the Weil or Tate pairings. The first of these schemes was developed by Dan Boneh and Matthew K. Franklin (2001), and performs probabilistic encryption of arbitrary ciphertexts using an Elgamal-like approach. Though the Boneh-Franklin scheme is provably secure, the security proof rests on relatively new assumptions about the hardness of problems in certain elliptic curve groups.

Another approach to identity-based encryption was proposed by Clifford Cocks in 2001. The Cocks IBE scheme is based on well-studied assumptions (the quadratic residuosity assumption) but encrypts messages one bit at a time with a high degree of ciphertext expansion. Thus it is highly inefficient and impractical for sending all but the shortest messages, such as a session key for use with a symmetric cipher.

A third approach to IBE is through the use of lattices.

Identity-based Encryption Algorithms

The following lists practical identity-based encryption algorithms

- Boneh–Franklin (BF-IBE).

- Sakai–Kasahara (SK-IBE).

- Boneh–Boyen (BB-IBE).

All these algorithms have security proofs.

Advantages

One of the major advantages of any identity-based encryption scheme is that if there are only a finite number of users, after all users have been issued with keys the third party's secret can be destroyed. This can take place because this system assumes that, once issued, keys are always valid (as this basic system lacks a method of key revocation). The majority of derivatives of this system which have key revocation lose this advantage.

Moreover, as public keys are derived from identifiers, IBE eliminates the need for a public key distribution infrastructure. The authenticity of the public keys is guaranteed implicitly as long as the transport of the private keys to the corresponding user is kept secure (Authenticity, Integrity, Confidentiality).

Apart from these aspects, IBE offers interesting features emanating from the possibility to encode additional information into the identifier. For instance, a sender might specify an expiration date for a message. He appends this timestamp to the actual recipient's identity (possibly using some binary format like X.509). When the receiver contacts the PKG to retrieve the private key for this public key, the PKG can evaluate the identifier and decline the extraction if the expiration date has passed. Generally, embedding data in the ID corresponds to opening an additional channel between sender and PKG with authenticity guaranteed through the dependency of the private key on the identifier.

Drawbacks

- If a Private Key Generator (PKG) is compromised, all messages protected over the entire lifetime of the public-private key pair used by that server are also compromised. This makes the PKG a high-value target to adversaries. To limit the exposure due to a compromised server, the master private-public key pair could be updated with a new independent key pair. However, this introduces a key-management problem where all users must have the most recent public key for the server.

- Because the Private Key Generator (PKG) generates private keys for users, it may decrypt and/or sign any message without authorization. This implies that IBE systems cannot be used for non-repudiation. This may not be an issue for organizations that host their own PKG and are willing to trust their system administrators and do not require non-repudiation.

- The issue of implicit key escrow does not exist with the current PKI system, wherein private keys are usually generated on the user's computer. Depending on the context key escrow can be seen as a positive feature (e.g., within Enterprises). A number of variant systems have been proposed which remove the escrow including certificate-based encryption, secret sharing, secure key issuing cryptography and certificateless cryptography.

- A secure channel between a user and the Private Key Generator (PKG) is required for transmitting the private key on joining the system. Here, a SSL-like connection is a common solution for a large-scale system. It is important to observe that users that hold accounts with the PKG must be able to authenticate themselves. In principle, this may be achieved through username, password or through public key pairs managed on smart cards.

- IBE solutions may rely on cryptographic techniques that are insecure against code breaking quantum computer attacks.

RSA (Cryptosystem)

RSA is one of the first practical public-key cryptosystems and is widely used for secure data transmission. In such a cryptosystem, the encryption key is public and differs from the decryption key which is kept secret. In RSA, this asymmetry is based on the practical difficulty of factoring the product of two large prime numbers, the factoring problem. RSA is made of the initial letters of the surnames of Ron Rivest, Adi Shamir, and Leonard Adleman, who first publicly described the algorithm in 1977. Clifford Cocks, an English mathematician working for the UK intelligence agency GCHQ, had developed an equivalent system in 1973, but it was not declassified until 1997.

A user of RSA creates and then publishes a public key based on two large prime numbers, along with an auxiliary value. The prime numbers must be kept secret. Anyone can use the public key to encrypt a message, but with currently published methods, if the public key is large enough, only someone with knowledge of the prime numbers can feasibly decode the message. Breaking RSA encryption is known as the RSA problem; whether it is as hard as the factoring problem remains an open question.

RSA is a relatively slow algorithm, and because of this it is less commonly used to directly encrypt user data. More often, RSA passes encrypted shared keys for symmetric key cryptography which in turn can perform bulk encryption-decryption operations at much higher speed.

History

Adi Shamir, one of the authors of RSA: Rivest, Shamir and Adleman

The idea of an asymmetric public-private key cryptosystem is attributed to Whitfield Diffie and Martin Hellman, who published the concept in 1976. They also introduced digital signatures and attempted to apply number theory; their formulation used a shared secret key created from exponentiation of some number, modulo a prime number. However, they left open the problem of realizing a one-way function, possibly because the difficulty of factoring was not well studied at the time.

Ron Rivest, Adi Shamir, and Leonard Adleman at MIT made several attempts over the course of a year to create a one-way function that is hard to invert. Rivest and Shamir, as computer scientists, proposed many potential functions while Adleman, as a mathematician, was responsible for finding their weaknesses. They tried many approaches including "knapsack-based" and "permutation polynomials". For a time they thought it was impossible for what they wanted to achieve due to contradictory requirements. In April 1977, they spent Passover at the house of a student and drank a good deal of Manischewitz wine before returning to their home at around midnight. Rivest, unable to sleep, lay on the couch with a math textbook and started thinking about their one-way function. He spent the rest of the night formalizing his idea and had much of the paper ready by daybreak. The algorithm is now known as RSA – the initials of their surnames in same order as their paper.

Clifford Cocks, an English mathematician working for the UK intelligence agency GCHQ, described an equivalent system in an internal document in 1973. However, given the relatively expensive computers needed to implement it at the time, it was mostly considered a curiosity and, as far as is publicly known, was never deployed. His discovery, however, was not revealed until 1997 due to its top-secret classification.

Kid-RSA (KRSA) is a simplified public-key cipher published in 1997, designed for educational purposes. Some people feel that learning Kid-RSA gives insight into RSA and other public-key ciphers, analogous to simplified DES.

Patent

MIT was granted U.S. Patent 4,405,829 for a "Cryptographic communications system and method" that used the algorithm, on September 20, 1983. Though the patent was going to expire on September 21, 2000 (the term of patent was 17 years at the time), the algorithm was released to the public domain by RSA Security on September 6, 2000, two weeks earlier. Since a paper describing the algorithm had been published in August 1977, prior to the December 1977 filing date of the patent application, regulations in much of the rest of the world precluded patents elsewhere and only the US patent was granted. Had Cocks' work been publicly known, a patent in the US would not have been possible either.

From the DWPI's abstract of the patent,

The system includes a communications channel coupled to at least one terminal having an encoding device and to at least one terminal having a decoding device. A message-to-be-transferred is enciphered to ciphertext at the encoding terminal by encoding the message as a number M in a predetermined set. That number is then raised to a first predetermined power (associated with the intended receiver) and finally computed. The remainder or residue, C, is... computed when the exponentiated number is divided by the product of two predetermined prime numbers (associated with the intended receiver).

Operation

The RSA algorithm involves four steps: key generation, key distribution, encryption and decryption.

RSA involves a *public key* and a *private key*. The public key can be known by everyone and is used for encrypting messages. The intention is that messages encrypted with the public key can only be decrypted in a reasonable amount of time using the private key.

The basic principle behind RSA is the observation that it is practical to find three very large positive integers e, d and n such that with modular exponentiation for all m:

$$(m^e)^d \equiv m \pmod{n}$$

and that even knowing e and n or even m it can be extremely difficult to find d.

Additionally, for some operations it is convenient that the order of the two exponentiations can be changed and that this relation also implies:

$$(m^d)^e \equiv m \pmod{n}$$

Key Distribution

To enable Bob to send his encrypted messages, Alice transmits her public key (n, e) to Bob via a reliable, but not necessarily secret route. The private key is never distributed.

Encryption

Suppose that Bob would like to send message M to Alice.

He first turns M into an integer m, such that $0 \le m < n$ and $\gcd(m, n) = 1$ (that is, m and n are co-prime integers) by using an agreed-upon reversible protocol known as a padding scheme. He then computes the ciphertext c, using Alice's public key e, corresponding to

$$c \equiv m^e \pmod{n}$$

This can be done reasonably quickly, even for 500-bit numbers, using modular exponentiation. Bob then transmits c to Alice.

Decryption

Alice can recover m from c by using her private key exponent d by computing

$$c^d \equiv (m^e)^d \equiv m \pmod{n}$$

Given m, she can recover the original message M by reversing the padding scheme.

Key Generation

The keys for the RSA algorithm are generated the following way:

1. Choose two distinct prime numbers p and q.

    o   For security purposes, the integers p and q should be chosen at random, and should be similar in magnitude but 'differ in length by a few digits' to make factoring harder. Prime integers can be efficiently found using a primality test.

2. Compute $n = pq$.

    o n is used as the modulus for both the public and private keys. Its length, usually expressed in bits, is the key length.

3. Compute $\varphi(n) = \varphi(p)\varphi(q) = (p-1)(q-1) = n - (p+q-1)$, where φ is Euler's totient function. This value is kept private.

4. Choose an integer e such that $1 < e < \varphi(n)$ and $\gcd(e, \varphi(n)) = 1$; i.e., e and $\varphi(n)$ are coprime.

5. Determine d as $d \equiv e^{-1} \pmod{\varphi(n)}$; i.e., d is the modular multiplicative inverse of e (modulo $\varphi(n)$)

    •   This is more clearly stated as: solve for d given $d{\cdot}e \equiv 1 \pmod{\varphi(n)}$

    • e having a short bit-length and small Hamming weight results in more efficient encryption – most commonly $2^{16} + 1 = 65{,}537$. However, much smaller values of e (such as 3) have been shown to be less secure in some settings.

    • e is released as the public key exponent.

    • d is kept as the private key exponent.

The *public key* consists of the modulus n and the public (or encryption) exponent e. The *private key* consists of the modulus n and the private (or decryption) exponent d, which must be kept secret. p, q, and $\varphi(n)$ must also be kept secret because they can be used to calculate d.

•   An alternative, used by PKCS#1, is to choose d matching $de \equiv 1 \pmod{\lambda}$ with $\lambda = \text{lcm}(p-1, q-1)$, where lcm is the least common multiple. Using λ instead of $\varphi(n)$ allows more choices for d. λ can also be defined using the Carmichael function, $\lambda(n)$.

Since any common factors of $(p-1)$ and $(q-1)$ are present in the factorisation of pq − 1, it is recommended that $(p-1)$ and $(q-1)$ have only very small common factors, if any besides the necessary 2.

Note: The authors of RSA carry out the key generation by choosing d and then computing e as the modular multiplicative inverse of d (modulo $\varphi(n)$). Since it is beneficial to use a small value for e (i.e. 65,537) in order to speed up the encryption function, current implementations of RSA, such as PKCS#1 choose e and compute d instead.

Example

Here is an example of RSA encryption and decryption. The parameters used here are artificially small, but one can also use OpenSSL to generate and examine a real keypair.

1. Choose two distinct prime numbers, such as

    $p = 61$ and $q = 53$

2. Compute $n = pq$ giving

$$n = 61 \times 53 = 3233$$

3. Compute the totient of the product as $\varphi(n) = (p-1)(q-1)$ giving

$$\varphi(3233) = (61-1)(53-1) = 3120$$

4. Choose any number $1 < e < 3120$ that is coprime to 3120. Choosing a prime number for e leaves us only to check that e is not a divisor of 3120.

Let $e = 17$

5. Compute d, the modular multiplicative inverse of e (mod $\varphi(n)$) yielding,

$$d = 2753$$

Worked example for the modular multiplicative inverse:

$$d \times e \bmod \varphi(n) = 1$$

$$2753 \times 17 \bmod 3120 = 1$$

The public key is (n = 3233, e = 17). For a padded plaintext message m, the encryption function is

$$m(c) = c^{2753} \bmod 3233$$

The private key is (d = 2753). For an encrypted ciphertext c, the decryption function is

$$m(c) = c^{2753} \bmod 3233$$

For instance, in order to encrypt m = 65, we calculate

$$c = 65^{17} \bmod 3233 = 2790$$

To decrypt c = 2790, we calculate

$$m = 2790^{2753} \bmod 3233 = 65$$

Both of these calculations can be computed efficiently using the square-and-multiply algorithm for modular exponentiation. In real-life situations the primes selected would be much larger; in our example it would be trivial to factor n, 3233 (obtained from the freely available public key) back to the primes p and q. e, also from the public key, is then inverted to get d, thus acquiring the private key.

Practical implementations use the Chinese remainder theorem to speed up the calculation using modulus of factors (mod pq using mod p and mod q).

The values d_p, d_q and q_{inv}, which are part of the private key are computed as follows:

$$d_p = d \bmod (p-1) = 2753 \bmod (61-1) = 53$$

$$d_q = d \bmod (q-1) = 2753 \bmod (53-1) = 49$$

$$q_{inv} = q^{-1} \bmod p = 53^{-1} \bmod 61 = 38$$

$$\Rightarrow (q_{\text{inv}} \times q) \bmod p = 38 \times 53 \bmod 61 = 1$$

Here is how d_p, d_q and q_{inv} are used for efficient decryption. (Encryption is efficient by choice of a suitable d and e pair)

$$m_1 = c^{d_p} \bmod p = 2790^{53} \bmod 61 = 4$$

$$m_2 = c^{d_q} \bmod q = 2790^{49} \bmod 53 = 12$$

$$h = (q_{\text{inv}} \times (m_1 - m_2)) \bmod p = (38 \times -8) \bmod 61 = 1$$

$$m = m_2 + h \times q = 12 + 1 \times 53 = 65$$

Code

A working example in JavaScript. This code should not be used in production, as numbers generated by JavaScript's Math.random() are not cryptographically secure.

```
'use strict';

/**
 * RSA hash function reference implementation.
 *
 * @namespace
 */

var RSA = {};

/**
 * Generates an RSA hash
 * https://en.wikipedia.org/wiki/RSA_(cryptosystem)#A_working_example
 *
 * @returns {array} Result of RSA generation
 */

RSA.generate = function(){
    /**
     * Calculate modular multiplicative inverse.
     * https://en.wikipedia.org/wiki/Modular_multiplicative_inverse
     * Function based on PHP variant on http://rosettacode.org/wiki/Modular_inverse
     *
     * @param   {a} int
     * @param   {n} int
     * @returns {int} Result of modular multiplicative inverse.
     */

    function modular_multiplicative_inverse(a, n){
        var t = 0,
```

```
      nt = 1,
       r  = n,
    if (n < 0){
        n = -n;
    }
    if (a < 0){
        a = n - (-a % n);
    }
    nr = a % n;
        while (nr !== 0) {
                var quot= (r/nr) | 0;
                var tmp = nt;  nt = t - quot*nt;  t = tmp;
                   tmp = nr;  nr = r - quot*nr;  r = tmp;
        }
        if (r > 1) { return -1; }
        if (t < 0) { t += n; }
        return t;
}
/**
 * Generates a random prime
 *
 * @param   {min} int, minimal value
 * @param   {max} int, maximal value
 * @returns {int} a random generated prime
 */
function random_prime(min, max){
   var p = Math.floor(Math.random() * ((max - 1) - min + 1)) + min;
   if(bigInt(p).isPrime()===true){
      return p;
   } else {
      return random_prime(min, max);
   }
}
// generate values
var p = random_prime(1, 255), // 8 bit
   q = random_prime(1, 255), // 8 bit
   n = p * q,
   t = (p - 1) * (q - 1), // totient as φ(n) = (p – 1)(q – 1)
   e = random_prime(1, t),
   d = modular_multiplicative_inverse(e, t);
return {
     n: n, // public key (part I)
   e: e, // public key (part II)
   d: d  // private key
};
```

```
};
/**
 * Encrypt
 * Uses BigInteger.js https://github.com/peterolson/BigInteger.js/tree/master
 *
 * @param   {m} int, the 'message' to be encoded
 * @param   {n} int, n value returned from generate_rsa() aka public key (part I)
 * @param   {e} int, e value returned from generate_rsa() aka public key (part II)
 * @returns {int} encrypted hash
 */
RSA.encrypt = function(m, n, e){
        return bigInt(m).pow(e).mod(n);
};
/**
 * Decrypt
 * Uses BigInteger.js https://github.com/peterolson/BigInteger.js/tree/master
 *
 * @param   {mEnc} int, the 'message' to be decoded (encoded with RSA_encrypt())
 * @param   {d} int, d value returned from generate_rsa() aka private key
 * @param   {n} int, n value returned from generate_rsa() aka public key (part I)
 * @returns {int} decrypted hash
 */
RSA.decrypt = function(mEnc, d, n){
        return bigInt(mEnc).pow(d).mod(n);
};
```

Signing Messages

Suppose Alice uses Bob's public key to send him an encrypted message. In the message, she can claim to be Alice but Bob has no way of verifying that the message was actually from Alice since anyone can use Bob's public key to send him encrypted messages. In order to verify the origin of a message, RSA can also be used to sign a message.

Suppose Alice wishes to send a signed message to Bob. She can use her own private key to do so. She produces a hash value of the message, raises it to the power of d (modulo n) (as she does when decrypting a message), and attaches it as a "signature" to the message. When Bob receives the signed message, he uses the same hash algorithm in conjunction with Alice's public key. He raises the signature to the power of e (modulo n) (as he does when encrypting a message), and compares the resulting hash value with the message's actual hash value. If the two agree, he knows that the author of the message was in possession of Alice's private key, and that the message has not been tampered with since.

Proofs of Correctness

Proof using Fermat's Little Theorem

The proof of the correctness of RSA is based on Fermat's little theorem. This theorem states that if

p is prime and p does not divide an integer a then

$$a^{p-1} \equiv 1 \pmod{p}$$

We want to show that $m^{ed} \equiv m$ (mod pq) for every integer m when p and q are distinct prime numbers and e and d are positive integers satisfying

$$ed \equiv 1 \pmod{\phi(pq)}.$$

Since $\phi(pq) = (p-1)(q-1)$, we can write

$$ed - 1 = h(p-1)(q-1)$$

for some nonnegative integer h.

To check whether two numbers, like m^{ed} and m, are congruent mod pq it suffices (and in fact is equivalent) to check they are congruent mod p and mod q separately. (This is part of the Chinese remainder theorem, although it is not the significant part of that theorem.) To show $m^{ed} \equiv m$ (mod p), we consider two cases: $m \equiv 0$ (mod p) and $m \not\equiv 0$ (mod p).

In the first case, m is a multiple of p, thus m^{ed} is a multiple of p, so $m^{ed} \equiv 0 \equiv m$ (mod p). In the second case

$$m^{ed} = m^{(ed-1)}m = m^{h(p-1)(q-1)}m = \left(m^{p-1}\right)^{h(q-1)}m \equiv 1^{h(q-1)}m \equiv m \pmod{p}$$

where we used Fermat's little theorem to replace m^{p-1} mod p with 1.

The verification that $m^{ed} \equiv m$ (mod q) proceeds in a similar way, treating separately the cases $m \equiv 0$ (mod q) and $m \not\equiv 0$ (mod q).

In the first case m^{ed} is a multiple of q, so $m^{ed} \equiv 0 \equiv m$ (mod q). In the second case

$$m^{ed} = m^{(ed-1)}m = m^{h(p-1)(q-1)}m = \left(m^{q-1}\right)^{h(p-1)}m \equiv 1^{h(p-1)}m \equiv m \pmod{q}$$

This completes the proof that, for any integer m, and integers e, d such that $ed \equiv 1 \pmod{\phi(pq)}$,

$$\left(m^e\right)^d \equiv m \pmod{pq}$$

Proof using Euler's Theorem

Although the original paper of Rivest, Shamir, and Adleman used Fermat's little theorem to explain why RSA works, it is common to find proofs that rely instead on Euler's theorem.

We want to show that $m^{ed} \equiv m$ (mod n), where $n = pq$ is a product of two different prime numbers and e and d are positive integers satisfying $ed \equiv 1$ (mod $\varphi(n)$). Since e and d are positive, we can write $ed = 1 + h\varphi(n)$ for some non-negative integer h. *Assuming* that m is relatively prime to n, we have

$$m^{ed} = m^{1+h\varphi(n)} = m\left(m^{\varphi(n)}\right)^{h} \equiv m(1)^h \equiv m \pmod{n}$$

where the second-last congruence follows from Euler's theorem.

When m is not relatively prime to n, the argument just given is invalid. This is highly improbable (only a proportion of $1/p + 1/q - 1/(pq)$ numbers have this property), but even in this case the desired congruence is still true. Either $m \equiv 0 \pmod p$ or $m \equiv 0 \pmod q$, and these cases can be treated using the previous proof.

Padding

Attacks Against Plain RSA

There are a number of attacks against plain RSA as described below.

- When encrypting with low encryption exponents (e.g., $e = 3$) and small values of the m, (i.e., $m < n^{1/e}$) the result of m^e is strictly less than the modulus n. In this case, ciphertexts can be easily decrypted by taking the eth root of the ciphertext over the integers.

- If the same clear text message is sent to e or more recipients in an encrypted way, and the receivers share the same exponent e, but different p, q, and therefore n, then it is easy to decrypt the original clear text message via the Chinese remainder theorem. Johan Håstad noticed that this attack is possible even if the cleartexts are not equal, but the attacker knows a linear relation between them. This attack was later improved by Don Coppersmith.

- Because RSA encryption is a deterministic encryption algorithm (i.e., has no random component) an attacker can successfully launch a chosen plaintext attack against the cryptosystem, by encrypting likely plaintexts under the public key and test if they are equal to the ciphertext. A cryptosystem is called semantically secure if an attacker cannot distinguish two encryptions from each other even if the attacker knows (or has chosen) the corresponding plaintexts. As described above, RSA without padding is not semantically secure.

- RSA has the property that the product of two ciphertexts is equal to the encryption of the product of the respective plaintexts. That is $m_1^e m_2^e \equiv (m_1 m_2)^e \pmod n$. Because of this multiplicative property a chosen-ciphertext attack is possible. E.g., an attacker, who wants to know the decryption of a ciphertext $c \equiv m^e \pmod n$ may ask the holder of the private key d to decrypt an unsuspicious-looking ciphertext $c' \equiv cr^e \pmod n$ for some value r chosen by the attacker. Because of the multiplicative property c' is the encryption of $mr \pmod n$. Hence, if the attacker is successful with the attack, he will learn $mr \pmod n$ from which he can derive the message m by multiplying mr with the modular inverse of r modulo n.

Padding Schemes

To avoid these problems, practical RSA implementations typically embed some form of structured, randomized padding into the value m before encrypting it. This padding ensures that m does not fall into the range of insecure plaintexts, and that a given message, once padded, will encrypt to one of a large number of different possible ciphertexts.

Standards such as PKCS#1 have been carefully designed to securely pad messages prior to RSA encryption. Because these schemes pad the plaintext m with some number of additional bits, the size of the un-padded message M must be somewhat smaller. RSA padding schemes must be carefully designed so as to prevent sophisticated attacks which may be facilitated by a predictable message structure. Early versions of the PKCS#1 standard (up to version 1.5) used a construction that appears to make RSA semantically secure. However, at Eurocrypt 2000, Coron et al. showed that for some types of messages, this padding does not provide a high enough level of security. Furthermore, at Crypto 1998, Bleichenbacher showed that this version is vulnerable to a practical adaptive chosen ciphertext attack. Later versions of the standard include Optimal Asymmetric Encryption Padding (OAEP), which prevents these attacks. As such, OAEP should be used in any new application, and PKCS#1 v1.5 padding should be replaced wherever possible. The PKCS#1 standard also incorporates processing schemes designed to provide additional security for RSA signatures, e.g. the Probabilistic Signature Scheme for RSA (RSA-PSS).

Secure padding schemes such as RSA-PSS are as essential for the security of message signing as they are for message encryption. Two US patents on PSS were granted (USPTO 6266771 and USPTO 70360140); however, these patents expired on 24 July 2009 and 25 April 2010, respectively. Use of PSS no longer seems to be encumbered by patents. Note that using different RSA key-pairs for encryption and signing is potentially more secure.

Security and Practical Considerations

Using the Chinese Remainder Algorithm

For efficiency many popular crypto libraries (like OpenSSL, Java and .NET) use the following optimization for decryption and signing based on the Chinese remainder theorem. The following values are precomputed and stored as part of the private key:

- p and q : the primes from the key generation,

- $d_P = d \pmod{p-1}$,

- $d_Q = d \pmod{q-1}$ and

- $q_{\text{inv}} = q^{-1} \pmod{p}$.

These values allow the recipient to compute the exponentiation $m = c^d \pmod{pq}$ more efficiently as follows:

- $m_1 = c^{d_P} \pmod{p}$

- $m_2 = c^{d_Q} \pmod{q}$

- $h = q_{\text{inv}}(m_1 - m_2) \pmod{p}$ (if $m_1 < m_2$ then some libraries compute h as)

- $m = m_2 + hq$

This is more efficient than computing exponentiation by squaring even though two modular exponentiations have to be computed. The reason is that these two modular exponentiations both use a smaller exponent and a smaller modulus.

Integer Factorization and RSA Problem

The security of the RSA cryptosystem is based on two mathematical problems: the problem of factoring large numbers and the RSA problem. Full decryption of an RSA ciphertext is thought to be infeasible on the assumption that both of these problems are hard, i.e., no efficient algorithm exists for solving them. Providing security against *partial* decryption may require the addition of a secure padding scheme.

The RSA problem is defined as the task of taking eth roots modulo a composite n: recovering a value m such that $c \equiv m^e \pmod{n}$, where (n, e) is an RSA public key and c is an RSA ciphertext. Currently the most promising approach to solving the RSA problem is to factor the modulus n. With the ability to recover prime factors, an attacker can compute the secret exponent d from a public key (n, e), then decrypt c using the standard procedure. To accomplish this, an attacker factors n into p and q, and computes $(p-1)(q-1)$ which allows the determination of d from e. No polynomial-time method for factoring large integers on a classical computer has yet been found, but it has not been proven that none exists.

Multiple polynomial quadratic sieve (MPQS) can be used to factor the public modulus n. The time taken to factor 128-bit and 256-bit n on a desktop computer (Processor: Intel Dual-Core i7-4500U 1.80GHz) are respectively 2 seconds and 35 minutes.

Bits	Time
128	Less than 2 seconds
192	16 seconds
256	35 minutes
260	1 hour

A tool called yafu can be used to optimize this process. The automation within YAFU is state-of-the-art, combining factorization algorithms in an intelligent and adaptive methodology that minimizes the time to find the factors of arbitrary input integers. Most algorithm implementations are multi-threaded, allowing YAFU to fully utilize multi- or many-core processors (including SNFS, GNFS, SIQS, and ECM). YAFU is primarily a command-line driven tool. The time taken to factor n using yafu on the same computer was reduced to 103.1746 seconds. Yafu requires the GGNFS binaries to factor N that are 320 bits or larger. It took about 5720s to factor *320bit-N* on the same computer.

Bits	Time	Memory used
128	0.4886 seconds	0.1 MiB
192	3.9979 seconds	0.5 MiB
256	103.1746 seconds	3 MiB
300	1175.7826 seconds	10.9 MiB

In 2009, Benjamin Moody has factored an RSA-512 bit key in 73 days using only public software (GGNFS) and his desktop computer (dual-core Athlon64 at 1,900 MHz). Just under 5 gigabytes of disk was required and about 2.5 gigabytes of RAM for the sieving process. The first RSA-512 factorization in 1999 required the equivalent of 8,400 MIPS years over an elapsed time of about 7 months.

Rivest, Shamir and Adleman note that Miller has shown that – assuming the Extended Riemann

Hypothesis – finding d from n and e is as hard as factoring n into p and q (up to a polynomial time difference). However, Rivest, Shamir and Adleman note (in section IX / D of their paper) that they have not found a proof that inverting RSA is equally hard as factoring.

As of 2010, the largest factored RSA number was 768 bits long. Its factorization, by a state-of-the-art distributed implementation, took around fifteen hundred CPU years (two years of real time, on many hundreds of computers). No larger RSA key is publicly known to have been factored. In practice, RSA keys are typically 1024 to 4096 bits long. Some experts believe that 1024-bit keys may become breakable in the near future or may already be breakable by a sufficiently well-funded attacker (though this is disputed); few see any way that 4096-bit keys could be broken in the foreseeable future. Therefore, it is generally presumed that RSA is secure if n is sufficiently large. If n is 300 bits or shorter, it can be factored in a few hours on a personal computer, using software already freely available. Keys of 512 bits have been shown to be practically breakable in 1999 when RSA-155 was factored by using several hundred computers and are now factored in a few weeks using common hardware. Exploits using 512-bit code-signing certificates that may have been factored were reported in 2011. A theoretical hardware device named TWIRL and described by Shamir and Tromer in 2003 called into question the security of 1024 bit keys. It is currently recommended that n be at least 2048 bits long.

In 1994, Peter Shor showed that a quantum computer (if one could ever be practically created for the purpose) would be able to factor in polynomial time, breaking RSA.

Faulty Key Generation

Finding the large primes p and q is usually done by testing random numbers of the right size with probabilistic primality tests which quickly eliminate virtually all non-primes.

Numbers p and q should not be 'too close', lest the Fermat factorization for n be successful, if $p - q$, for instance is less than $2n^{1/4}$ (which for even small 1024-bit values of n is 3×10^{77}) solving for p and q is trivial. Furthermore, if either $p - 1$ or $q - 1$ has only small prime factors, n can be factored quickly by Pollard's $p - 1$ algorithm, and these values of p or q should therefore be discarded as well.

It is important that the private exponent d be large enough. Michael J. Wiener showed that if p is between q and $2q$ (which is quite typical) and $d < n^{1/4}/3$, then d can be computed efficiently from n and e.

There is no known attack against small public exponents such as $e = 3$, provided that proper padding is used. Coppersmith's Attack has many applications in attacking RSA specifically if the public exponent e is small and if the encrypted message is short and not padded. 65537 is a commonly used value for e; this value can be regarded as a compromise between avoiding potential small exponent attacks and still allowing efficient encryptions (or signature verification). The NIST Special Publication on Computer Security (SP 800-78 Rev 1 of August 2007) does not allow public exponents e smaller than 65537, but does not state a reason for this restriction.

Importance of Strong Random Number Generation

A cryptographically strong random number generator, which has been properly seeded with adequate entropy, must be used to generate the primes p and q. An analysis comparing millions of public keys gathered from the Internet was carried out in early 2012 by Arjen K. Lenstra, James P. Hughes, Maxime Augier, Joppe W. Bos, Thorsten Kleinjung and Christophe Wachter. They were able to factor 0.2% of the keys using only Euclid's algorithm.

They exploited a weakness unique to cryptosystems based on integer factorization. If $n = pq$ is one public key and $n' = p'q'$ is another, then if by chance $p = p'$ (but q is not equal to q'), then a simple computation of $\gcd(n,n') = p$ factors both n and n', totally compromising both keys. Lenstra et al. note that this problem can be minimized by using a strong random seed of bit-length twice the intended security level, or by employing a deterministic function to choose q given p, instead of choosing p and q independently.

Nadia Heninger was part of a group that did a similar experiment. They used an idea of Daniel J. Bernstein to compute the GCD of each RSA key n against the product of all the other keys n' they had found (a 729 million digit number), instead of computing each $\gcd(n,n')$ separately, thereby achieving a very significant speedup since after one large division the GCD problem is of normal size.

Heninger says in her blog that the bad keys occurred almost entirely in embedded applications, including "firewalls, routers, VPN devices, remote server administration devices, printers, projectors, and VOIP phones" from over 30 manufacturers. Heninger explains that the one-shared-prime problem uncovered by the two groups results from situations where the pseudorandom number generator is poorly seeded initially and then reseeded between the generation of the first and second primes. Using seeds of sufficiently high entropy obtained from key stroke timings or electronic diode noise or atmospheric noise from a radio receiver tuned between stations should solve the problem.

Strong random number generation is important throughout every phase of public key cryptography. For instance, if a weak generator is used for the symmetric keys that are being distributed by RSA, then an eavesdropper could bypass the RSA and guess the symmetric keys directly.

Timing Attacks

Kocher described a new attack on RSA in 1995: if the attacker Eve knows Alice's hardware in sufficient detail and is able to measure the decryption times for several known ciphertexts, she can deduce the decryption key d quickly. This attack can also be applied against the RSA signature scheme. In 2003, Boneh and Brumley demonstrated a more practical attack capable of recovering RSA factorizations over a network connection (e.g., from a Secure Sockets Layer (SSL)-enabled webserver) This attack takes advantage of information leaked by the Chinese remainder theorem optimization used by many RSA implementations.

One way to thwart these attacks is to ensure that the decryption operation takes a constant amount of time for every ciphertext. However, this approach can significantly reduce performance. Instead, most RSA implementations use an alternate technique known as cryptographic blinding. RSA blinding makes use of the multiplicative property of RSA. Instead of computing c^d (mod n), Alice first chooses a secret random value r and computes $(r^e c)^d$ (mod n). The result of this computation after applying Euler's Theorem is rc^d (mod n) and so the effect of r can be removed by multiplying by its inverse. A new value of r is chosen for each ciphertext. With blinding applied, the decryption time is no longer correlated to the value of the input ciphertext and so the timing attack fails.

Adaptive Chosen Ciphertext Attacks

In 1998, Daniel Bleichenbacher described the first practical adaptive chosen ciphertext attack, against RSA-encrypted messages using the PKCS #1 v1 padding scheme (a padding scheme randomizes and adds structure to an RSA-encrypted message, so it is possible to determine whether a decrypted message is valid). Due to flaws with the PKCS #1 scheme, Bleichenbacher was able to mount a practical attack against RSA implementations of the Secure Socket Layer protocol, and to recover session keys. As a result of this work, cryptographers now recommend the use of provably secure padding schemes such as Optimal Asymmetric Encryption Padding, and RSA Laboratories has released new versions of PKCS #1 that are not vulnerable to these attacks.

Side-channel Analysis Attacks

A side-channel attack using branch prediction analysis (BPA) has been described. Many processors use a branch predictor to determine whether a conditional branch in the instruction flow of a program is likely to be taken or not. Often these processors also implement simultaneous multithreading (SMT). Branch prediction analysis attacks use a spy process to discover (statistically) the private key when processed with these processors.

Simple Branch Prediction Analysis (SBPA) claims to improve BPA in a non-statistical way. In their paper, "On the Power of Simple Branch Prediction Analysis", the authors of SBPA (Onur Aciicmez and Cetin Kaya Koc) claim to have discovered 508 out of 512 bits of an RSA key in 10 iterations.

A power fault attack on RSA implementations has been described in 2010. The authors recovered the key by varying the CPU power voltage outside limits; this caused multiple power faults on the server.

Elliptic Curve Cryptography

Elliptic curve cryptography (ECC) is an approach to public-key cryptography based on the algebraic structure of elliptic curves over finite fields. ECC requires smaller keys compared to non-ECC cryptography (based on plain Galois fields) to provide equivalent security.

Elliptic curves are applicable for encryption, digital signatures, pseudo-random generators and other tasks. They are also used in several integer factorization algorithms that have applications in cryptography, such as Lenstra elliptic curve factorization.

Rationale

Public-key cryptography is based on the intractability of certain mathematical problems. Early public-key systems are secure assuming that it is difficult to factor a large integer composed of two or more large prime factors. For elliptic-curve-based protocols, it is assumed that finding the discrete logarithm of a random elliptic curve element with respect to a publicly known base point is infeasible: this is the "elliptic curve discrete logarithm problem" or ECDLP. The security of ECC depends on the ability to compute a point multiplication and the inability to compute the multiplicand given the original and product points. The size of the elliptic curve determines the difficulty of the problem.

The primary benefit promised by ECC is a smaller key size, reducing storage and transmission requirements, i.e. that an elliptic curve group could provide the same level of security afforded by an RSA-based system with a large modulus and correspondingly larger key: for example, a 256-bit ECC public key should provide comparable security to a 3072-bit RSA public key.

The U.S. National Institute of Standards and Technology (NIST) has endorsed ECC in its Suite B set of recommended algorithms, specifically Elliptic Curve Diffie–Hellman (ECDH) for key exchange and Elliptic Curve Digital Signature Algorithm (ECDSA) for digital signature. The U.S. National Security Agency (NSA) allows their use for protecting information classified up to top secret with 384-bit keys. However, in August 2015, the NSA announced that it plans to replace Suite B with a new cipher suite due to concerns about quantum computing attacks on ECC.

While the RSA patent expired in 2000, there may be patents in force covering certain aspects of ECC technology, though some (including RSA Laboratories and Daniel J. Bernstein) argue that the Federal elliptic curve digital signature standard (ECDSA; NIST FIPS 186-3) and certain practical ECC-based key exchange schemes (including ECDH) can be implemented without infringing them.

History

The use of elliptic curves in cryptography was suggested independently by Neal Koblitz and Victor S. Miller in 1985. Elliptic curve cryptography algorithms entered wide use in 2004 to 2005.

Theory

For current cryptographic purposes, an *elliptic curve* is a plane curve over a finite field (rather than the real numbers) which consists of the points satisfying the equation

$$y^2 = x^3 + ax + b,$$

along with a distinguished point at infinity, denoted ∞. (The coordinates here are to be chosen from a fixed finite field of characteristic not equal to 2 or 3, or the curve equation will be somewhat more complicated.)

This set together with the group operation of elliptic curves is an Abelian group, with the point at infinity as identity element. The structure of the group is inherited from the divisor group of the underlying algebraic variety.

$$\mathrm{Div}^0(E) \rightarrow \mathrm{Pic}^0(E) \simeq E,$$

As is the case for other popular public key cryptosystems, no mathematical proof of security has been published for ECC as of 2009.

Cryptographic Schemes

Several discrete logarithm-based protocols have been adapted to elliptic curves, replacing the group $(\mathbb{Z}_p)^{\times}$ with an elliptic curve:

- The elliptic curve Diffie–Hellman (ECDH) key agreement scheme is based on the Diffie–Hellman scheme,

- The Elliptic Curve Integrated Encryption Scheme (ECIES), also known as Elliptic Curve Augmented Encryption Scheme or simply the Elliptic Curve Encryption Scheme,

- The Elliptic Curve Digital Signature Algorithm (ECDSA) is based on the Digital Signature Algorithm,

- The Edwards-curve Digital Signature Algorithm (EdDSA) is based on Schnorr signature and uses twisted Edwards curves,

- The ECMQV key agreement scheme is based on the MQV key agreement scheme,

- The ECQV implicit certificate scheme.

At the RSA Conference 2005, the National Security Agency (NSA) announced Suite B which exclusively uses ECC for digital signature generation and key exchange. The suite is intended to protect both classified and unclassified national security systems and information.

Recently, a large number of cryptographic primitives based on bilinear mappings on various elliptic curve groups, such as the Weil and Tate pairings, have been introduced. Schemes based on these primitives provide efficient identity-based encryption as well as pairing-based signatures, signcryption, key agreement, and proxy re-encryption.

Implementation

Some common implementation considerations include:

Domain Parameters

To use ECC, all parties must agree on all the elements defining the elliptic curve, that is, the *domain parameters* of the scheme. The field is defined by p in the prime case and the pair of m and f in the binary case. The elliptic curve is defined by the constants a and b used in its defining equation. Finally, the cyclic subgroup is defined by its *generator* (a.k.a. *base point*) G. For cryptographic application the order of G, that is the smallest positive number n such that $nG = \infty$, is normally prime. Since n is the size of a subgroup of it follows from Lagrange's theorem that the number $h = \frac{1}{n} | E(\mathbb{F}_p) |$ is an integer. In cryptographic applications this number h, called the *cofactor*, must be small ($h \leq 4$) and, preferably, $h = 1$. To summarize: in the prime case, the domain parameters are (p, a, b, G, n, h); in the binary case, they are (m, f, a, b, G, n, h).

Unless there is an assurance that domain parameters were generated by a party trusted with respect to their use, the domain parameters *must* be validated before use.

The generation of domain parameters is not usually done by each participant because this involves computing the number of points on a curve which is time-consuming and troublesome to implement. As a result, several standard bodies published domain parameters of elliptic curves for several common field sizes. Such domain parameters are commonly known as "standard curves" or "named curves"; a named curve can be referenced either by name or by the unique object identifier defined in the standard documents:

- NIST, Recommended Elliptic Curves for Government Use

- SECG, SEC 2: Recommended Elliptic Curve Domain Parameters

- ECC Brainpool (RFC 5639), ECC Brainpool Standard Curves and Curve Generation

SECG test vectors are also available. NIST has approved many SECG curves, so there is a significant overlap between the specifications published by NIST and SECG. EC domain parameters may be either specified by value or by name.

If one (despite the above) wants to construct one's own domain parameters, one should select the underlying field and then use one of the following strategies to find a curve with appropriate (i.e., near prime) number of points using one of the following methods:

- Select a random curve and use a general point-counting algorithm, for example, Schoof's algorithm or Schoof–Elkies–Atkin algorithm,

- Select a random curve from a family which allows easy calculation of the number of points (e.g., Koblitz curves), or

- Select the number of points and generate a curve with this number of points using *complex multiplication* technique.

Several classes of curves are weak and should be avoided:

- Curves over $\mathbb{F}_{2^m}$ with non-prime m are vulnerable to Weil descent attacks.

- Curves such that n divides $p^B - 1$ (where p is the characteristic of the field − q for a prime field, or 2 for a binary field) for sufficiently small B are vulnerable to Menezes–Okamoto–Vanstone (MOV) attack which applies usual Discrete Logarithm Problem (DLP) in a small degree extension field of $\mathbb{F}_p$ to solve ECDLP. The bound B should be chosen so that discrete logarithms in the field $\mathbb{F}_{p^B}$ are at least as difficult to compute as discrete logs on the elliptic curve $E(\mathbb{F}_q)$.

- Curves such that $|E(\mathbb{F}_q)| = q$ are vulnerable to the attack that maps the points on the curve to the additive group of $\mathbb{F}_q$

Key Sizes

Because all the fastest known algorithms that allow one to solve the ECDLP (baby-step giant-step, Pollard's rho, etc.), need $O(\sqrt{n})$ steps, it follows that the size of the underlying field should be roughly twice the security parameter. For example, for 128-bit security one needs a curve over $\mathbb{F}_q$, , where $q \approx 2^{256}$. This can be contrasted with finite-field cryptography (e.g., DSA) which requires 3072-bit public keys and 256-bit private keys, and integer factorization cryptography (e.g., RSA) which requires a 3072-bit value of n, where the private key should be just as large. However the public key may be smaller to accommodate efficient encryption, especially when processing power is limited.

The hardest ECC scheme (publicly) broken to date had a 112-bit key for the prime field case and a 109-bit key for the binary field case. For the prime field case, this was broken in July 2009 using a cluster of over 200 PlayStation 3 game consoles and could have been finished in 3.5 months using this cluster when running continuously. The binary field case was broken in April 2004 using 2600 computers over 17 months.

A current project is aiming at breaking the ECC2K-130 challenge by Certicom, by using a wide range of different hardware: CPUs, GPUs, FPGA.

Projective Coordinates

A close examination of the addition rules shows that in order to add two points, one needs not only several additions and multiplications in $\mathbb{F}_q$ but also an inversion operation. The inversion (for given $x \in \mathbb{F}_q$ find $y \in \mathbb{F}_q$ such that $xy = 1$) is one to two orders of magnitude slower than multiplication. Fortunately, points on a curve can be represented in different coordinate systems which do not require an inversion operation to add two points. Several such systems were proposed: in the *projective* system each point is represented by three coordinates (X, Y, Z) using the following relation: $x = \dfrac{X}{Z}$, $y = \dfrac{Y}{Z}$; in the *Jacobian system* a point is also represented with three coordinates (X, Y, Z), but a different relation is used: $x = \dfrac{X}{Z^2}$, $y = \dfrac{Y}{Z^3}$; in the *López–Dahab system* the relation is $x = \dfrac{X}{Z}$, $y = \dfrac{Y}{Z^2}$; in the *modified Jacobian* system the same relations are used but four coordinates are stored and used for calculations (X, Y, Z, aZ^4); and in the *Chudnovsky Jacobian* system five coordinates are used (X, Y, Z, Z^2, Z^3). Note that there may be different naming conventions, for example, IEEE P1363-2000 standard uses "projective coordinates" to refer to what is commonly called Jacobian coordinates. An additional speed-up is possible if mixed coordinates are used.

Fast Reduction (NIST Curves)

Reduction modulo p (which is needed for addition and multiplication) can be executed much faster if the prime p is a pseudo-Mersenne prime, that is $p \approx 2^d$; for example, $p = 2^{521} - 1$ or $p = 2^{256} - 2^{32} - 2^9 - 2^8 - 2^7 - 2^6 - 2^4 - 1$. Compared to Barrett reduction, there can be an order of magnitude speed-up. The speed-up here is a practical rather than theoretical one, and derives from the fact that the moduli of numbers against numbers near powers of two can be performed efficiently by computers operating on binary numbers with bitwise operations.

The curves over $\mathbb{F}_p$ with pseudo-Mersenne p are recommended by NIST. Yet another advantage of the NIST curves is that they use $a = -3$, which improves addition in Jacobian coordinates.

Many of the efficiency-related decisions in NIST FIPS 186-2 are sub-optimal. Other curves are more secure and run just as fast.

Applications

Elliptic curves are applicable for encryption, digital signatures, pseudo-random generators and other tasks. They are also used in several integer factorization algorithms that have applications in cryptography, such as Lenstra elliptic curve factorization.

NIST recommended 15 elliptic curves. Specifically, FIPS 186-3 has 10 recommended finite fields:

- Five prime fields $\mathbb{F}_p$ for certain primes p of sizes 192, 224, 256, 384, and 521 bits. For each of the prime fields, one elliptic curve is recommended.

- Five binary fields   for m equal 163, 233, 283, 409, and 571. For each of the binary fields, one elliptic curve and one Koblitz curve was selected.

The NIST recommendation thus contains a total of 5 prime curves and 10 binary curves. The curves were ostensibly chosen for optimal security and implementation efficiency.

In 2013, the *New York Times* stated that Dual Elliptic Curve Deterministic Random Bit Generation (or Dual_EC_DRBG) had been included as a NIST national standard due to the influence of NSA, which had included a deliberate weakness in the algorithm and the recommended elliptic curve. RSA Security in September 2013 issued an advisory recommending that its customers discontinue using any software based on Dual_EC_DRBG. In the wake of the exposure of Dual_EC_DRBG as "an NSA undercover operation", cryptography experts have also expressed concern over the security of the NIST recommended elliptic curves, suggesting a return to encryption based on non-elliptic-curve groups.

Security

Side-channel Attacks

Unlike most other DLP systems (where it is possible to use the same procedure for squaring and multiplication), the EC addition is significantly different for doubling ($P = Q$) and general addition ($P \neq Q$) depending on the coordinate system used. Consequently, it is important to counteract side channel attacks (e.g., timing or simple/differential power analysis attacks) using, for example, fixed pattern window (a.k.a. comb) methods (note that this does not increase computation time). Alternatively one can use an Edwards curve; this is a special family of elliptic curves for which doubling and addition can be done with the same operation. Another concern for ECC-systems is the danger of fault attacks, especially when running on smart cards.

Backdoors

Cryptographic experts have expressed concerns that the National Security Agency has inserted a kleptographic backdoor into at least one elliptic curve-based pseudo random generator. Internal memos leaked by former NSA contractor, Edward Snowden, suggest that the NSA put a backdoor in the Dual EC DRBG standard. One analysis of the possible backdoor concluded that an adversary in possession of the algorithm's secret key could obtain encryption keys given only 32 bytes of ciphertext.

Quantum Computing Attacks

In contrast with its current standing over RSA, elliptic curve cryptography is expected to be more vulnerable to an attack based on Shor's algorithm. In theory, making a practical attack feasible many years before an attack on an equivalently secure RSA scheme is possible. This is because smaller elliptic curve keys are needed to match the classical security of RSA. The work of Proos and Zalka show how a quantum computer for breaking 2048-bit RSA requires roughly 4096 qubits, while a quantum computer to break the equivalently secure 224-bit Elliptic Curve Cryptography requires between 1300 and 1600 qubits.

To avoid quantum computing concerns, an elliptic curve-based alternative to Elliptic Curve Diffie Hellman which is not susceptible to Shor's attack is the Supersingular Isogeny Diffie–Hellman Key Exchange of De Feo, Jao and Plut. It uses elliptic curve isogenies to create a drop-in replacement for the quantum attackable Diffie–Hellman and Elliptic curve Diffie–Hellman key exchanges. This key exchange uses the same elliptic curve computational primitives of existing elliptic curve cryptography and requires computational and transmission overhead similar to many currently used public key systems.

In August, 2015, NSA announced that it planned to transition "in the not distant future" to a new cipher suite that is resistant to quantum attacks. "Unfortunately, the growth of elliptic curve use has bumped up against the fact of continued progress in the research on quantum computing, necessitating a re-evaluation of our cryptographic strategy."

Patents

At least one ECC scheme (ECMQV) and some implementation techniques are covered by patents.

Alternative Representations

Alternative representations of elliptic curves include:

- Hessian curves

- Edwards curves

- Twisted curves

- Twisted Hessian curves

- Twisted Edwards curve

- Doubling-oriented Doche–Icart–Kohel curve

- Tripling-oriented Doche–Icart–Kohel curve

- Jacobian curve

- Montgomery curve

References

- Delfs, Hans & Knebl, Helmut (2007). "Symmetric-key encryption". Introduction to cryptography: principles and applications. Springer. ISBN 9783540492436.

- Stallings, William (1990-05-03). Cryptography and Network Security: Principles and Practice. Prentice Hall. p. 165. ISBN 9780138690175.

- Stallings, William (1999-01-01). Cryptography and Network Security: Principles and Practice. Prentice Hall. p. 164. ISBN 9780138690175.

- Miller, V. (1985). "Use of elliptic curves in cryptography". CRYPTO. Lecture Notes in Computer Science. 85: 417–426. doi:10.1007/3-540-39799-X_31. ISBN 978-3-540-16463-0.

- Cohen, H.; Miyaji, A.; Ono, T. (1998). "Efficient Elliptic Curve Exponentiation Using Mixed Coordinates". Advances in Cryptology – AsiaCrypt '98. Lecture Notes in Computer Science. 1514: 51–65. doi:10.1007/3-540-49649-1_6. ISBN 978-3-540-65109-3.

- Brown, M.; Hankerson, D.; Lopez, J.; Menezes, A. (2001). "Software Implementation of the NIST Elliptic Curves Over Prime Fields". Topics in Cryptology – CT-RSA 2001. Lecture Notes in Computer Science. 2020: 250–265. doi:10.1007/3-540-45353-9_19. ISBN 978-3-540-41898-6.

- See, for example, Biehl, Ingrid; Meyer, Bernd; Müller, Volker (2000). "Differential Fault Attacks on Elliptic Curve Cryptosystems". Advances in Cryptology – CRYPTO 2000. Lecture Notes in Computer Science. 1880: 131–146. doi:10.1007/3-540-44598-6_8. ISBN 978-3-540-67907-3.

- Michael A. Nielsen; Isaac L. Chuang (9 December 2010). Quantum Computation and Quantum Information: 10th Anniversary Edition. Cambridge University Press. pp. 202–. ISBN 978-1-139-49548-6.

- Selinger, Peter. "MD5 Collision Demo". Peter Selinger / Department of Mathematics and Statistics. Dalhousie University. Retrieved 23 June 2015.

- Proos, John; Zalka. "Shor's discrete logarithm quantum algorithm for elliptic curves". QIC. arXiv:quantph/0301141. Archived from the original on 2004. Retrieved 3 May 2014.

- Daniel J. Bernstein and Tanja Lange. "SafeCurves: choosing safe curves for elliptic-curve cryptography". Retrieved 1 December 2013.

4

Technologies Related to Cryptography

This chapter guides the reader on the technologies related to cryptography. It elaborately explains technologies such as the rotor machine, cryptographically secure pseudorandom number generator, disk encryption, onion routing and secure multi-party computation. The major components of cryptographic technology are discussed in this chapter.

Rotor Machine

In cryptography, a rotor machine is an electro-mechanical stream cipher device used for encrypting and decrypting secret messages. Rotor machines were the cryptographic state-of-the-art for a prominent period of history; they were in widespread use in the 1920s–1970s. The most famous example is the German Enigma machine, whose messages were deciphered by the Allies during World War II, producing intelligence code-named *Ultra*.

A series of three rotors from an Enigma machine, used by Germany during World War II

The primary component is a set of *rotors*, also termed *wheels* or *drums*, which are rotating disks with an array of electrical contacts on either side. The wiring between the contacts implements a fixed substitution of letters, replacing them in some complex fashion. On its own, this would offer little security; however, after encrypting each letter, the rotors advance positions, changing the substitution. By this means, a rotor machine produces a complex polyalphabetic substitution cipher, which changes with every keypress.

Background

In classical cryptography, one of the earliest encryption methods was the simple substitution cipher, where letters in a message were systematically replaced using some secret scheme. *Monoalphabetic* substitution ciphers used only a single replacement scheme — sometimes termed an "alphabet"; this could be easily broken, for example, by using frequency analysis. Somewhat more secure were schemes involving multiple alphabets, polyalphabetic ciphers. Because such schemes were implemented by hand, only a handful of different alphabets could be used; anything more complex would be impractical. However, using only a few alphabets left the ciphers vulnerable to attack. The invention of rotor machines mechanised polyalphabetic encryption, providing a practical way to use a much larger number of alphabets.

40-point rotors from a machine made by Tatjana van Vark

The earliest cryptanalytic technique was frequency analysis, in which letter patterns unique to every language could be used to discover information about the substitution alphabet(s) in use in a mono-alphabetic substitution cipher. For instance, in English, the plaintext letters E, T, A, O, I, N and S, are usually easy to identify in ciphertext on the basis that since they are very frequent, their corresponding ciphertext letters will also be as frequent. In addition, bigram combinations like NG, ST and others are also very frequent, while others are rare indeed (Q followed by anything other than U for instance). The simplest frequency analysis relies on one ciphertext letter always being substituted for a plaintext letter in the cipher: if this is not the case, deciphering the message is more difficult. For many years, cryptographers attempted to hide the telltale frequencies by using several different substitutions for common letters, but this technique was unable to fully hide patterns in the substitutions for plaintext letters. Such schemes were being widely broken by the 16th century.

In the mid-15th century, a new technique was invented by Alberti, now known generally as poly-alphabetic ciphers, which recognised the virtue of using more than a single substitution alphabet; he also invented a simple technique for "creating" a multitude of substitution patterns for use in a message. Two parties exchanged a small amount of information (referred to as the *key*) and used it to create many substitution alphabets, and so many different substitutions for each plaintext letter over the course of a single plaintext. The idea is simple and effective, but proved more difficult to use than might have been expected. Many ciphers were only partial implementations of Alberti's, and so were easier to break than they might have been (e.g. the Vigenère cipher).

Not until the 1840s (Babbage) was any technique known which could reliably break any of the polyalphabetic ciphers. His technique also looked for repeating patterns in the ciphertext, which provide clues about the length of the key. Once this is known, the message essentially becomes a series of messages, each as long as the length of the key, to which normal frequency analysis can be applied. Charles Babbage, Friedrich Kasiski, and William F. Friedman are among those who did most to develop these techniques.

Cipher designers tried to get users to use a different substitution for every letter, but this usually meant a very long key, which was a problem in several ways. A long key takes longer to convey (securely) to the parties who need it, and so mistakes are more likely in key distribution. Also, many users do not have the patience to carry out lengthy, letter perfect evolutions, and certainly not under time pressure or battlefield stress. The 'ultimate' cipher of this type would be one in which such a 'long' key could be generated from a simple pattern (ideally automatically), producing a cipher in which there are so many substitution alphabets that frequency counting and statistical attacks would be effectively impossible. Enigma, and the rotor machines generally, were just what was needed since they were seriously polyalphabetic, using a different substitution alphabet for each letter of plaintext, and automatic, requiring no extraordinary abilities from their users. Their messages were, generally, much harder to break than any previous ciphers.

Mechanization

It is relatively straightforward to create a machine for performing simple substitution. We can consider an electrical system with 26 switches attached to 26 light bulbs; when you turn on any one of the switches, one of the light bulbs is illuminated. If each switch is operated by a key on a typewriter, and the bulbs are labelled with letters, then such a system can be used for encryption by choosing the wiring between the keys and the bulb: for example, typing the letter A would make the bulb labelled Q light up. However, the wiring is fixed, providing little security.

Rotor machines build on this idea by, in effect, changing the wiring with each key stroke. The wiring is placed inside a rotor, and then rotated with a gear every time a letter was pressed. So while pressing A the first time might generate a Q, the next time it might generate a J. Every letter pressed on the keyboard would spin the rotor and get a new substitution, implementing a polyalphabetic substitution cipher.

Depending on the size of the rotor, this may or may not be more secure than hand ciphers. If the rotor has only 26 positions on it, one for each letter, then all messages will have a (repeating) key 26 letters long. Although the key itself (mostly hidden in the wiring of the rotor) might not be known, the methods for attacking these types of ciphers don't need that information. So while such a *single rotor* machine is certainly easy to use, it's no more secure than any other partial polyalphabetic cipher system.

But this is easy to correct. Simply stack more rotors next to each other, and gear them together. After the first rotor spins "all the way", make the rotor beside it spin one position. Now you would have to type $26 \times 26 = 676$ letters (for the Latin alphabet) before the key repeats, and yet it still only requires you to communicate a key of two letters/numbers to set things up. If a key of 676 length is not long enough, another rotor can be added, resulting in a period 17,576 letters long.

In order to be as easy to decipher as encipher, some rotor machines, most notably the Enigma machine, were designed to be *symmetrical*, i.e., encrypting twice with the same settings recovers the original message.

History

Invention

The concept of a rotor machine occurred to a number of inventors independently at a similar time.

In 2003, it emerged that the first inventors were two Dutch naval officers, Theo A. van Hengel (1875 – 1939) and R. P. C. Spengler (1875 – 1955) in 1915 (De Leeuw, 2003). Previously, the invention had been ascribed to four inventors working independently and at much the same time: Edward Hebern, Arvid Damm, Hugo Koch and Arthur Scherbius.

In the United States Edward Hugh Hebern built a rotor machine using a single rotor in 1917. He became convinced he would get rich selling such a system to the military, the Hebern Rotor Machine, and produced a series of different machines with one to five rotors. His success was limited, however, and he went bankrupt in the 1920s. He sold a small number of machines to the US Navy in 1931.

In Hebern's machines the rotors could be opened up and the wiring changed in a few minutes, so a single mass-produced system could be sold to a number of users who would then produce their own rotor keying. Decryption consisted of taking out the rotor(s) and turning them around to reverse the circuitry. Unknown to Hebern, William F. Friedman of the US Army's SIS promptly demonstrated a flaw in the system that allowed the ciphers from it, and from any machine with similar design features, to be cracked with enough work.

Another early rotor machine inventor was Dutchman Hugo Koch, who filed a patent on a rotor machine in 1919. At about the same time in Sweden, Arvid Gerhard Damm invented and patented another rotor design. However, the rotor machine was ultimately made famous by Arthur Scherbius, who filed a rotor machine patent in 1918. Scherbius later went on to design and market the Enigma machine.

The Enigma Machine

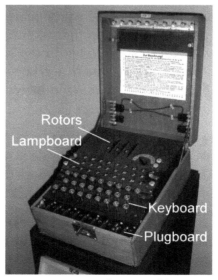

A German Enigma machine

The most widely known rotor cipher device is the German Enigma machine used during World War II, of which there were a number of variants.

The standard Enigma model, Enigma I, used three rotors. At the end of the stack of rotors was an additional, non-rotating disk, the "reflector," wired such that the input was connected electrically back out to another contact on the same side and thus was "reflected" back through the three-rotor stack to produce the ciphertext.

When current was sent into most other rotor cipher machines, it would travel through the rotors and out the other side to the lamps. In the Enigma, however, it was "reflected" back through the disks before going to the lamps. The advantage of this was that there was nothing that had to be done to the setup in order to decipher a message; the machine was "symmetrical" at all times.

The Enigma's reflector guaranteed that no letter could be enciphered as itself, so an *A* could never turn back into an *A*. This helped Polish and, later, British efforts to break the cipher.

Scherbius joined forces with a mechanical engineer named Ritter and formed Chiffriermaschinen AG in Berlin before demonstrating Enigma to the public in Bern in 1923, and then in 1924 at the World Postal Congress in Stockholm. In 1927 Scherbius bought Koch's patents, and in 1928 they added a *plugboard*, essentially a non-rotating manually rewireable fourth rotor, on the front of the machine. After the death of Scherbius in 1929, Willi Korn was in charge of further technical development of Enigma.

As with other early rotor machine efforts, Scherbius had limited commercial success. However, the German armed forces, responding in part to revelations that their codes had been broken during World War I, adopted the Enigma to secure their communications. The *Reichsmarine* adopted Enigma in 1926, and the German Army began to use a different variant around 1928.

The Enigma (in several variants) was the rotor machine that Scherbius's company and its successor, Heimsoth & Reinke, supplied to the German military and to such agencies as the Nazi party security organization, the *SD*.

The Poles broke the German Army Enigma beginning in December 1932, not long after it had been put into service. On July 25, 1939, just five weeks before Hitler's invasion of Poland, the Polish General Staff's Cipher Bureau shared its Enigma-decryption methods and equipment with the French and British as the Poles' contribution to the common defense against Nazi Germany. Dilly Knox had already broken Spanish Nationalist messages on a commercial Enigma machine in 1937 during the Spanish Civil War.

A few months later, using the Polish techniques, the British began reading Enigma ciphers in collaboration with Polish Cipher Bureau cryptologists who had escaped Poland, overrun by the Germans, to reach Paris. The Poles continued breaking German Army Enigma — along with Luftwaffe Enigma traffic — until work at Station *PC Bruno* in France was shut down by the German invasion of May–June 1940.

The British continued breaking Enigma and, assisted eventually by the United States, extended the work to German Naval Enigma traffic (which the Poles had been reading before the war), most especially to and from U-boats during the Battle of the Atlantic.

Various Machines

The rotor stack from an Enigma rotor machine. The rotors of this machine contain 26 contacts.

During World War II (WWII), both the Germans and Allies developed additional rotor machines. The Germans used the Lorenz SZ 40/42 and Siemens and Halske T52 machines to encipher tele-printer traffic which used the Baudot code; this traffic was known as Fish to the Allies. The Allies developed the Typex (British) and the SIGABA (American). During the War the Swiss began development on an Enigma improvement which became the NEMA machine which was put into service after WWII. There was even a Japanese developed variant of the Enigma in which the rotors sat horizontally; it was apparently never put into service. The Japanese PURPLE machine was not a rotor machine, being built around electrical stepping switches, but was conceptually similar.

Rotor machines continued to be used even in the computer age. The KL-7 (ADONIS), an encryption machine with 8 rotors, was widely used by the U.S. and its allies from the 1950s until the 1980s. The last Canadian message encrypted with a KL-7 was sent on June 30, 1983. The Soviet Union and its allies used a 10-rotor machine called Fialka well into the 1970s.

Typex was a printing rotor machine used by the United Kingdom and its Commonwealth, and was based on the Enigma patents.

A unique rotor machine was constructed in 2002 by Netherlands-based Tatjana van Vark. This unusual device is inspired by Enigma, but makes use of 40-point rotors, allowing letters, numbers and some punctuation; each rotor contains 509 parts.

A software implementation of a rotor machine was used in the crypt command that was part of early UNIX operating systems. It was among the first software programs to run afoul of U.S. export regulations which classified cryptographic implementations as munitions.

List of Rotor Machines

- Combined Cipher Machine
- Enigma machine
- Lorenz SZ 40/42
- Siemens and Halske T52
- Fialka
- Hebern rotor machine
- HX-63
- KL-7
- Lacida
- M-325
- Mercury
- NEMA
- OMI cryptograph
- Portex
- RED
- SIGABA
- SIGCUM
- Hagelin's family of machines including the C-36, the C-52 the CD-57 and the M-209
- BID/60 (Singlet)
- Typex

Cryptographically Secure Pseudorandom Number Generator

A cryptographically secure pseudo-random number generator (CSPRNG) or cryptographic pseudo-random number generator (CPRNG) is a pseudo-random number generator (PRNG) with properties that make it suitable for use in cryptography.

Many aspects of cryptography require random numbers, for example:

- key generation

- nonces

- one-time pads

- salts in certain signature schemes, including ECDSA, RSASSA-PSS

The "quality" of the randomness required for these applications varies. For example, creating a nonce in some protocols needs only uniqueness. On the other hand, generation of a master key requires a higher quality, such as more entropy. And in the case of one-time pads, the information-theoretic guarantee of perfect secrecy only holds if the key material comes from a true random source with high entropy.

Ideally, the generation of random numbers in CSPRNGs uses entropy obtained from a high-quality source, generally the operating system's randomness API. However, unexpected correlations have been found in several such ostensibly independent processes. From an information-theoretic point of view, the amount of randomness, the entropy that can be generated, is equal to the entropy provided by the system. But sometimes, in practical situations, more random numbers are needed than there is entropy available. Also the processes to extract randomness from a running system are slow in actual practice. In such instances, a CSPRNG can sometimes be used. A CSPRNG can "stretch" the available entropy over more bits.

Requirements

The requirements of an ordinary PRNG are also satisfied by a cryptographically secure PRNG, but the reverse is not true. CSPRNG requirements fall into two groups: first, that they pass statistical randomness tests; and secondly, that they hold up well under serious attack, even when part of their initial or running state becomes available to an attacker.

- Every CSPRNG should satisfy the next-bit test. That is, given the first k bits of a random sequence, there is no polynomial-time algorithm that can predict the $(k+1)$th bit with probability of success better than 50%. Andrew Yao proved in 1982 that a generator passing the next-bit test will pass all other polynomial-time statistical tests for randomness.

- Every CSPRNG should withstand "state compromise extensions". In the event that part or all of its state has been revealed (or guessed correctly), it should be impossible to reconstruct the stream of random numbers prior to the revelation. Additionally, if there is an entropy input while running, it should be infeasible to use knowledge of the input's state to predict future conditions of the CSPRNG state.

  Example: If the CSPRNG under consideration produces output by computing bits of π in sequence, starting from some unknown point in the binary expansion, it may well satisfy the next-bit test and thus be statistically random, as π appears to be a random sequence. (This would be guaranteed if π is a normal number, for example.) However, this algorithm is not cryptographically secure; an attacker who determines which bit of pi (i.e. the state of the algorithm) is currently in use will be able to calculate all preceding bits as well.

Most PRNGs are not suitable for use as CSPRNGs and will fail on both counts. First, while most

PRNGs outputs appear random to assorted statistical tests, they do not resist determined reverse engineering. Specialized statistical tests may be found specially tuned to such a PRNG that shows the random numbers not to be truly random. Second, for most PRNGs, when their state has been revealed, all past random numbers can be retrodicted, allowing an attacker to read all past messages, as well as future ones.

CSPRNGs are designed explicitly to resist this type of cryptanalysis.

Definitions

In the asymptotic setting, a family of deterministic polynomial time computable functions $G_k : \{0, 1\}^k \to \{0, 1\}^{p(k)}$ for some polynomial p, is a pseudorandom number generator (PRG), if it stretches the length of its input ($p(k) > k$ for any k), and if its output is computationally indistinguishable from true randomess, i.e. for any probabilistic polynomial time algorithm A, which outputs 1 or 0 as a distinguisher,

$$\left| \Pr_{x \leftarrow \{0,1\}^k}[A(G(x)) = 1] - \Pr_{r \leftarrow \{0,1\}^{p(k)}}[A(r) = 1] \right| < \quad (k)$$

for some negligible function μ. (The notation $x \leftarrow X$ means that x is chosen uniformly at random from the set X.)

There is an equivalent characterization: For any function family $G_k : \{0, 1\}^k \to \{0, 1\}^{p(k)}$, G is a PRG if and only if the next output bit of G cannot be predicted by a polynomial time algorithm.

A forward-secure PRG with block length $t(k)$ is a PRG $G_k : \{0, 1\}^k \to \{0, 1\}^k \times \{0, 1\}^{t(k)}$ polynomial time computable function, where the input string s_i with length k is the current state at period i, and the output (s_{i+1}, y_i) consists of the next state s_{i+1} and the pseudorandom output block y_i of period i. Such a PRG is called forward secure if it withstands state compromise extensions in the following sense. If the initial state s_1 is chosen at uniformly random from $\{0, 1\}^k$, for any i, $(y_1 y_2 \cdots y_i, s_{i+1})$ must be computationally indistinguishable from $(r_{i \cdot t(k)}, s_{i+1})$, in which $r_{i \cdot t(k)}$ is chosen at uniformly random from $\{0, 1\}^{i \cdot t(k)}$.

Any PRG $G : \{0, 1\}^k \to \{0, 1\}^{p(k)}$ can be turned into a forward secure PRG with block length $p(k)$ - k by splitting its output into the next state and the actual output. This is done by setting $G(s) = (G_0(s), G_1(s))$, in which $|G_0(s)| = |s| = k$ and $|G_1(s)| = p(k) - k$; then G is a forward secure PRG with G_0 as the next state and G_1 as the pseudorandom output block of the current period.

Entropy Extraction

Santha and Vazirani proved that several bit streams with weak randomness can be combined to produce a higher-quality quasi-random bit stream. Even earlier, John von Neumann proved that a simple algorithm can remove a considerable amount of the bias in any bit stream which should be applied to each bit stream before using any variation of the Santha-Vazirani design.

Designs

In the discussion below, CSPRNG designs are divided into three classes:

1. those based on cryptographic primitives such as ciphers and cryptographic hashes,

2. those based upon mathematical problems thought to be hard, and

3. special-purpose designs.

The last often introduce additional entropy when available and, strictly speaking, are not "pure" pseudorandom number generators, as their output is not completely determined by their initial state. This addition can prevent attacks even if the initial state is compromised.

Designs based on Cryptographic Primitives

- A secure block cipher can be converted into a CSPRNG by running it in counter mode. This is done by choosing a random key and encrypting a 0, then encrypting a 1, then encrypting a 2, etc. The counter can also be started at an arbitrary number other than zero. Assuming an n-bit block cipher the output can be distinguished from random data after around $2^{n/2}$ blocks since, following the birthday problem, colliding blocks should become likely at that point, whereas a block cipher in CTR mode will never output identical blocks. For 64 bit block ciphers this limits the safe output size to a few gigabytes, with 128 bit blocks the limitation is large enough not to impact typical applications.

- A cryptographically secure hash of a counter might also act as a good CSPRNG in some cases. In this case, it is also necessary that the initial value of this counter is random and secret. However, there has been little study of these algorithms for use in this manner, and at least some authors warn against this use.

- Most stream ciphers work by generating a pseudorandom stream of bits that are combined (almost always XORed) with the plaintext; running the cipher on a counter will return a new pseudorandom stream, possibly with a longer period. The cipher can only be secure if the original stream is a good CSPRNG, although this is not necessarily the case. Again, the initial state must be kept secret.

Number Theoretic Designs

- The Blum Blum Shub algorithm has a security proof based on the difficulty of the quadratic residuosity problem. Since the only known way to solve that problem is to factor the modulus, it is generally regarded that the difficulty of integer factorization provides a conditional security proof for the Blum Blum Shub algorithm. However the algorithm is very inefficient and therefore impractical unless extreme security is needed.

- The Blum-Micali algorithm has an unconditional security proof based on the difficulty of the discrete logarithm problem but is also very inefficient.

- Daniel Brown of Certicom has written a 2006 security proof for Dual_EC_DRBG, based on the assumed hardness of the *Decisional Diffie–Hellman assumption*, the *x-logarithm problem*, and the *truncated point problem*. The 2006 proof explicitly assumes a lower *outlen* than in the Dual_EC_DRBG standard, and that the P and Q in the Dual_EC_DRBG standard (which were revealed in 2013 to be probably backdoored by NSA) are replaced with non-backdoored values.

Special Designs

There are a number of practical PRNGs that have been designed to be cryptographically secure, including

- the Yarrow algorithm which attempts to evaluate the entropic quality of its inputs. Yarrow is used in FreeBSD, OpenBSD and Mac OS X (also as /dev/random).

- the Fortuna algorithm, the successor to Yarrow, which does not attempt to evaluate the entropic quality of its inputs.

- the function CryptGenRandom provided in Microsoft's Cryptographic Application Programming Interface

- ISAAC based on a variant of the RC4 cipher

- Evolutionary algorithm based on NIST Statistical Test Suite.

- arc4random

- AES-CTR DRBG is often used as a random number generator in systems that use AES encryption.

- ANSI X9.17 standard (*Financial Institution Key Management (wholesale)*), which has been adopted as a FIPS standard as well. It takes as input a TDEA (keying option 2) key bundle k and (the initial value of) a 64 bit random seed s. Each time a random number is required it:

    o   Obtains the current date/time D to the maximum resolution possible.

    o   Computes a temporary value $t = \text{TDEA}_k(D)$

    o   Computes the random value $x = \text{TDEA}_k(s \oplus t)$, where $\oplus$ denotes bitwise exclusive or.

    o   Updates the seed $s = \text{TDEA}_k(x \oplus t)$

    Obviously, the technique is easily generalized to any block cipher; AES has been suggested (Young and Yung, op cit, sect 3.5.1).

Standards

Several CSPRNGs have been standardized. For example,

- FIPS 186-4

- NIST SP 800-90A: This standard has three uncontroversial CSPRNGs named Hash_DRBG, HMAC_DRBG, and CTR_DRBG; and a PRNG named Dual_EC_DRBG which has been shown to not be cryptographically secure and probably has a kleptographic NSA backdoor.

- ANSI X9.17-1985 Appendix C

- ANSI X9.31-1998 Appendix A.2.4

- ANSI X9.62-1998 Annex A.4, obsoleted by ANSI X9.62-2005, Annex D (HMAC_DRBG)

A good reference is maintained by NIST.

There are also standards for statistical testing of new CSPRNG designs:

- *A Statistical Test Suite for Random and Pseudorandom Number Generators*, NIST Special Publication 800-22.

NSA Kleptographic Backdoor in the Dual_EC_DRBG PRNG

The Guardian and *The New York Times* have reported that the National Security Agency (NSA) inserted a PRNG into NIST SP 800-90A that had a backdoor which allows the NSA to readily decrypt material that was encrypted with the aid of Dual_EC_DRBG. Both papers report that, as independent security experts long suspected, the NSA has been introducing weaknesses into CSPRNG standard 800-90; this being confirmed for the first time by one of the top secret documents leaked to the Guardian by Edward Snowden. The NSA worked covertly to get its own version of the NIST draft security standard approved for worldwide use in 2006. The leaked document states that "eventually, NSA became the sole editor." In spite of the known potential for a kleptographic backdoor and other known significant deficiencies with Dual_EC_DRBG, several companies such as RSA Security continued using Dual_EC_DRBG until the backdoor was confirmed in 2013. RSA Security received a $10 million payment from the NSA to do so.

Disk Encryption

Disk encryption is a technology which protects information by converting it into unreadable code that cannot be deciphered easily by unauthorized people. Disk encryption uses disk encryption software or hardware to encrypt every bit of data that goes on a disk or disk volume. Disk encryption prevents unauthorized access to data storage.

Expressions *full disk encryption (FDE)* or *whole disk encryption* often signify that everything on disk is encrypted – including the programs that can encrypt bootable operating system partitions – when part of the disk is necessarily not encrypted. On systems that use a master boot record (MBR), that part of the disk remains non encrypted. Some hardware-based full disk encryption systems can truly encrypt an entire boot disk, including the MBR.

Transparent Encryption

Transparent encryption, also known as real-time encryption and on-the-fly encryption (OTFE), is a method used by some disk encryption software. "Transparent" refers to the fact that data is automatically encrypted or decrypted as it is loaded or saved.

With transparent encryption, the files are accessible immediately after the key is provided, and the entire volume is typically mounted as if it were a physical drive, making the files just as accessible as any unencrypted ones. No data stored on an encrypted volume can be read (decrypted) without using the correct password/keyfile(s) or correct encryption keys. The entire file system within the volume is encrypted (including file names, folder names, file contents, and other meta-data).

To be transparent to the end user, transparent encryption usually requires the use of device drivers to enable the encryption process. Although administrator access rights are normally required to install such drivers, encrypted volumes can typically be used by normal users without these rights .

In general, every method in which data is transparently encrypted on write and decrypted on read can be called transparent encryption.

Disk Encryption vs. Filesystem-level Encryption

Disk encryption does not replace file encryption in all situations. Disk encryption is sometimes used in conjunction with filesystem-level encryption with the intention of providing a more secure implementation. Since disk encryption generally uses the same key for encrypting the whole volume, all data is decryptable when the system runs. However, some disk encryption solutions use multiple keys for encrypting different partitions. If an attacker gains access to the computer at run-time, the attacker has access to all files. Conventional file and folder encryption instead allows different keys for different portions of the disk. Thus an attacker cannot extract information from still-encrypted files and folders.

Unlike disk encryption, filesystem-level encryption does not typically encrypt filesystem metadata, such as the directory structure, file names, modification timestamps or sizes.

Disk Encryption and Trusted Platform Module

Trusted Platform Module (TPM) is a secure cryptoprocessor embedded in the motherboard that can be used to authenticate a hardware device. Since each TPM chip is unique to a particular device, it is capable of performing platform authentication. It can be used to verify that the system seeking the access is the expected system.

A limited number of disk encryption solutions have support for TPM. These implementations can wrap the decryption key using the TPM, thus tying the hard disk drive (HDD) to a particular device. If the HDD is removed from that particular device and placed in another, the decryption process will fail. Recovery is possible with the decryption password or token.

Although this has the advantage that the disk cannot be removed from the device, it might create a single point of failure in the encryption. For example, if something happens to the TPM or the motherboard, a user would not be able to access the data by connecting the hard drive to another computer, unless that user has a separate recovery key.

Implementations

There are multiple tools available in the market that allow for disk encryption. However, they vary greatly in features and security. They are divided into three main categories: software-based, hardware-based within the storage device, and hardware-based elsewhere (such as CPU or host bus adaptor). Hardware-based full disk encryption within the storage device are called self-encrypting drives and have no impact on performance whatsoever. Furthermore, the media-encryption key never leaves the device itself and is therefore not available to any virus in the operating system.

The Trusted Computing Group Opal drive provides industry accepted standardization for self-encrypting drives. External hardware is considerably faster than the software-based solutions although CPU versions may still have a performance impact, and the media encryption keys are not as well protected.

All solutions for the boot drive require a Pre-Boot Authentication component which is available for all types of solutions from a number of vendors. It is important in all cases that the authentication credentials are usually a major potential weakness since the symmetric cryptography is usually strong.

Password/Data Recovery Mechanism

Secure and safe recovery mechanisms are essential to the large-scale deployment of any disk encryption solutions in an enterprise. The solution must provide an easy but secure way to recover passwords (most importantly data) in case the user leaves the company without notice or forgets the password.

Challenge/Response Password Recovery Mechanism

Challenge/Response password recovery mechanism allows the password to be recovered in a secure manner. It is offered by a limited number of disk encryption solutions.

Some benefits of challenge/response password recovery:

1. No need for the user to carry a disc with recovery encryption key.

2. No secret data is exchanged during the recovery process.

3. No information can be sniffed.

4. Does not require a network connection, i.e. it works for users that are at a remote location.

Emergency Recovery Information (ERI) File Password Recovery Mechanism

An Emergency Recovery Information (ERI) file provides an alternative for recovery if a challenge response mechanism is unfeasible due to the cost of helpdesk operatives for small companies or implementation challenges.

Some benefits of ERI file recovery:

1. Small companies can use it without implementation difficulties

2. No secret data is exchanged during the recovery process.

3. No information can be sniffed.

4. Does not require a network connection, i.e. it works for users that are at a remote location.

Security Concerns

Most full disk encryption schemes are vulnerable to a cold boot attack, whereby encryption keys can be stolen by cold-booting a machine already running an operating system, then dumping the contents of memory before the data disappears. The attack relies on the data remanence property of computer memory, whereby data bits can take up to several minutes to degrade after power has been removed. Even a Trusted Platform Module (TPM) is not effective against the attack, as the operating system needs to hold the decryption keys in memory in order to access the disk.

Full disk encryption is also vulnerable when a computer is stolen when suspended. As wake-up does not involve a BIOS boot sequence, it typically does not ask for the FDE password. Hibernation, in contrast goes via a BIOS boot sequence, and is safe.

All software-based encryption systems are vulnerable to various side channel attacks such as acoustic cryptanalysis and hardware keyloggers. In contrast, self-encrypting drives are not vulnerable to these attacks since the hardware encryption key never leaves the disk controller.

Full Disk Encryption

Benefits

Full disk encryption has several benefits compared to regular file or folder encryption, or encrypted vaults. The following are some benefits of disk encryption:

1. Nearly everything including the swap space and the temporary files is encrypted. Encrypting these files is important, as they can reveal important confidential data. With a software implementation, the bootstrapping code cannot be encrypted however. (For example, Bit-Locker Drive Encryption leaves an unencrypted volume to boot from, while the volume containing the operating system is fully encrypted.)

2. With full disk encryption, the decision of which individual files to encrypt is not left up to users' discretion. This is important for situations in which users might not want or might forget to encrypt sensitive files.

3. Immediate data destruction, such as simply destroying the cryptographic keys, renders the contained data useless. However, if security towards future attacks is a concern, purging or physical destruction is advised.

The Boot Key Problem

One issue to address in full disk encryption is that the blocks where the operating system is stored must be decrypted before the OS can boot, meaning that the key has to be available before there is a user interface to ask for a password. Most Full Disk Encryption solutions utilize Pre-Boot Authentication by loading a small, highly secure operating system which is strictly locked down and hashed versus system variables to check for the integrity of the Pre-Boot kernel. Some implementations such as BitLocker Drive Encryption can make use of hardware such as a Trusted Platform Module to ensure the integrity of the boot environment, and thereby frustrate attacks that target the boot loader by replacing it with a modified version. This ensures that authentication can take place in a controlled environment without the possibility of a bootkit being used to subvert the pre-boot decryption.

With a Pre-Boot Authentication environment, the key used to encrypt the data is not decrypted until an external key is input into the system.

Solutions for storing the external key include:

- Username / password

- Using a smartcard in combination with a PIN

- Using a biometric authentication method such as a fingerprint

- Using a dongle to store the key, assuming that the user will not allow the dongle to be stolen with the laptop or that the dongle is encrypted as well.

- Using a boot-time driver that can ask for a password from the user

- Using a network interchange to recover the key, for instance as part of a PXE boot

- Using a TPM to store the decryption key, preventing unauthorized access of the decryption key or subversion of the boot loader.

- Use a combination of the above

All these possibilities have varying degrees of security; however, most are better than an unencrypted disk.

Cryptosystem

In cryptography, a cryptosystem is a suite of cryptographic algorithms needed to implement a particular security service, most commonly for achieving confidentiality (encryption).

Typically, a cryptosystem consists of three algorithms: one for key generation, one for encryption, and one for decryption. The term *cipher* (sometimes *cypher*) is often used to refer to a pair of algorithms, one for encryption and one for decryption. Therefore, the term *cryptosystem* is most often used when the key generation algorithm is important. For this reason, the term *cryptosystem* is commonly used to refer to public key techniques; however both "cipher" and "cryptosystem" are used for symmetric key techniques.

Formal Definition

Mathematically, a cryptosystem or encryption scheme can be defined as a tuple $(\mathcal{P}, \mathcal{C}, \mathcal{K}, \mathcal{E}, \mathcal{D})$ with the following properties.

1. $\mathcal{P}$ is a set called the "plaintext space". Its elements are called plaintexts.

2. $\mathcal{C}$ is a set called the "ciphertext space". Its elements are called ciphertexts.

3. $\mathcal{K}$ is a set called the "key space". Its elements are called keys.

4. $\mathcal{E} = \{E_k : k \in \mathcal{K}\}$ is a set of functions $E_k : \mathcal{P} \to \mathcal{C}.$. Its elements are called "encryption functions".

5. $\mathcal{D} = \{D_k : k \in \mathcal{K}\}$ is a set of functions $D_k : \mathcal{C} \to \mathcal{P}.$ Its elements are called "decryption functions".

For each $e \in \mathcal{K}$, there is $d \in \mathcal{K}$ such that $D_d(E_e(p)) = p$ for all $p \in \mathcal{P}$.

Note; typically this definition is modified in order to distinguish an encryption scheme as being either a symmetric-key or public-key type of cryptosystem.

Examples

A classical example of a cryptosystem is the Caesar cipher. A more contemporary example is the RSA cryptosystem.

Hybrid Cryptosystem

In cryptography, a hybrid cryptosystem is one which combines the convenience of a public-key cryptosystem with the efficiency of a symmetric-key cryptosystem. Public-key cryptosystems are convenient in that they do not require the sender and receiver to share a common secret in order to communicate securely (among other useful properties). However, they often rely on complicated mathematical computations and are thus generally much more inefficient than comparable symmetric-key cryptosystems. In many applications, the high cost of encrypting long messages in a public-key cryptosystem can be prohibitive. This is addressed by hybrid systems by using a combination of both.

A hybrid cryptosystem can be constructed using any two separate cryptosystems:

- a key encapsulation scheme, which is a public-key cryptosystem, and

- a data encapsulation scheme, which is a symmetric-key cryptosystem.

The hybrid cryptosystem is itself a public-key system, whose public and private keys are the same as in the key encapsulation scheme.

Note that for very long messages the bulk of the work in encryption/decryption is done by the more efficient symmetric-key scheme, while the inefficient public-key scheme is used only to encrypt/decrypt a short key value.

All practical implementations of public key cryptography today employ the use of a hybrid system. Examples include the TLS protocol which uses a public-key mechanism for key exchange (such as Diffie-Hellman) and a symmetric-key mechanism for data encapsulation (such as AES). The OpenPGP (RFC 4880) file format and the PKCS #7 (RFC 2315) file format are other examples.

Example

To encrypt a message addressed to Alice in a hybrid cryptosystem, Bob does the following:

1. Obtains Alice's public key.

2. Generates a fresh symmetric key for the data encapsulation scheme.

3. Encrypts the message under the data encapsulation scheme, using the symmetric key just generated.

4. Encrypt the symmetric key under the key encapsulation scheme, using Alice's public key.

5. Send both of these encryptions to Alice.

To decrypt this hybrid ciphertext, Alice does the following:

1. Uses her private key to decrypt the symmetric key contained in the key encapsulation segment.

2. Uses this symmetric key to decrypt the message contained in the data encapsulation segment.

Security

If both the key encapsulation and data encapsulation schemes are secure against adaptive chosen ciphertext attacks, then the hybrid scheme inherits that property as well. However, it is possible to construct a hybrid scheme secure against adaptive chosen ciphertext attack even if the key encapsulation has a slightly weakened security definition (though the security of the data encapsulation must be slightly stronger).

Onion Routing

Onion routing is a technique for anonymous communication over a computer network. In an onion network, messages are encapsulated in layers of encryption, analogous to layers of an onion. The encrypted data is transmitted through a series of network nodes called onion routers, each of which "peels" away a single layer, uncovering the data's next destination. When the final layer is decrypted, the message arrives at its destination. The sender remains anonymous because each intermediary knows only the location of the immediately preceding and following nodes.

Development and Implementation

Onion routing was developed in the mid-1990s at the U.S. Naval Research Laboratory by employees Paul Syverson, Michael G. Reed, and David Goldschlag to protect U.S. intelligence communications online. It was further developed by the Defense Advanced Research Projects Agency (DARPA) and patented by the Navy in 1998.

Computer scientists Roger Dingledine and Nick Mathewson joined Syverson in 2002 to develop what would become the largest and best known implementation of onion routing, Tor, then called The Onion Routing project or TOR project. After the Naval Research Laboratory released the code for Tor under a free license, Dingledine, Mathewson and five others founded The Tor Project as a non-profit organization in 2006, with the financial support of the Electronic Frontier Foundation and several other organizations.

Data Structure

In this example onion, the source of the data sends the onion to Router A, which removes a layer of encryption to learn only where to send it next and where it came from (though it does not know if the sender is the origin or just another node). Router A sends it to Router B, which decrypts another layer to learn its next destination. Router B sends it to Router C, which removes the final layer of encryption and transmits the original message to its destination.

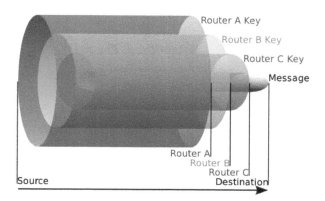

An onion is the data structure formed by "wrapping" a message with successive layers of encryption to be decrypted ("peeled" or "unwrapped") by as many intermediary computers as there are layers before arriving at its destination. The original message remains hidden as it is transferred from one node to the next, and no intermediary knows both the origin and final destination of the data, allowing the sender to remain anonymous.

Onion Creation and Transmission

To create and transmit an onion, the originator selects a set of nodes from a list provided by a "directory node". The chosen nodes are arranged into a path, called a "chain" or "circuit", through which the message will be transmitted. To preserve the anonymity of the sender, no node in the circuit is able to tell whether the node before it is the originator or another intermediary like itself. Likewise, no node in the circuit is able to tell how many other nodes are in the circuit and only the final node, the "exit node", is able to determine its own location in the chain.

Using asymmetric key cryptography, the originator obtains a public key from the directory node to send an encrypted message to the first ("entry") node, establishing a connection and a shared secret ("session key"). Using the established encrypted link to the entry node, the originator can then relay a message through the first node to a second node in the chain using encryption that only the second node, and not the first, can decrypt. When the second node receives the message, it establishes a connection with the first node. While this extends the encrypted link from the originator, the second node cannot determine whether the first node is the originator or just another node in the circuit. The originator can then send a message through the first and second nodes to a third node, encrypted such that only the third node is able to decrypt it. The third, as with the second, becomes linked to the originator but connects only with the second. This process can be repeated to build larger and larger chains, but is typically limited to preserve performance.

When the chain is complete, the originator can send data over the Internet anonymously. When the final recipient of the data sends data back, the intermediary nodes maintain the same link back to the originator, with data again layered, but in reverse such that the final node this time removes the first layer of encryption and the first node removes the last layer of encryption before sending the data, for example a web page, to the originator.

Weaknesses

Timing Analysis

One of the reasons typical Internet connections are not considered anonymous is the ability of Internet service providers to trace and log connections between computers. For example, when a person accesses a particular website, the data itself may be secured through a connection like HTTPS such that your password, emails, or other content is not visible to an outside party, but there is a record of the connection itself, what time it occurred, and the amount of data transferred. Onion routing creates and obscures a path between two computers such that there's no discernible connection directly from a person to a website, but there still exist records of connections between computers. Traffic analysis searches those records of connections made by a potential originator and tries to match timing and data transfers to connections made to a potential recipient. For example, a person may be seen to have transferred exactly 51 kilobytes of data to an unknown computer just three seconds before a different unknown computer transferred exactly 51 kilobytes of data to a particular website. Factors that may facilitate traffic analysis include nodes failing or leaving the network and a compromised node keeping track of a session as it occurs when chains are periodically rebuilt.

Garlic routing is a variant of onion routing associated with the I2P network that encrypts multiple messages together to make it more difficult for attackers to perform traffic analysis.

Exit Node Vulnerability

Although the message being sent is transmitted inside several layers of encryption, the job of the exit node, as the final node in the chain, is to decrypt the final layer and deliver the message to the recipient. A compromised exit node is thus able to acquire the raw data being transmitted, potentially including passwords, private messages, bank account numbers, and other forms of personal information. Dan Egerstad, a Swedish researcher, used such an attack to collect the passwords of over 100 email accounts related to foreign embassies.

Exit node vulnerabilities are similar to those on unsecured wireless networks, where the data being transmitted by a user on the network may be intercepted by another user or by the router operator. Both issues are solved by using a secure end-to-end connection like SSL or secure HTTP (S-HTTP). If there is end-to-end encryption between the sender and the recipient, then not even the last intermediary can view the original message.

Secure Multi-party Computation

Secure multi-party computation (also known as secure computation or multi-party computation/ MPC) is a subfield of cryptography with the goal of creating methods for parties to jointly compute a function over their inputs while keeping those inputs private.

Definition and Overview

In an MPC, a given number of participants, p_1, p_2, ..., p_N, each have private data, respectively d_1, d_2, ..., d_N. Participants want to compute the value of a public function on that private data: $F(d_1, d_2, ..., d_N)$ while keeping their own inputs secret.

For example, suppose we have three parties Alice, Bob and Charlie, with respective inputs x, y and z denoting their salaries. They want to find out the highest of the three salaries, without revealing to each other how much each of them makes. Mathematically, this translates to them computing:

$$F(x,y,z) = max(x,y,z)$$

If there were some trusted outside party (say, they had a mutual friend Tony who they knew could keep a secret), they could each tell their salary to Tony, he could compute the maximum, and tell that number to all of them. The goal of MPC is to design a protocol, where, by exchanging messages only with each other, Alice, Bob, and Charlie can still learn F(x, y, z) without revealing who makes what and without having to rely on Tony. They should learn no more by engaging in their protocol than they would learn by interacting with an incorruptible, perfectly trustworthy Tony.

In particular, all that the parties can learn is what they can learn from the output and their own input. So in the above example, if the output is z, then Charlie learns that his z is the maximum value, whereas Alice and Bob learn (if x, y and z are distinct), that their input is not equal to the maximum, and that the maximum held is equal to z. The basic scenario can be easily generalised to where the parties have several inputs and outputs, and the function outputs different values to different parties.

Informally speaking, the most basic properties that a multi-party computation protocol aims to ensure are:

- Input privacy: No information about the private data held by the parties can be inferred from the messages sent during the execution of the protocol. The only information that can be inferred about the private data is whatever could be inferred from seeing the output of the function alone.

- Correctness: Any proper subset of adversarial colluding parties willing to share information or deviate from the instructions during the protocol execution should not be able to force honest parties to output an incorrect result. This correctness goal comes in two flavours: either the honest parties are guaranteed to compute the correct output (a "robust" protocol), or they abort if they find an error (an MPC protocol "with abort").

There are a wide range of practical applications, varying from simple tasks such as coin tossing to more complex ones like electronic auctions (e.g. compute the market clearing price), electronic voting, or privacy-preserving data mining. A classical example is the Millionaire's Problem: two millionaires want to know who is richer, in such a way that neither of them learns the net worth of the other. A solution to this situation is essentially to securely evaluate the comparison function.

Security Definitions

A key question to ask is; when is such a multiparty computation protocol secure? In modern cryptography, a protocol can only be deemed to be secure if it comes equipped with a "security proof". This is a mathematical proof that the security of the protocol reduces to that of the security of the underlying primitives. But this means we need a definition of what it means for a protocol to be secure. This is hard to formalize, in the case of MPC, since we cannot say that the parties should "learn nothing" since they need to learn the output and this depends on the inputs. In addition, we cannot just say that the output must be "correct" since the correct output depends on the parties' inputs, and we do not know what inputs corrupted parties will use. A formal mathematical definition of security for MPC protocols follows the ideal-real-world paradigm, described below.

The ideal-real-world paradigm imagines two worlds. In the ideal world, there exists an incorruptible trusted party to whom each protocol participant sends its input. This trusted party computes the function on its own and sends back the appropriate output to each party. (In the Alice, Bob, and Charlie example above, Tony performed the role of trusted outside party.) In contrast, in the real-world model, there is no trusted party and all the parties can do is to exchange messages with each other. We say a protocol is secure if one can learn no more about each party's private inputs in the real world than one could learn in the ideal world. Since no messages between the parties are exchanged in the ideal world, this security definition implies that the real-world messages that were exchanged cannot have revealed any secret information.

We stress that the ideal-real-world paradigm provides a simple abstraction of the complexities of MPC that is of great use to anyone using an MPC protocol. Namely, it suffices to construct an application under the pretense that the MPC protocol at its core is actually an ideal execution. If the application is secure in this case, then it is also secure when a real protocol is run instead.

The security requirements on an MPC protocol are so stringent that it may seem that it is rarely possible to actually achieve. Surprisingly, in the late 1980s it was already shown that any function can be securely computed, with security for malicious adversaries. This is encouraging news, but it took a long time until MPC became efficient enough to be used in practice. Unconditionally or information-theoretically secure MPC is closely related to the problem of secret sharing, and more specifically verifiable secret sharing (VSS), which many secure MPC protocols that protect against active adversaries use.

Unlike in traditional cryptographic applications, such as encryption or signatures, the adversary in an MPC protocol can be one of the players engaged in the protocol. In fact, in MPC we assume that corrupted parties may collude in order to breach the security of the protocol. If the number of parties in the protocol is n, then the number of parties who can be adversarial is usually denoted by t. The protocols and solutions for the case of $t < n/2$ (i.e., when an honest majority is assumed) are very different to those where no such assumption is made. This latter case includes the important case of two-party computation where one of the participants may be corrupted, and the general case where an unlimited number of participants are corrupted and collude to attack the honest participants.

Different protocols can deal with different adversarial powers. We can categorize adversaries according to how willing they are to deviate from the protocol. There are essentially two types of adversaries, each giving rise to different forms of security:

- Semi-Honest (Passive) Security: In this case, we assume that corrupted parties merely cooperate to gather information out of the protocol, but do not deviate from the protocol specification. This is a naive adversary model, yielding weak security in real situations. However, protocols achieving this level of security prevent inadvertent leakage of information between parties, and are thus useful if this is the only concern. In addition, protocols in the semi-honest model are very efficient, and are often an important first step for achieving higher levels of security.

- Malicious (Active) Security: In this case, the adversary may arbitrarily deviate from the protocol execution in its attempt to cheat. Protocols that achieve security in this model provide a very high security guarantee. The only thing that an adversary can do in the case of dishonest majority is to cause the honest parties to "abort" having detected cheating. If the honest parties do obtain output, then they are guaranteed that it is correct. Of course, their privacy is always preserved.

Since security against active adversaries is often only possible at the cost of reducing efficiency one is led to consider a relaxed form of active security called covert security, proposed by Aumann and Lindell. Covert security captures more realistic situations, where active adversaries are willing to cheat but only if they are not caught. For example, their reputation could be damaged, preventing future collaboration with other honest parties. Thus, protocols that are covertly secure provide mechanisms to ensure that, if some of the parties do not follow the instructions, then it will be noticed with high probability, say 75% or 90%. In a way, covert adversaries are active ones forced to act passively due to external non-cryptographic (e.g. business) concerns. This sets a bridge between the two models in the hope of finding protocols, which are efficient yet secure enough for practice.

Like many cryptographic protocols, the security of an MPC protocol can rely on different assumptions:

- It can be computational (i.e. based on some mathematical problem, like factoring) or unconditional (usually with some probability of error which can be made arbitrarily small).

- The model might assume that participants use a synchronized network, where a message sent at a "tick" always arrives at the next "tick", or that a secure and reliable broadcast channel exists, or that a secure communication channel exists between every pair of participants where an adversary cannot read, modify or generate messages in the channel, etc.

The set of honest parties that can execute a computational task is related to the concept of access structure. "Adversary structures" can be static, i.e. the adversary chooses its victims before the start of the multi-party computation, or dynamic, i.e. it chooses its victims during the course of execution of the multiparty computation. Attaining security against a dynamic adversary is often much harder than security against a static adversary. An adversary structure can be defined as a "threshold structure" meaning that it can corrupt or simply read the memory of a number of participants up to some threshold, or be defined as a more complex structure, where it can affect certain predefined subsets of participants, modeling different possible collusions.

History

Secure computation was formally introduced as secure two-party computation (2PC) in 1982 by

Andrew Yao, the first recipient of the Knuth Prize. It is also referred to as Secure function evaluation (SFE), and is concerned with the question: 'Can two party computation be achieved more efficiently and under weaker security assumptions than general MPC?'. The millionaire problem solution gave way to a generalization to multi-party protocols.

Increasingly efficient protocols for MPC have been proposed, and MPC can be now used as a practical solution to various real-life problems such as distributed voting, private bidding and auctions, sharing of signature or decryption functions and private information retrieval. The first large-scale and practical application of multiparty computation took place in Denmark in January 2008.

Protocols used

There are major differences between the protocols proposed for two party computation (2PC) and multiparty computation (MPC).

Two-party Computation

The two party setting is particularly interesting, not only from an applications perspective but also because special techniques can be applied in the two party setting which do not apply in the multi-party case. Indeed, secure multi-party computation (in fact the restricted case of secure function evaluation, where only a single function is evaluated) was first presented in the two-party setting. The original work is often cited as being from one of the two papers of Yao; although the papers do not actually contain what is now known as Yao's protocol.

Yao's basic protocol is secure against semi-honest adversaries and is extremely efficient in terms of number of rounds, which is constant, and independent of the target function being evaluated. The function is viewed as a Boolean circuit, with inputs in binary of fixed length. A Boolean circuit is a collection of gates connected with three different types of wires: circuit-input wires, circuit-output wires and intermediate wires. Each gate receives two input wires and it has a single output wire which might be fan-out (i.e. be passed to multiple gates at the next level). Plain evaluation of the circuit is done by evaluating each gate in turn; assuming the gates have been lexicographically ordered. The gate is represented as a truth table such that for each possible pair of bits (those coming from the input wires' gate) the table assigns a unique output bit; which is the value of the output wire of the gate. The results of the evaluation are the bits obtained in the circuit-output wires.

Yao explained how to garble a circuit (hide its structure) so that two parties, sender and receiver, can learn the output of the circuit and nothing else. At a high level, the sender prepares the garbled circuit and sends it to the receiver, who obliviously evaluates the circuit, learning the encodings corresponding to both his and the senders output. He then just sends back the senders encodings, allowing the sender to compute his part of the output. The sender sends the mapping from the receivers output encodings to bits to the receiver, allowing the receiver to obtain their output.

In more detail, the garbled circuit is computed as follows. The main ingredient is a double-keyed symmetric encryption scheme. Given a gate of the circuit, each possible value of its input wires (either 0 or 1) is encoded with a random number (label). The values resulting from the evaluation of the gate at each of the four possible pair of input bits are also replaced with random labels. The garbled truth table of the gate consists of encryptions of each output label using its inputs labels as keys. The position of these four encryptions in the truth table is randomized so no information on the gate is leaked.

To correctly evaluate each garbled gate the encryption scheme has the following two properties. Firstly, the ranges of the encryption function under any two distinct keys are disjoint (with overwhelming probability). The second property says that it can be checked efficiently whether a given ciphertext has been encrypted under a given key. With these two properties the receiver, after obtaining the labels for all circuit-input wires, can evaluate each gate by first finding out which of the four ciphertexts has been encrypted with his label keys, and then decrypting to obtain the label of the output wire. This is done obliviously as all the receiver learns during the evaluation are encodings of the bits.

The sender's (i.e. circuit creators) input bits can be just sent as encodings to the evaluator; whereas the receiver's (i.e. circuit evaluators) encodings corresponding to his input bits are obtained via a 1-out-of-2 Oblivious Transfer (OT) protocol. A 1-out-of-2 OT protocol, enables the sender, in possession of two values C1 and C2, to send the one requested by the receiver (b a value in {1,2}) in such a way that the sender does not know what value has been transferred, and the receiver only learns the queried value.

If one is considering malicious adversaries, further mechanisms to ensure correct behaviour of both parties need to be provided. By construction it is easy to show security for the sender, as all the receiver can do is to evaluate a garbled circuit that would fail to reach the circuit-output wires if he deviated from the instructions. The situation is very different on the sender's side. For example, he may send an incorrect garbled circuit that computes a function revealing the receiver's input. This would mean that privacy no longer holds, but since the circuit is garbled the receiver would not be able to detect this.

Multiparty Protocols

Most MPC protocols, as opposed to 2PC protocols, make use of secret sharing. In the secret sharing based methods, the parties do not play special roles (as in Yao, of creator and evaluator). Instead the data associated to each wire is shared amongst the parties; and a protocol is then used to evaluate each gate. The function is now defined as a "circuit" over $GF(p)$, as opposed to the binary circuits used for Yao. Such a circuit is called an arithmetic circuit in the literature, and it consists of addition and multiplication "gates" where the values operated on are defined over $GF(p)$.

Secret sharing allows one to distribute a secret among a number of parties by distributing shares to each party. Three types of secret sharing schemes are commonly used; Shamir Secret Sharing, Replicated Secret Sharing and Additive Secret Sharing. In all three cases the shares are random elements of $GF(p)$ that add up to the secret in $GF(p)$; intuitively, security steams because any non-qualifying set shares looks randomly distributed. All three secret sharing schemes are linear, so the sum of two shared secrets, or multiplication a secret by a public constant, can be done locally. Thus linear functions can be evaluated for free.

Replicated Secret Sharing schemes are usually associated with passively secure MPC systems consisting of three parties, of which at most one can be adversarial; such as used in the Sharemind system. MPC systems based on Shamir Secret Sharing are generally associated with systems which can tolerate up to t adversaries out of n, so called threshold systems. In the case of information theoretic protocols actively secure protocols can be realised with Shamir Secret Sharing sharing if $t<n/3$, whilst passively secure ones are available if $t<n/2$. In the case of computationally secure protocols one can tolerate a threshold of $t<n/2$ for actively secure protocols. A practical system adopting this approach is the VIFF framework. Additive secret sharing is used when one wants to tolerate a dishonest majority, i.e. $t<n$, in which case we can only obtain MPC protocols "with abort", this later type is typified by the SPDZ and (multi-party variant) of the TinyOT protocol.

Other Protocols

Virtual Party Protocol is a protocol which uses virtual parties and complex mathematics to hide the identity of the parties.

Secure sum protocols allow multiple cooperating parties to compute sum function of their individual data without revealing the data to one another.

In 2014 a "model of fairness in secure computation in which an adversarial party that aborts on receiving output is forced to pay a mutually predefined monetary penalty" has been described for the Bitcoin network or for fair lottery.

Scalable MPC

Recently, several multi-party computation techniques have been proposed targeting resource-efficiency (in terms of bandwidth, computation, and latency) for large networks. Although much theoretical progress has been made to achieve scalability, practical progress is slower. In particular, most known schemes suffer from either poor or unknown communication and computation costs in practice.

Practical MPC Systems

Many advances have been made on 2PC and MPC systems in recent years.

Yao-based Protocols

One of the main issues when working with Yao-based protocols is that the function to be securely evaluated (which could be an arbitrary program) must be represented as a circuit, usually consisting of XOR and AND gates. Since most real-world programs contain loops and complex data structures, this is a highly non-trivial task. The Fairplay system was the first tool designed to tackle this problem. Fairplay comprises two main components. The first of these is a compiler enabling users to write programs in a simple high-level language, and output these programs in a Boolean circuit representation. The second component can then garble the circuit and execute a protocol to securely evaluate the garbled circuit. As well as two-party computation based on Yao's protocol, Fairplay can also carry out multi-party protocols. This is done using the BMR protocol, which extends Yao's passively secure protocol to the active case.

In the years following the introduction of Fairplay, many improvements to Yao's basic protocol have been created, in the form of both efficiency improvements and techniques for active security. These include techniques such as the free XOR method, which allows for much simpler evaluation of XOR gates, and garbled row reduction, reducing the size of garbled tables with two inputs by 25%.

The approach that so far seems to be the most fruitful in obtaining active security comes from a combination of the garbling technique and the "cut-and-choose" paradigm. This combination seems to render more efficient constructions. To avoid the aforementioned problems with respect to dishonest behaviour, many garblings of the same circuit are sent from the constructor to the evaluator. Then around half of them (depending on the specific protocol) are opened to check consistency, and if so a vast majority of the unopened ones are correct with high probability. The output is the majority vote of all the evaluations. Note that here the majority output is needed. If there is disagreement on the outputs the receiver knows the sender is cheating, but he cannot complain as otherwise this would leak information on his input.

This approach for active security was initiated by Lindell and Pinkas. This technique was implemented by Pinkas et al. in 2009, This provided the first actively secure two-party evaluation of the Advanced Encryption Standard (AES) circuit, regarded as a highly complex (consisting of around 30,000 AND and XOR gates), non-trivial function (also with some potential applications), taking around 20 minutes to compute and requiring 160 circuits to obtain a 2-40 cheating probability.

As many circuits are evaluated, the parties (including the receiver) need to commit to their inputs to ensure that in all the iterations the same values are used. The experiments of Pinkas et al. reported show that the bottleneck of the protocol lies in the consistency checks. They had to send over the net about 6,553,600 commitments to various values to evaluate the AES circuit. In recent results the efficiency of actively secure Yao-based implementations was improved even further, requiring only 40 circuits, and much less commitments, to obtain 2-40 cheating probability. The improvements come from new methodologies for performing cut-and-choose on the transmitted circuits.

More recently, there has been a focus on highly parallel implementations based on garbled circuits, designed to be run on CPUs with many cores. Kreuter, et al. describe an implementation running on 512 cores of a powerful cluster computer. Using these resources they could evaluate the 4095-bit edit distance function, whose circuit comprises almost 6 billion gates. To accomplish this they developed a custom, better optimized circuit compiler than Fairplay and several new optimizations such as pipelining, whereby transmission of the garbled circuit across the network begins while the rest of the circuit is still being generated. The time to compute AES was reduced to 1.4 seconds per block in the active case, using a 512-node cluster machine, and 115 seconds using one node. shelat and Shen improve this, using commodity hardware, to 0.52 seconds per block. The same paper reports on a throughput of 21 blocks per second, but with a latency of 48 seconds per block.

Meanwhile, another group of researchers has investigated using consumer-grade GPUs to achieve similar levels of parallelism. They utilize OT extensions and some other novel techniques to design their GPU-specific protocol. This approach seems to achieve comparable efficiency to the cluster computing implementation, using a similar number of cores. However, the authors only report on an implementation of the AES circuit, which has around 50,000 gates. On the other hand, the hardware required here is far more accessible, as similar devices may already be found in many people's desktop computers or games consoles. The authors obtain a timing of 2.7 seconds per AES block on a standard desktop, with a standard GPU. If they allow security to decrease to something akin to covert security, they obtain a run time of 0.30 seconds per AES block.It should be noted that in the passive security case there are reports of processing of circuits with 250 million gates, and at a rate of 75 million gates per second.

References

- Fagoyinbo, Joseph Babatunde (2013-05-24). The Armed Forces: Instrument of Peace, Strength, Development and Prosperity. AuthorHouse. ISBN 9781477226476. Retrieved August 29, 2014.

- Leigh, David; Harding, Luke (2011-02-08). WikiLeaks: Inside Julian Assange's War on Secrecy. PublicAffairs. ISBN 1610390628. Retrieved August 29, 2014.

- Pathak Rohit, Joshi Satyadhar, Advances in Information Security and Assurance, Springer Berlin / Heidelberg, ISSN 0302-9743 (Print) 1611-3349 (Online), ISBN 978-3-642-02616-4.

- Jared Saia and Mahdi Zamani. Recent Results in Scalable Multi-Party Computation. SOFSEM 2015: Theory and Practice of Computer Science. Springer Berlin Heidelberg. Volume 8939. pp 24–44. 2015. ISBN 978-3-662-46078-8

- Webster, A. F.; Tavares, Stafford E. (1985). "On the design of S-boxes". Advances in Cryptology - Crypto '85. Lecture Notes in Computer Science. 218. New York, NY,: Springer-Verlag New York, Inc. pp. 523–534. ISBN 0-387-16463-4.

- David A. King, The ciphers of the monks - A forgotten number notation of the Middle Ages, Stuttgart: Franz Steiner, 2001 (ISBN 3-515-07640-9)

- Abraham Sinkov, Elementary Cryptanalysis: A Mathematical Approach, Mathematical Association of America, 1966. ISBN 0-88385-622-0

- van Tilborg, Henk C. A.; Jajodia, Sushil, eds. (2011). Encyclopedia of Cryptography and Security. Springer. ISBN 978-1-4419-5905-8. , p. 455.

- Menezes, Alfred J.; van Oorschot, Paul C.; Vanstone, Scott A. (1996). "Chapter 7: Block Ciphers". Handbook of Applied Cryptography. CRC Press. ISBN 0-8493-8523-7.

- Chakraborty, D. & Rodriguez-Henriquez F. (2008). "Block Cipher Modes of Operation from a Hardware Implementation Perspective". In Koç, Çetin K. Cryptographic Engineering. Springer. p. 321. ISBN 9780387718163.

- Junod, Pascal & Canteaut, Anne (2011). Advanced Linear Cryptanalysis of Block and Stream Ciphers. IOS Press. p. 2. ISBN 9781607508441.

- Keliher, Liam et al. (2000). "Modeling Linear Characteristics of Substitution-Permutation Networks". In Hays, Howard & Carlisle, Adam. Selected areas in cryptography: 6th annual international workshop, SAC'99, Kingston, Ontario, Canada, August 9-10, 1999 : proceedings. Springer. p. 79. ISBN 9783540671855.

- Baigneres, Thomas & Finiasz, Matthieu (2007). "Dial 'C' for Cipher". In Biham, Eli & Yousseff, Amr. Selected areas in cryptography: 13th international workshop, SAC 2006, Montreal, Canada, August 17-18, 2006 : revised selected papers. Springer. p. 77. ISBN 9783540744610.

- Cusick, Thomas W. & Stanica, Pantelimon (2009). Cryptographic Boolean functions and applications. Academic Press. p. 164. ISBN 9780123748904.

- Martin, Keith M. (2012). Everyday Cryptography: Fundamental Principles and Applications. Oxford University Press. p. 114. ISBN 9780199695591.

- Menezes, Alfred J.; Oorschot, Paul C. van; Vanstone, Scott A. (2001). Handbook of Applied Cryptography (Fifth ed.). p. 251. ISBN 0849385237.

- Menezes, Alfred; van Oorschot, Paul; Vanstone, Scott (1997). Handbook of Applied Cryptography Boca Raton, Florida: CRC Press. ISBN 0-8493-8523-7.

- Singh, Simon (1999) The Code Book: the evolution of secrecy from Mary Queen of Scots to quantum cryptography New York: Doubleday ISBN 0-385-49531-5

- Mark Bando (2007). 101st Airborne: The Screaming Eagles in World War II. Mbi Publishing Company. ISBN 978-0-7603-2984-9. Retrieved 20 May 2012.

- "Modern Cryptography: Theory & Practice", Wenbo Mao, Prentice Hall Professional Technical Reference, New Jersey, 2004, pg. 308. ISBN 0-13-066943-1

- Lund, Paul (2009). The Book of Codes. Berkeley and Los Angeles, California: University of California Press. pp. 106–107. ISBN 9780520260139.

5

Various Aspects of Cryptography

The process of encoding information in such a way that only the person authorized can read it is known as encryption. Other topics included in this chapter are key schedule, block size, avalanche effect, secure channels, etc. The topics discussed in the chapter are of great importance to broaden the existing knowledge on cryptography.

Encryption

In cryptography, encryption is the process of encoding messages or information in such a way that only authorized parties can read it. Encryption does not of itself prevent interception, but denies the message content to the interceptor. In an encryption scheme, the intended communication information or message, referred to as plaintext, is encrypted using an encryption algorithm, generating ciphertext that can only be read if decrypted. For technical reasons, an encryption scheme usually uses a pseudo-random encryption key generated by an algorithm. It is in principle possible to decrypt the message without possessing the key, but, for a well-designed encryption scheme, large computational resources and skill are required. An authorized recipient can easily decrypt the message with the key provided by the originator to recipients, but not to unauthorized interceptors.

Purpose

The purpose of encryption is to ensure that only somebody who is authorized to access data (e.g. a text message or a file), will be able to read it, using the decryption key. Somebody who is not authorized can be excluded, because he or she does not have the required key, without which it is impossible to read the encrypted information.

Types

Symmetric Key

In symmetric-key schemes, the encryption and decryption keys are the same. Communicating parties must have the same key before they can achieve secure communication.

Public Key

In public-key encryption schemes, the encryption key is published for anyone to use and encrypt messages. However, only the receiving party has access to the decryption key that enables messages to be read. Public-key encryption was first described in a secret document in 1973; before then all encryption schemes were symmetric-key (also called private-key).

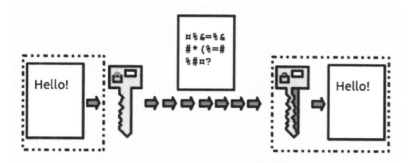

Illustration of how encryption is used within servers Public key encryption.

A publicly available public key encryption application called Pretty Good Privacy (PGP) was written in 1991 by Phil Zimmermann, and distributed free of charge with source code; it was purchased by Symantec in 2010 and is regularly updated.

Uses

Encryption has long been used by military and governments to facilitate secret communication. It is now commonly used in protecting information within many kinds of civilian systems. For example, the Computer Security Institute reported that in 2007, 71% of companies surveyed utilized encryption for some of their data in transit, and 53% utilized encryption for some of their data in storage. Encryption can be used to protect data "at rest", such as information stored on computers and storage devices (e.g. USB flash drives). In recent years there have been numerous reports of confidential data such as customers' personal records being exposed through loss or theft of laptops or backup drives. Encrypting such files at rest helps protect them should physical security measures fail. Digital rights management systems, which prevent unauthorized use or reproduction of copyrighted material and protect software against reverse engineering, is another somewhat different example of using encryption on data at rest.

Encryption is also used to protect data in transit, for example data being transferred via networks (e.g. the Internet, e-commerce), mobile telephones, wireless microphones, wireless intercom systems, Bluetooth devices and bank automatic teller machines. There have been numerous reports of data in transit being intercepted in recent years. Data should also be encrypted when transmitted across networks in order to protect against eavesdropping of network traffic by unauthorized users.

Message Verification

Encryption, by itself, can protect the confidentiality of messages, but other techniques are still needed to protect the integrity and authenticity of a message; for example, verification of a message authentication code (MAC) or a digital signature. Standards for cryptographic software and hardware to perform encryption are widely available, but successfully using encryption to ensure security may be a challenging problem. A single error in system design or execution can allow successful attacks. Sometimes an adversary can obtain unencrypted information without directly undoing the encryption.

Digital signature and encryption must be applied to the ciphertext when it is created (typically on the same device used to compose the message) to avoid tampering; otherwise any node between the sender and the encryption agent could potentially tamper with it. Encrypting at the time of creation is only secure if the encryption device itself has not been tampered with.

Plaintext

In cryptography, plaintext is information a sender wishes to transmit to a receiver. *Cleartext* is often used as a synonym. Plaintext has reference to the operation of cryptographic algorithms, usually encryption algorithms, and is the input upon which they operate. *Cleartext*, by contrast, refers to data that is transmitted or stored unencrypted (that is, 'in the clear').

Overview

With the advent of computing the definition of plaintext expanded to include any data, including binary files, in addition to simple messages and human-readable documents, in a form that can be interpreted or used without needing to be processed using information not generally available (a key). The information, which would normally be called a message, document, file, etc., if to be communicated or stored in encrypted form is referred to as plaintext.

Plaintext is used as input to an encryption algorithm; the output is usually termed ciphertext, particularly when the algorithm is a cipher. Codetext is less often used, and almost always only when the algorithm involved is actually a code. In some systems multiple layers of encryption are used, with the output of one encryption algorithm become the "plaintext" input for the next.

Secure Handling of Plaintext

Weaknesses can be introduced into a cryptosystem through insecure handling of plaintext, allowing an attacker to bypass the cryptography altogether. Plaintext is vulnerable in use and in storage, whether in electronic or paper format. Physical security deals with methods of securing information and its storage media from local, physical, attacks, for instance by entering a building and gaining access to papers, storage media, or computers. Discarded material, if not disposed of securely, may be a security risk; even shredded documents and erased magnetic media can often be reconstructed with sufficient effort.

If plaintext is stored in a computer file , the storage media, the computer and its components, and all backups must be secure. Sensitive data is sometimes processed on computers whose mass storage is removable, in which case physical security of the removed disk is separately vital. In the case of securing a computer, useful (as opposed to handwaving) security must be physical (e.g., against burglary, brazen removal under cover of supposed repair, installation of covert monitoring devices, etc.), as well as virtual (e.g., operating system modification, illicit network access, Trojan programs, ...). The wide availability of keydrives, which can plug into most modern computers and store large quantities of data, poses another severe security headache. A spy (perhaps posing as a cleaning person) could easily conceal one and even swallow it, if necessary.

Discarded computers, disk drives and media are also a potential source of plaintexts. Most operating systems do not actually erase anything — they simply mark the disk space occupied by a deleted file as 'available for use', and remove its entry from the file system directory. The information in a file deleted in this way remains fully present until overwritten at some later time when the operating system reuses the disk space. With even low-end computers commonly sold with many gigabytes of disk space and rising monthly, this 'later time' may be months later, or never. Even overwriting the portion of a disk surface occupied by a deleted file is insufficient in many cases. Peter Gutmann of the University of Auckland wrote a celebrated 1996 paper on the recovery of overwritten information from magnetic disks; areal storage densities have gotten much higher since then, so this sort of recovery is likely to be more difficult than it was when Gutmann wrote.

Also, independently, modern hard drives automatically remap sectors that are starting to fail; those sectors no longer in use will contain information that is entirely invisible to the file system (and all software which uses it for access to disk data), but is nonetheless still present on the physical drive platter. It may, of course, be sensitive plaintext. Some government agencies (e.g., US NSA) require that all disk drives be physically pulverized when they are discarded, and in some cases, chemically treated with corrosives before or after. This practice is not widespread outside of the government, however. For example, Garfinkel and Shelat (2003) analyzed 158 second-hand hard drives acquired at garage sales and the like and found that less than 10% had been sufficiently sanitized. A wide variety of personal and confidential information was found readable from the others.

Laptop computers are a special problem. Laptops containing secret information, some perhaps in plaintext form, belonging to the US State Department, Department of Defense, and the British Secret Service have been stolen or lost. Announcements of similar losses are becoming a common item in news reports. Appropriate disk encryption techniques can safeguard data on misappropriated computers or media.

On occasion, even when the data on the host systems is itself encrypted, the media used to transfer data between such systems is nevertheless plaintext due to poorly designed data policy. An incident in October 2007 in which HM Revenue and Customs lost CDs containing the records of 25 million child benefit recipients in the United Kingdom — the data apparently being entirely unencrypted — is a case in point.

Modern cryptographic systems are designed to resist known plaintext or even chosen plaintext attacks and so may not be entirely compromised when plaintext is lost or stolen. Older systems used techniques such as padding and Russian copulation to obscure information in plaintext that could be easily guessed, and to resist the effects of loss of plaintext on the security of the cryptosystem.

Web Browser Saved Password Security Controversy

Several popular web browsers which offer to store a user's passwords do so in plaintext form. Even though most of them initially hide the saved passwords, it is possible for anyone to view all passwords in cleartext with a few clicks of the mouse, by going into the browsers' security settings options menus. In 2010, it emerged that this is the case with Firefox (still the case as of end-2014), and in Aug 2013 it emerged that Google Chrome does so as well. When a software developer raised the issue with the Chrome security team, a company representative responded that Google would not change the feature, and justified the refusal by saying that hiding the passwords would "provide users with a false sense of security" and "that's just not how we approach security on Chrome".

RSA Problem

In cryptography, the RSA problem summarizes the task of performing an RSA private-key operation given only the public key. The RSA algorithm raises a *message* to an *exponent*, modulo a composite number N whose factors are not known. Thus, the task can be neatly described as finding the eth roots of an arbitrary number, modulo N. For large RSA key sizes (in excess of 1024 bits), no efficient method for solving this problem is known; if an efficient method is ever developed, it would threaten the current or eventual security of RSA-based cryptosystems—both for public-key encryption and digital signatures.

More specifically, the RSA problem is to efficiently compute P given an RSA public key (N, e) and a ciphertext $C \equiv P^e$ (mod N). The structure of the RSA public key requires that N be a large semiprime (i.e., a product of two large prime numbers), that $2 < e < N$, that e be coprime to $\varphi(N)$, and that $0 \le C < N$. C is chosen randomly within that range; to specify the problem with complete precision, one must also specify how N and e are generated, which will depend on the precise means of RSA random keypair generation in use.

The most efficient method known to solve the RSA problem is by first factoring the modulus N. A task believed to be impractical, if N is sufficiently large. The RSA key setup routine already turns the public exponent e, with this prime factorization, into the private exponent d, and so exactly the same algorithm allows anyone who factors N to obtain the *private key*. Any C can then be decrypted with the private key.

Just as there are no proofs that integer factorization is computationally difficult, there are also no proofs that the RSA problem is similarly difficult. By the above method, the RSA problem is at least as easy as factoring, but it might well be easier. Indeed, there is strong evidence pointing to this conclusion: that a method to break the RSA method cannot be converted necessarily into a method for factoring large semiprimes. This is perhaps easiest to see by the sheer overkill of the factoring approach: the RSA problem asks us to decrypt *one* arbitrary ciphertext, whereas the factoring method reveals the private key: thus decrypting *all* arbitrary ciphertexts, and it also allows one to perform arbitrary RSA private-key encryptions. Along these same lines, finding the decryption exponent d indeed *is* computationally equivalent to factoring N, even though the RSA problem does not ask for d.

In addition to the RSA problem, RSA also has a particular mathematical structure that can potentially be exploited *without* solving the RSA problem directly. To achieve the full strength of the RSA problem, an RSA-based cryptosystem must also use a padding scheme like OAEP, to protect against such structural problems in RSA.

Key Schedule

In cryptography, the so-called product ciphers are a certain kind of ciphers, where the (de-)ciphering of data is done in "rounds". The general setup of each round is the same, except for some hard-coded parameters and a part of the cipher key, called a subkey. A key schedule is an algorithm that, given the key, calculates the subkeys for these rounds.

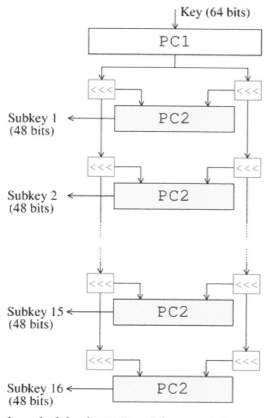

The key schedule of DES ("<<<" denotes a left rotation)

Some Types of Key Schedules

- Some ciphers have simple key schedules. For example, the block cipher TEA simply splits the 128-bit key into four 32-bit pieces and uses them repeatedly in successive rounds.

- DES uses a key schedule where the 56 bit key is divided into two 28-bit halves; each half is thereafter treated separately. In successive rounds, both halves are rotated left by one or two bits (specified for each round), and then 48 subkey bits are selected by Permuted Choice 2 (PC-2) — 24 bits from the left half, and 24 from the right. The rotations mean that a different set of bits is used in each subkey; each bit is used in approximately 14 out of the 16 subkeys.

- In an effort to avoid simple relationships between the cipher key and the subkeys, to resist such forms of cryptanalysis as related-key attacks and slide attacks, many modern ciphers use much more elaborate key schedules, algorithms that use a one-way function to generate an "expanded key" from which subkeys are drawn. Some ciphers, such as Rijndael (AES) and Blowfish, use parts of the cipher algorithm itself for this key expansion, sometimes initialized with some "nothing up my sleeve numbers". Other ciphers, such as RC5, expand keys with functions that are somewhat or completely different from the encryption functions.

Block Size (Cryptography)

In modern cryptography, symmetric key ciphers are generally divided into stream ciphers and block ciphers. Block ciphers operate on a fixed length string of bits. The length of this bit string is the block size. Both the input (plaintext) and output (ciphertext) are the same length; the output cannot be shorter than the input — this follows logically from the Pigeonhole principle and the fact that the cipher must be reversible — and it is undesirable for the output to be longer than the input.

Until the announcement of NIST's AES contest, the majority of block ciphers followed the example of the DES in using a block size of 64 bits (8 bytes). However the Birthday paradox tells us that after accumulating a number of blocks equal to the square root of the total number possible, there will be an approximately 50% chance of two or more being the same, which would start to leak information about the message contents. Thus even when used with a proper encryption mode (e.g. CBC or OFB), only 2^{32} x 8 B = 32 GB of data can be safely sent under one key. In practice a greater margin of security is desired, restricting a single key to the encryption of much less data - say a few hundred megabytes. Once that seemed like a fair amount of data, but today it is easily exceeded. If the cipher mode does not properly randomise the input, the limit is even lower.

Consequently, AES candidates were required to support a block length of 128 bits (16 bytes). This should be acceptable for up to 2^{64} x 16 B = 256 Exabytes of data, and should suffice for quite a few years to come. The winner of the AES contest, Rijndael, supports block and key sizes of 128, 192, and 256 bits, but in AES the block size is always 128 bits. The extra block sizes were not adopted by the AES standard.

Many block ciphers, such as RC5, support a variable block size. The Luby-Rackoff construction and the Outerbridge construction can both increase the effective block size of a cipher.

Joan Daemen's 3-Way and BaseKing have unusual block sizes of 96 and 192 bits, respectively.

Avalanche Effect

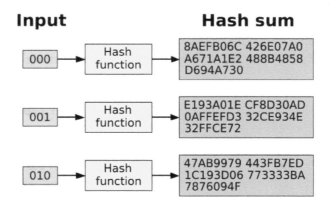

The SHA-1 hash function exhibits good avalanche effect. When a single bit is changed the hash sum becomes completely different.

In cryptography, the avalanche effect refers to a desirable property of cryptographic algorithms, typically block ciphers and cryptographic hash functions. The avalanche effect is evident if, when an input is changed slightly (for example, flipping a single bit) the output changes significantly (e.g., half the output bits flip). In the case of high-quality block ciphers, such a small change in either the key or the plaintext should cause a drastic change in the ciphertext. The actual term was first used by Horst Feistel, although the concept dates back to at least Shannon's *diffusion*.

If a block cipher or cryptographic hash function does not exhibit the avalanche effect to a significant degree, then it has poor randomization, and thus a cryptanalyst can make predictions about the input, being given only the output. This may be sufficient to partially or completely break the algorithm. Thus, the avalanche effect is a desirable condition from the point of view of the designer of the cryptographic algorithm or device.

Constructing a cipher or hash to exhibit a substantial avalanche effect is one of the primary design objectives. This is why most block ciphers are product ciphers. It is also why hash functions have large data blocks. Both of these features allow small changes to propagate rapidly through iterations of the algorithm, such that every bit of the output should depend on every bit of the input before the algorithm terminates.

Strict Avalanche Criterion

The strict avalanche criterion (SAC) is a formalization of the avalanche effect. It is satisfied if, whenever a single input bit is complemented, each of the output bits changes with a 50% probability. The SAC builds on the concepts of completeness and avalanche and was introduced by Webster and Tavares in 1985.

Higher-order generalizations of SAC involve multiple input bits. Boolean functions which satisfy the highest order SAC are always bent functions, also called maximally nonlinear functions, also called "perfect nonlinear" functions.

Bit independence criterion

The bit independence criterion (BIC) states that output bits j and k should change independently when any single input bit i is inverted, for all i, j and k.

Optimal Asymmetric Encryption Padding

In cryptography, Optimal Asymmetric Encryption Padding (OAEP) is a padding scheme often used together with RSA encryption. OAEP was introduced by Bellare and Rogaway, and subsequently standardized in PKCS#1 v2 and RFC 2437.

The OAEP algorithm is a form of Feistel network which uses a pair of random oracles G and H to process the plaintext prior to asymmetric encryption. When combined with any secure trapdoor one-way permutation f, this processing is proved in the random oracle model to result in a combined scheme which is semantically secure under chosen plaintext attack (IND-CPA). When implemented with certain trapdoor permutations (e.g., RSA), OAEP is also proved secure against chosen ciphertext attack. OAEP can be used to build an all-or-nothing transform.

OAEP satisfies the following two goals:

1. Add an element of randomness which can be used to convert a deterministic encryption scheme (e.g., traditional RSA) into a probabilistic scheme.

2. Prevent partial decryption of ciphertexts (or other information leakage) by ensuring that an adversary cannot recover any portion of the plaintext without being able to invert the trapdoor one-way permutation f.

The original version of OAEP (Bellare/Rogaway, 1994) showed a form of "plaintext awareness" (which they claimed implies security against chosen ciphertext attack) in the random oracle model when OAEP is used with any trapdoor permutation. Subsequent results contradicted this claim, showing that OAEP was only IND-CCA1 secure. However, the original scheme was proved in the random oracle model to be IND-CCA2 secure when OAEP is used with the RSA permutation using standard encryption exponents, as in the case of RSA-OAEP. An improved scheme (called OAEP+) that works with any trapdoor one-way permutation was offered by Victor Shoup to solve this problem. More recent work has shown that in the standard model (that is, when hash functions are not modeled as random oracles) it is impossible to prove the IND-CCA2 security of RSA-OAEP under the assumed hardness of the RSA problem.

Diagram of OAEP

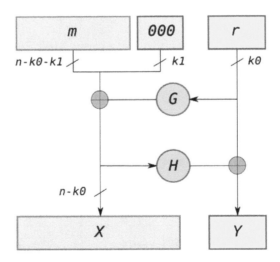

OAEP Diagram

In the diagram,

-   n is the number of bits in the RSA modulus.

-   k_0 and k_1 are integers fixed by the protocol.

-   m is the plaintext message, an $(n - k_0 - k_1)$-bit string

- G and H are typically some cryptographic hash functions fixed by the protocol.
- $\oplus$ is an xor operation.

To encode,

1. messages are padded with k_1 zeros to be $n - k_0$ bits in length.
2. r is a randomly generated k_0-bit string
3. G expands the k_0 bits of r to $n - k_0$ bits.
4. $X = m00..0 \oplus G(r)$
5. H reduces the $n - k_0$ bits of X to k_0 bits.
6. $Y = r \oplus H(X)$
7. The output is $X \parallel Y$ where X is shown in the diagram as the leftmost block and Y as the rightmost block.

To decode,

1. recover the random string as $r = Y \oplus H(X)$
2. recover the message as $m00..0 = X \oplus G(r)$

The "all-or-nothing" security is from the fact that to recover m, you must recover the entire X and the entire Y; X is required to recover r from Y, and r is required to recover m from X. Since any changed bit of a cryptographic hash completely changes the result, the entire X, and the entire Y must both be completely recovered.

Message Authentication Code

In cryptography, a message authentication code (MAC) is a short piece of information used to authenticate a message—in other words, to confirm that the message came from the stated sender (its authenticity) and has not been changed in transit (its integrity).

A MAC algorithm, sometimes called a keyed (cryptographic) hash function (which is somewhat misleading, since a cryptographic hash function is only one of the possible ways to generate a MAC), accepts as input a secret key and an arbitrary-length message to be authenticated, and outputs a MAC (sometimes known as a *tag*). The MAC value protects both a message's data integrity as well as its authenticity, by allowing verifiers (who also possess the secret key) to detect any changes to the message content.

Definitions

Informally, message authentication code consists of three algorithms:

- A key generation algorithm selects a key from the key space uniformly at random.

- A signing algorithm efficiently returns a tag given the key and the message.
- A verifying algorithm efficiently verifies the authenticity of the message given the key and the tag. That is, return *accepted* when the message and tag are not tampered with or forged, and otherwise return *rejected*.

For a secure unforgeable message authentication code, it should be computationally infeasible to compute a valid tag of the given message without knowledge of the key, even if for the worst case, we assume the adversary can forge the tag of any message except the given one.

Formally, A Message Authentication Code (MAC) is a triple of efficient algorithms (G, S, V) satisfying:

- G (key-generator) gives the key k on input 1^n, where n is the security parameter.

- S (Signing) outputs a tag t on the key k and the input string x.

- V (Verifying) outputs *accepted* or *rejected* on inputs: the key k, the string x and the tag t. S and V must satisfy.

  $\Pr[\,k \leftarrow G(1^n),\, V(\,k, x, S(k, x)\,) = accepted\,] = 1.$

A MAC is unforgeable if for every efficient adversary A

$$Pr\left[k \leftarrow G\left(1^n\right),\ (x,t) \leftarrow A^{S(k,\,\cdot\,)}\left(1^n\right), x \notin Query\left(A^{S(k,\,\cdot\,)},\ 1^n\right), V\left(k,x,t\right) = accepted\right] < negl\left(n\right),$$

where $A^{S(k,\,\cdot\,)}$ denotes that A has access to the oracle $S(k, \cdot)$, and $\text{Query}(A^{S(k,\,\cdot\,)}, 1^n)$ denotes the set of the queries on S made by A, which knows n. Clearly we require that any adversary cannot directly query the string x on S, since otherwise she can easily obtain a valid tag.

Security

While MAC functions are similar to cryptographic hash functions, they possess different security requirements. To be considered secure, a MAC function must resist existential forgery under chosen-plaintext attacks. This means that even if an attacker has access to an oracle which possesses the secret key and generates MACs for messages of the attacker's choosing, the attacker cannot guess the MAC for other messages (which were not used to query the oracle) without performing infeasible amounts of computation.

MACs differ from digital signatures as MAC values are both generated and verified using the same secret key. This implies that the sender and receiver of a message must agree on the same key before initiating communications, as is the case with symmetric encryption. For the same reason, MACs do not provide the property of non-repudiation offered by signatures specifically in the case of a network-wide shared secret key: any user who can verify a MAC is also capable of generating MACs for other messages. In contrast, a digital signature is generated using the private key of a key pair, which is public-key cryptography. Since this private key is only accessible to its holder, a digital signature proves that a document was signed by none other than that holder. Thus, digital signatures do offer non-repudiation. However, non-repudiation can be provided by systems that securely bind key usage information to the MAC key; the same key is in the possession of two people, but one has a copy of the key that can be used for MAC generation while the other has a copy of the key in a hardware security module that only permits MAC verification. This is commonly done in the finance industry.

Message Integrity Codes

The term message integrity code (MIC) is frequently substituted for the term MAC, especially in communications, where the acronym MAC traditionally stands for Media Access Control address. However, some authors use MIC to refer to a message digest, which is different from a MAC -- a message digest does not use secret keys. This lack of security means that any message digest intended for use gauging message integrity should be encrypted or otherwise be protected against tampering. Message digest algorithms are created such that a given message will always produce the same message digest assuming the same algorithm is used to generate both. Conversely, MAC algorithms are designed to produce matching MACs only if the same message, secret key and initialization vector are input to the same algorithm. Message digests do not use secret keys and, when taken on their own, are therefore a much less reliable gauge of message integrity than MACs. Because MACs use secret keys, they do not necessarily need to be encrypted to provide the same level of assurance.

RFC 4949 recommends avoiding the term "message integrity code" (MIC), and instead using "checksum", "error detection code", "hash", "keyed hash", "Message Authentication Code", or "protected checksum".

Implementation

MAC algorithms can be constructed from other cryptographic primitives, such as cryptographic hash functions (as in the case of HMAC) or from block cipher algorithms (OMAC, CBC-MAC and PMAC). However many of the fastest MAC algorithms such as UMAC and VMAC are constructed based on universal hashing.

Additionally, the MAC algorithm can deliberately combine two or more cryptographic primitives, so as to maintain protection even if one of them is later found to be vulnerable. For instance, in Transport Layer Security (TLS), the input data is split in halves that are each processed with a different hashing primitive (MD5 and SHA-1) then XORed together to output the MAC.

Standards

Various standards exist that define MAC algorithms. These include:

- FIPS PUB 113 *Computer Data Authentication*, withdrawn in 2002, defines an algorithm based on DES.

- FIPS PUB 198-1 *The Keyed-Hash Message Authentication Code (HMAC)*

- ISO/IEC 9797-1 *Mechanisms using a block cipher*

- ISO/IEC 9797-2 *Mechanisms using a dedicated hash-function*

ISO/IEC 9797-1 and -2 define generic models and algorithms that can be used with any block cipher or hash function, and a variety of different parameters. These models and parameters allow more specific algorithms to be defined by nominating the parameters. For example, the FIPS PUB

113 algorithm is functionally equivalent to ISO/IEC 9797-1 MAC algorithm 1 with padding method 1 and a block cipher algorithm of DES.

An Example of Message Authentication Code Algorithm

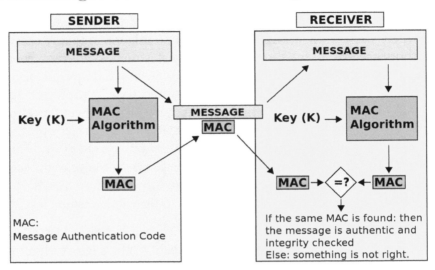

In this example, the sender of a message runs it through a MAC algorithm to produce a MAC data tag. The message and the MAC tag are then sent to the receiver. The receiver in turn runs the message portion of the transmission through the same MAC algorithm using the same key, producing a second MAC data tag. The receiver then compares the first MAC tag received in the transmission to the second generated MAC tag. If they are identical, the receiver can safely assume that the integrity of the message was not compromised, and the message was not altered or tampered with during transmission.

However, to allow the receiver to be able to detect replay attacks, the message itself must contain data that assures that this same message can only be sent once (e.g. time stamp, sequence number or use of a one-time MAC). Otherwise an attacker could — without even understanding its content — record this message and play it back at a later time, producing the same result as the original sender.

One-time MAC

Universal hashing and in particular pairwise independent hash functions provide a message authentication code as long as the key is used at most once (or less than k-times for k-wise independent hash functions. This can be seen as of the one-time pad for authentication.

The simplest such pairwise independent hash function is defined by the random key $key = (a,b)$, and the MAC tag for a message m is computed as $tag = (am + b) \bmod p$, where p is prime.

Secure Channel

In cryptography, a secure channel is a way of transferring data that is resistant to overhearing and tampering. A confidential channel is a way of transferring data that is resistant to overhearing (i.e., reading the content), but not necessarily resistant to tampering. An authentic channel is a way of transferring data that is resistant to tampering but not necessarily resistant to overhearing.

Secure Channels in the Real World

There are no perfectly secure channels in the real world. There are, at best, only ways to make insecure channels (e.g., couriers, homing pigeons, diplomatic bags, etc.) less insecure: padlocks (between courier wrists and a briefcase), loyalty tests, security investigations, and guns for courier personnel, diplomatic immunity for diplomatic bags, and so forth.

In 1976, two researchers proposed a key exchange technique (now named after them) — Diffie–Hellman key exchange (D-H). This protocol allows two parties to generate a key only known to them, under the assumption that a certain mathematical problem (e.g., the Diffie–Hellman problem in their proposal) is computationally infeasible (i.e., very very hard) to solve, and that the two parties have access to an authentic channel. In short, that an eavesdropper—conventionally termed 'Eve', who can listen to all messages exchanged by the two parties, but who can not modify the messages—will not learn the exchanged key. Such a key exchange was impossible with any previously known cryptographic schemes based on symmetric ciphers, because with these schemes it is necessary that the two parties exchange a secret key at some prior time, hence they require a confidential channel at that time which is just what we are attempting to build.

It is important to note that most cryptographic techniques are trivially breakable if keys are not exchanged securely or, if they actually were so exchanged, if those keys become known in some other way — burglary or extortion, for instance. An actually secure channel will not be required if an insecure channel can be used to securely exchange keys, and if burglary, bribery, or threat aren't used. The eternal problem has been and of course remains — even with modern key exchange protocols — how to know when an insecure channel worked securely (or alternatively, and perhaps more importantly, when it did not), and whether anyone has actually been bribed or threatened or simply lost a notebook (or a notebook computer) with key information in it. These are hard problems in the real world and no solutions are known — only expedients, jury rigs, and workarounds.

Future Possibilities

Researchers have proposed and demonstrated quantum cryptography in order to create a secure channel. If the current understanding of this subject of quantum physics is adequate, quantum cryptography facilitates the exchange of theoretically uneavesdroppable, non-interceptable, non-tamperable data. The mechanism is related to the uncertainty relation.

It is not clear whether the special conditions under which it can be made to work are practical in the real world of noise, dirt, and imperfection in which most everything is required to function. Thus far, actual implementation of the technique is exquisitely finicky and expensive, limiting it to very special purpose applications. It may also be vulnerable to attacks specific to particular implementations and imperfections in the optical components of which the quantum cryptographic equipment is built. While implementations of classical cryptographic algorithms have received worldwide scrutiny over the years, only a limited amount of public research has been done to assess security of the present-day implementations of quantum cryptosystems, mostly because they are not in widespread use as of 2014.

Modeling a Secure Channel

Security definitions for a secure channel try to model its properties independently from its concrete instantiation. A good understanding of these properties is needed before designing a secure channel, and before being able to assess its appropriateness of employment in a cryptographic protocol. This is a topic of provable security. A definition of a secure channel that remains secure, even when used in arbitrary cryptographic protocols is an important building block for universally composable cryptography.

A universally composable authenticated channel can be built using digital signatures and a public key infrastructure.

Universally composable confidential channels are known to exist under computational hardness assumptions based on hybrid encryption and a public key infrastructure.

References

- Webster, A. F.; Tavares, Stafford E. (1985). "On the design of S-boxes". Advances in Cryptology - Crypto '85. Lecture Notes in Computer Science. 218. New York, NY,: Springer-Verlag New York, Inc. pp. 523–534. ISBN 0-387-16463-4.

- Simmons, Gustavus (1985). "Authentication theory/coding theory". Advances in Cryptology: Proceedings of CRYPTO 84. Berlin: Springer. pp. 411–431. ISBN 0387156585.

- Google Chrome security representative statement, (2)HYPERLINK "https://twitter.com/justinschuh/status/364818561694302209" (3), Y Combinator (company). 6 Aug 2013. Retrieved 7 Aug 2013.

- "VMAC: Message Authentication Code using Universal Hashing". CFRG Working Group. CFRG Working Group. Retrieved 16 March 2010.

6

Cipher and its Types

The algorithm used for performing encryptions or decryptions in cryptography is known as a cipher. The major types of ciphers that this chapter elucidates are, among others, block cipher, product cipher, feistal cipher and substitution cipher. The topics discussed are of great importance to broaden the existing knowledge on ciphers.

Cipher

In cryptography, a cipher (or cypher) is an algorithm for performing encryption or decryption—a series of well-defined steps that can be followed as a procedure. An alternative, less common term is *encipherment*. To encipher or encode is to convert information into cipher or code. In common parlance, 'cipher' is synonymous with 'code', as they are both a set of steps that encrypt a message; however, the concepts are distinct in cryptography, especially classical cryptography.

Edward Larsson's rune cipher resembling that found on the Kensington Runestone. Also includes runically unrelated blackletter writing style and pigpen cipher.

Codes generally substitute different length strings of characters in the output, while ciphers generally substitute the same number of characters as are input. There are exceptions and some cipher systems may use slightly more, or fewer, characters when output versus the number that were input.

Codes operated by substituting according to a large codebook which linked a random string of characters or numbers to a word or phrase. For example, "UQJHSE" could be the code for "Proceed to the following coordinates." When using a cipher the original information is known as plaintext, and the encrypted form as ciphertext. The ciphertext message contains all the information of the plaintext message, but is not in a format readable by a human or computer without the proper mechanism to decrypt it.

The operation of a cipher usually depends on a piece of auxiliary information, called a key (or, in traditional NSA parlance, a *cryptovariable*). The encrypting procedure is varied depending on the key, which changes the detailed operation of the algorithm. A key must be selected before using a cipher to encrypt a message. Without knowledge of the key, it should be extremely difficult, if not impossible, to decrypt the resulting ciphertext into readable plaintext.

Most modern ciphers can be categorized in several ways

- By whether they work on blocks of symbols usually of a fixed size (block ciphers), or on a continuous stream of symbols (stream ciphers).

- By whether the same key is used for both encryption and decryption (symmetric key algorithms), or if a different key is used for each (asymmetric key algorithms). If the algorithm is symmetric, the key must be known to the recipient and sender and to no one else. If the algorithm is an asymmetric one, the enciphering key is different from, but closely related to, the deciphering key. If one key cannot be deduced from the other, the asymmetric key algorithm has the public/private key property and one of the keys may be made public without loss of confidentiality.

Etymology

The word "cipher" (minority spelling "cypher") in former times meant "zero" and had the same origin: Middle French as *cifre* and Medieval Latin as *cifra,* from the Arabic صفر *ṣifr* = zero. "Cipher" was later used for any decimal digit, even any number. There are many theories about how the word "cipher" may have come to mean "encoding".

- Encoding often involved numbers.

- The Roman number system was very cumbersome because there was no concept of zero (or empty space). The concept of zero (which was also called "cipher"), which is now common knowledge, was alien to medieval Europe, so confusing and ambiguous to common Europeans that in arguments people would say "talk clearly and not so far fetched as a cipher". Cipher came to mean concealment of clear messages or encryption.

  o The French formed the word "chiffre" and adopted the Italian word "zero".

  o The English used "zero" for "o", and "cipher" from the word "ciphering" as a means of computing.

  o The Germans used the words "Ziffer" (digit) and "Chiffre".

  o The Dutch still use the word "cijfer" to refer to a numerical digit.

o   The Serbians use the word "cifra", which refers to a digit, or in some cases, any number. Besides "cifra", they use word "broj" for a number.

o   The Italians and the Spanish also use the word "cifra" to refer to a number.

o   The Swedes use the word "siffra" which refers to a digit and "nummer" to refer to a combination of "siffror".

Ibrahim Al-Kadi concluded that the Arabic word *sifr*, for the digit zero, developed into the European technical term for encryption.

As the decimal zero and its new mathematics spread from the Arabic world to Europe in the Middle Ages, words derived from □*ifr* and *zephyrus* came to refer to calculation, as well as to privileged knowledge and secret codes. According to Ifrah, "in thirteenth-century Paris, a 'worthless fellow' was called a '… cifre en algorisme', i.e., an 'arithmetical nothing'." Cipher was the European pronunciation of sifr, and cipher came to mean a message or communication not easily understood.

Versus Codes

In non-technical usage, a "(secret) code" typically means a "cipher". Within technical discussions, however, the words "code" and "cipher" refer to two different concepts. Codes work at the level of meaning—that is, words or phrases are converted into something else and this chunking generally shortens the message.

An example of this is the Telegraph Code which was used to shorten long telegraph messages which resulted from entering into commercial contracts using exchanges of Telegrams.

Another example is given by whole words cipher s, which allow the user to replace an entire word with a symbol or character, much like the way Japanese utilize Kanji (Japanese) characters to supplement their language. ex "The quick brown fox jumps over the lazy dog" becomes "The quick brown 狐 jumps 过 the lazy 狗".

Ciphers, on the other hand, work at a lower level: the level of individual letters, small groups of letters, or, in modern schemes, individual bits and blocks of bits. Some systems used both codes and ciphers in one system, using superencipherment to increase the security. In some cases the terms codes and ciphers are also used synonymously to substitution and transposition.

Historically, cryptography was split into a dichotomy of codes and ciphers; and coding had its own terminology, analogous to that for ciphers: "*encoding, codetext, decoding*" and so on.

However, codes have a variety of drawbacks, including susceptibility to cryptanalysis and the difficulty of managing a cumbersome codebook. Because of this, codes have fallen into disuse in modern cryptography, and ciphers are the dominant technique.

Types

There are a variety of different types of encryption. Algorithms used earlier in the history of cryptography are substantially different from modern methods, and modern ciphers can be classified according to how they operate and whether they use one or two keys.

Historical

Historical pen and paper ciphers used in the past are sometimes known as classical ciphers. They include simple substitution ciphers (such as Rot 13) and transposition ciphers (such as a Rail Fence Cipher). For example, "GOOD DOG" can be encrypted as "PLLX XLP" where "L" substitutes for "O", "P" for "G", and "X" for "D" in the message. Transposition of the letters "GOOD DOG" can result in "DGOGDOO". These simple ciphers and examples are easy to crack, even without plaintext-ciphertext pairs.

Simple ciphers were replaced by polyalphabetic substitution ciphers (such as the Vigenère) which changed the substitution alphabet for every letter. For example, "GOOD DOG" can be encrypted as "PLSX TWF" where "L", "S", and "W" substitute for "O". With even a small amount of known or estimated plaintext, simple polyalphabetic substitution ciphers and letter transposition ciphers designed for pen and paper encryption are easy to crack. It is possible to create a secure pen and paper cipher based on a one-time pad though, but the usual disadvantages of one-time pads apply.

During the early twentieth century, electro-mechanical machines were invented to do encryption and decryption using transposition, polyalphabetic substitution, and a kind of "additive" substitution. In rotor machines, several rotor disks provided polyalphabetic substitution, while plug boards provided another substitution. Keys were easily changed by changing the rotor disks and the plugboard wires. Although these encryption methods were more complex than previous schemes and required machines to encrypt and decrypt, other machines such as the British Bombe were invented to crack these encryption methods.

Modern

Modern encryption methods can be divided by two criteria: by type of key used, and by type of input data.

By type of key used ciphers are divided into:

- symmetric key algorithms (Private-key cryptography), where the same key is used for encryption and decryption, and

- asymmetric key algorithms (Public-key cryptography), where two different keys are used for encryption and decryption.

In a symmetric key algorithm (e.g., DES and AES), the sender and receiver must have a shared key set up in advance and kept secret from all other parties; the sender uses this key for encryption, and the receiver uses the same key for decryption. The Feistel cipher uses a combination of substitution and transposition techniques. Most block cipher algorithms are based on this structure. In an asymmetric key algorithm (e.g., RSA), there are two separate keys: a *public key* is published and enables any sender to perform encryption, while a *private key* is kept secret by the receiver and enables only him to perform correct decryption.

Ciphers can be distinguished into two types by the type of input data:

- block ciphers, which encrypt block of data of fixed size, and

- stream ciphers, which encrypt continuous streams of data

Key Size and Vulnerability

In a pure mathematical attack, (i.e., lacking any other information to help break a cipher) two factors above all count:

- Computational power available, i.e., the computing power which can be brought to bear on the problem. It is important to note that average performance/capacity of a single computer is not the only factor to consider. An adversary can use multiple computers at once, for instance, to increase the speed of exhaustive search for a key (i.e., "brute force" attack) substantially.

- Key size, i.e., the size of key used to encrypt a message. As the key size increases, so does the complexity of exhaustive search to the point where it becomes impracticable to crack encryption directly.

Since the desired effect is computational difficulty, in theory one would choose an algorithm and desired difficulty level, thus decide the key length accordingly.

An example of this process can be found at Key Length which uses multiple reports to suggest that a symmetric cipher with 128 bits, an asymmetric cipher with 3072 bit keys, and an elliptic curve cipher with 512 bits, all have similar difficulty at present.

Claude Shannon proved, using information theory considerations, that any theoretically unbreakable cipher must have keys which are at least as long as the plaintext, and used only once: one-time pad.

Block Cipher

In cryptography, a block cipher is a deterministic algorithm operating on fixed-length groups of bits, called *blocks*, with an unvarying transformation that is specified by a symmetric key. Block ciphers operate as important elementary components in the design of many cryptographic protocols, and are widely used to implement encryption of bulk data.

The modern design of block ciphers is based on the concept of an *iterated* product cipher. In his seminal 1949 publication, *Communication Theory of Secrecy Systems*, Claude Shannon analyzed product ciphers and suggested them as a means of effectively improving security by combining simple operations such as substitutions and permutations. Iterated product ciphers carry out encryption in multiple rounds, each of which uses a different subkey derived from the original key. One widespread implementation of such ciphers, named a Feistel network after Horst Feistel, is notably implemented in the DES cipher. Many other realizations of block ciphers, such as the AES, are classified as substitution-permutation networks.

The publication of the DES cipher by the United States National Bureau of Standards (subsequently the U.S. National Institute of Standards and Technology, NIST) in 1977 was fundamental in the public understanding of modern block cipher design. It also influenced the academic development of cryptanalytic attacks. Both differential and linear cryptanalysis arose out of studies on the DES design. As of 2016 there is a palette of attack techniques against which a block cipher must be secure, in addition to being robust against brute force attacks.

Even a secure block cipher is suitable only for the encryption of a single block under a fixed key. A multitude of modes of operation have been designed to allow their repeated use in a secure way, commonly to achieve the security goals of confidentiality and authenticity. However, block ciphers may also feature as building-blocks in other cryptographic protocols, such as universal hash functions and pseudo-random number generators.

Definition

A block cipher consists of two paired algorithms, one for encryption, E, and the other for decryption, D. Both algorithms accept two inputs: an input block of size n bits and a key of size k bits; and both yield an n-bit output block. The decryption algorithm D is defined to be the inverse function of encryption, i.e., $D = E^{-1}$. More formally, a block cipher is specified by an encryption function

$$E_K(P) := E(K, P) : \{0,1\}^k \times \{0,1\}^n \to \{0,1\}^n,$$

which takes as input a key K of bit length k, called the *key size*, and a bit string P of length n, called the *block size*, and returns a string C of n bits. P is called the plaintext, and C is termed the ciphertext. For each K, the function $E_K(P)$ is required to be an invertible mapping on $\{0,1\}^n$. The inverse for E is defined as a function

$$E_K^{-1}(C) := D_K(C) = D(K, C) : \{0,1\}^k \times \{0,1\}^n \to \{0,1\}^n,$$

taking a key K and a ciphertext C to return a plaintext value P, such that

$$\forall K : D_K(E_K(P)) = P.$$

For example, a block cipher encryption algorithm might take a 128-bit block of plaintext as input, and output a corresponding 128-bit block of ciphertext. The exact transformation is controlled using a second input – the secret key. Decryption is similar: the decryption algorithm takes, in this example, a 128-bit block of ciphertext together with the secret key, and yields the original 128-bit block of plain text.

For each key K, E_K is a permutation (a bijective mapping) over the set of input blocks. Each key selects one permutation from the possible set of $(2^n)!$.

Design

Iterated Block Ciphers

Most block cipher algorithms are classified as *iterated block ciphers* which means that they transform fixed-size blocks of plain-text into identical size blocks of ciphertext, via the repeated application of an invertible transformation known as the *round function*, with each iteration referred to as a *round*.

Usually, the round function R takes different *round keys* K_i as second input, which are derived

from the original key:
$$M_i = R_{K_i}(M_{i-1})$$

where M_0 is the plaintext and M_r the ciphertext, with r being the round number.

Frequently, key whitening is used in addition to this. At the beginning and the end, the data is modified with key material (often with XOR, but simple arithmetic operations like adding and subtracting are also used):

$$M_0 = M \oplus K_0$$

$$M_i = R_{K_i}(M_{i-1}) ; i = 1 \ldots r$$

$$C = M_r \oplus K_{r+1}$$

Given one of the standard iterated block cipher design schemes, it is fairly easy to construct a block cipher that is cryptographically secure, simply by using a large number of rounds. However, this will make the cipher inefficient. Thus, efficiency is the most important additional design criterion for professional ciphers. Further, a good block cipher is designed to avoid side-channel attacks, such as input-dependent memory accesses that might leak secret data via the cache state or the execution time. In addition, the cipher should be concise, for small hardware and software implementations. Finally, the cipher should be easily cryptanalyzable, such that it can be shown to how many rounds the cipher needs to be reduced such that the existing cryptographic attacks would work and, conversely, that the number of actual rounds is large enough to protect against them.

Substitution-permutation Networks

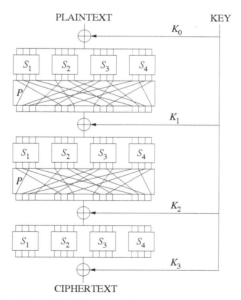

A sketch of a Substitution-Permutation Network with 3 rounds, encrypting a plaintext block of 16 bits into a ciphertext block of 16 bits. The S-boxes are the S_i's, the P-boxes are the same P, and the round keys are the K_i's.

One important type of iterated block cipher known as a *substitution-permutation network* (SPN) takes a block of the plaintext and the key as inputs, and applies several alternating rounds consisting of a substitution stage followed by a permutation stage—to produce each block of ciphertext output. The non-linear substitution stage mixes the key bits with those of the plaintext, creating Shannon's *confusion*. The linear permutation stage then dissipates redundancies, creating *diffusion*.

A *substitution box* (S-box) substitutes a small block of input bits with another block of output bits. This substitution must be one-to-one, to ensure invertibility (hence decryption). A secure S-box will have the property that changing one input bit will change about half of the output bits on average, exhibiting what is known as the avalanche effect—i.e. it has the property that each output bit will depend on every input bit.

A *permutation box* (P-box) is a permutation of all the bits: it takes the outputs of all the S-boxes of one round, permutes the bits, and feeds them into the S-boxes of the next round. A good P-box has the property that the output bits of any S-box are distributed to as many S-box inputs as possible.

At each round, the round key (obtained from the key with some simple operations, for instance, using S-boxes and P-boxes) is combined using some group operation, typically XOR.

Decryption is done by simply reversing the process (using the inverses of the S-boxes and P-boxes and applying the round keys in reversed order).

Feistel Ciphers

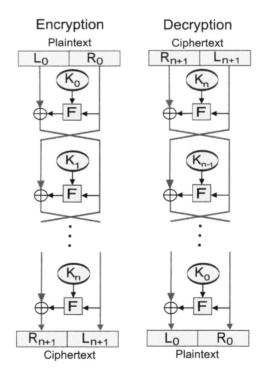

Many block ciphers, such as DES and Blowfish utilize structures known as *Feistel ciphers*

In a *Feistel cipher*, the block of plain text to be encrypted is split into two equal-sized halves. The round function is applied to one half, using a subkey, and then the output is XORed with the other half. The two halves are then swapped.

Let F be the round function and let $K_0, K_1, \ldots, K_n$ be the sub-keys for the rounds $0, 1, \ldots, n$ respectively.

Then the basic operation is as follows:

Split the plaintext block into two equal pieces, (L_0, R_0)

For each round $i = 0, 1, \ldots, n$, compute

$$L_{i+1} = R_i$$

$$R_{i+1} = L_i \oplus F(R_i, K_i).$$

Then the ciphertext is (R_{n+1}, L_{n+1}).

Decryption of a ciphertext (R_{n+1}, L_{n+1}) is accomplished by computing for $i = n, n-1, \ldots, 0$

$$R_i = L_{i+1}$$

$$L_i = R_{i+1} \oplus F(L_{i+1}, K_i).$$

Then (L_0, R_0) is the plaintext again.

One advantage of the Feistel model compared to a substitution-permutation network is that the round function F does not have to be invertible.

Lai-massey Ciphers

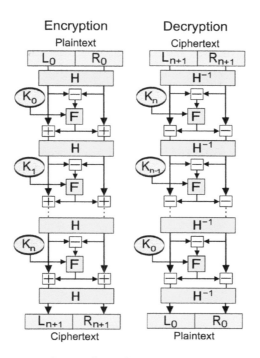

The Lai-Massey scheme. The archetypical cipher utilizing it is IDEA.

The Lai-Massey scheme offers security properties similar to those of the Feistel structure. It also shares its advantage that the round function F does not have to be invertible. Another similarity is that is also splits the input block into two equal pieces. However, the round function is applied to the difference between the two, and the result is then added to both half blocks.

Let F be the round function and H a half-round function and let $K_0, K_1, \ldots, K_n$ be the sub-keys for the rounds $0, 1, \ldots, n$ respectively.

Then the basic operation is as follows:

Split the plaintext block into two equal pieces, (L_0, R_0)

For each round $i = 0, 1, \ldots, n,$, compute

$$(L'_{i+1}, R'_{i+1}) = H(L'_i + T_i, R'_i + T_i)$$

where $T_i = F(L'_i - R'_i, K_i)$ and $(L'_0, R'_0) = H(L_0, R_0)$

Then the ciphertext is $(L_{n+1}, R_{n+1}) = (L'_{n+1}, R'_{n+1})$

Decryption of a ciphertext (L_{n+1}, R_{n+1}) is accomplished by computing for $i = n, n-1, \ldots, 0$

$$(L'_i, R') = H^{-1}(L'_{i+1} - T_i, R'_{i+1} - T_i)$$

where $T_i = F(L'_{i+1} - R'_{i+1}, K_i)$ and $(L'_{i+1} - R'_{i+1}) = H^{-1}(L_{n+1}, R_{n+1})$

Then $(L_o, R_o) = (L'_o, R'_o)$ is the plaintext again.

Operations

ARX Add-rotate-xor

Many modern block ciphers and hashes are ARX algorithms—their round function involves only three operations: modular addition, rotation with fixed rotation amounts, and XOR (ARX). Examples include Salsa20 and Speck and BLAKE. Many authors draw an ARX network, a kind of data flow diagram, to illustrate such a round function.

These ARX operations are popular because they are relatively fast and cheap in hardware and software, and also because they run in constant time, and are therefore immune to timing attacks. The rotational cryptanalysis technique attempts to attack such round functions.

Other Operations

Other operations often used in block ciphers include data-dependent rotations as in RC5 and RC6, a substitution box implemented as a lookup table as in Data Encryption Standard and Advanced Encryption Standard, a permutation box, and multiplication as in IDEA.

Modes of Operation

A block cipher by itself allows encryption only of a single data block of the cipher's block length. For a variable-length message, the data must first be partitioned into separate cipher blocks. In the simplest case, known as the electronic codebook (ECB) mode, a message is first split into separate blocks of the cipher's block size (possibly extending the last block with padding bits), and then each block is encrypted and decrypted independently. However, such a naive method is generally insecure because equal plaintext blocks will always generate equal ciphertext blocks (for the same key), so patterns in the plaintext message become evident in the ciphertext output.

Insecure encryption of an image as a result of electronic codebook mode encoding.

To overcome this limitation, several so-called block cipher modes of operation have been designed and specified in national recommendations such as NIST 800-38A and BSI TR-02102 and international standards such as ISO/IEC 10116. The general concept is to use randomization of the plaintext data based on an additional input value, frequently called an initialization vector, to create what is termed probabilistic encryption. In the popular cipher block chaining (CBC) mode, for encryption to be secure the initialization vector passed along with the plaintext message must be a random or pseudo-random value, which is added in an exclusive-or manner to the first plaintext block before it is being encrypted. The resultant ciphertext block is then used as the new initialization vector for the next plaintext block. In the cipher feedback (CFB) mode, which emulates a self-synchronizing stream cipher, the initialization vector is first encrypted and then added to the plaintext block. The output feedback (OFB) mode repeatedly encrypts the initialization vector to create a key stream for the emulation of a synchronous stream cipher. The newer counter (CTR) mode similarly creates a key stream, but has the advantage of only needing unique and not (pseudo-)random values as initialization vectors; the needed randomness is derived internally by using the initialization vector as a block counter and encrypting this counter for each block.

From a security-theoretic point of view, modes of operation must provide what is known as semantic security. Informally, it means that given some ciphertext under an unknown key one cannot practically derive any information from the ciphertext (other than the length of the message) over what one would have known without seeing the ciphertext. It has been shown that all of the modes discussed above, with the exception of the ECB mode, provide this property under so-called chosen plaintext attacks.

Padding

Some modes such as the CBC mode only operate on complete plaintext blocks. Simply extending the last block of a message with zero-bits is insufficient since it does not allow a receiver to easily distinguish messages that differ only in the amount of padding bits. More importantly, such a simple solution gives rise to very efficient padding oracle attacks. A suitable padding scheme is therefore needed to extend the last plaintext block to the cipher's block size. While many popular schemes described in standards and in the literature have been shown to be vulnerable to padding oracle attacks, a solution which adds a one-bit and then extends the last block with zero-bits, standardized as "padding method 2" in ISO/IEC 9797-1, has been proven secure against these attacks.

Cryptanalysis

Brute Force Attacks

Due to a block cipher's characteristic as an invertible function, its output becomes distinguishable from a truly random output string over time due to the birthday attack. This property results in the cipher's security degrading quadratically, and needs to be taken into account when selecting a block size. There is a trade-off though as large block sizes can result in the algorithm becoming inefficient to operate. Earlier block ciphers such as the DES have typically selected a 64-bit block size, while newer designs such as the AES support block sizes of 128 bits or more, with some ciphers supporting a range of different block sizes.

Differential Cryptanalysis

Linear Cryptanalysis

Linear cryptanalysis is a form of cryptanalysis based on finding affine approximations to the action of a cipher. Linear cryptanalysis is one of the two most widely used attacks on block ciphers; the other being differential cryptanalysis.

The discovery is attributed to Mitsuru Matsui, who first applied the technique to the FEAL cipher (Matsui and Yamagishi, 1992).

Integral Cryptanalysis

Integral cryptanalysis is a cryptanalytic attack that is particularly applicable to block ciphers based on substitution-permutation networks. Unlike differential cryptanalysis, which uses pairs of chosen plaintexts with a fixed XOR difference, integral cryptanalysis uses sets or even multisets of chosen plaintexts of which part is held constant and another part varies through all possibilities. For example, an attack might use 256 chosen plaintexts that have all but 8 of their bits the same, but all differ in those 8 bits. Such a set necessarily has an XOR sum of 0, and the XOR sums of the corresponding sets of ciphertexts provide information about the cipher's operation. This contrast between the differences of pairs of texts and the sums of larger sets of texts inspired the name "integral cryptanalysis", borrowing the terminology of calculus.

Other Techniques

In addition to linear and differential cryptanalysis, there is a growing catalog of attacks: truncated differential cryptanalysis, partial differential cryptanalysis, integral cryptanalysis, which encompasses square and integral attacks, slide attacks, boomerang attacks, the XSL attack, impossible differential cryptanalysis and algebraic attacks. For a new block cipher design to have any credibility, it must demonstrate evidence of security against known attacks.

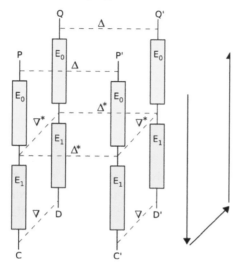

The development of the boomerang attack enabled differential cryptanalysis techniques to be applied to many ciphers that had previously been deemed secure against differential attacks

Provable Security

When a block cipher is used in a given mode of operation, the resulting algorithm should ideally be about as secure as the block cipher itself. ECB (discussed above) emphatically lacks this property: regardless of how secure the underlying block cipher is, ECB mode can easily be attacked. On the other hand, CBC mode can be proven to be secure under the assumption that the underlying block cipher is likewise secure. Note, however, that making statements like this requires formal mathematical definitions for what it means for an encryption algorithm or a block cipher to "be secure". This section describes two common notions for what properties a block cipher should have. Each corresponds to a mathematical model that can be used to prove properties of higher level algorithms, such as CBC.

This general approach to cryptography---proving higher-level algorithms (such as CBC) are secure under explicitly stated assumptions regarding their components (such as a block cipher)---is known as *provable security*.

Standard Model

Informally, a block cipher is secure in the standard model if an attacker cannot tell the difference between the block cipher (equipped with a random key) and a random permutation.

To be a bit more precise, let E be an n-bit block cipher. We imagine the following game:

The person running the game flips a coin.

   o   If the coin lands on heads, he chooses a random key K and defines the function $f = E_K$.

o   If the coin lands on tails, he chooses a random permutation π on the set of *n*-bit strings, and defines the function *f* = π.

The attacker chooses an *n*-bit string *X*, and the person running the game tells him the value of *f(X)*.

o   Step 2 is repeated a total of *q* times. (Each of these *q* interactions is a *query*.)

o   The attacker guesses how the coin landed. He wins if his guess is correct.

The attacker, which we can model as an algorithm, is called an *adversary*. The function *f* (which the adversary was able to query) is called an *oracle*.

Note that an adversary can trivially ensure a 50% chance of winning simply by guessing at random (or even by, for example, always guessing "heads"). Therefore, let $P_E(A)$ denote the probability that the adversary *A* wins this game against *E*, and define the *advantage* of *A* as $2(P_E(A) - 1/2)$. It follows that if *A* guesses randomly, its advantage will be 0; on the other hand, if *A* always wins, then its advantage is 1. The block cipher *E* is a *pseudo-random permutation* (PRP) if no adversary has an advantage significantly greater than 0, given specified restrictions on *q* and the adversary's running time. If in Step 2 above adversaries have the option of learning $f^{-1}(X)$ instead of *f(X)* (but still have only small advantages) then *E* is a *strong* PRP (SPRP). An adversary is *non-adaptive* if it chooses all *q* values for *X* before the game begins (that is, it does not use any information gleaned from previous queries to choose each *X* as it goes).

These definitions have proven useful for analyzing various modes of operation. For example, one can define a similar game for measuring the security of a block cipher-based encryption algorithm, and then try to show (through a reduction argument) that the probability of an adversary winning this new game is not much more than $P_E(A)$ for some *A*. (The reduction typically provides limits on *q* and the running time of *A*.) Equivalently, if $P_E(A)$ is small for all relevant *A*, then no attacker has a significant probability of winning the new game. This formalizes the idea that the higher-level algorithm inherits the block cipher's security.

Ideal Cipher Model

Practical Evaluation

Block ciphers may be evaluated according to multiple criteria in practice. Common factors include:

*   Key parameters, such as its key size and block size, both which provide an upper bound on the security of the cipher.

*   The *estimated security level*, which is based on the confidence gained in the block cipher design after it has largely withstood major efforts in cryptanalysis over time, the design's mathematical soundness, and the existence of practical or certificational attacks.

*   The cipher's *complexity* and its suitability for implementation in hardware or software. Hardware implementations may measure the complexity in terms of gate count or energy consumption, which are important parameters for resource-constrained devices.

*   The cipher's *performance* in terms of processing throughput on various platforms, including its memory requirements.

- The *cost* of the cipher, which refers to licensing requirements that may apply due to intellectual property rights.

- The *flexibility* of the cipher, which includes its ability to support multiple key sizes and block lengths.

Notable Block Ciphers

Lucifer / DES

Lucifer is generally considered to be the first civilian block cipher, developed at IBM in the 1970s based on work done by Horst Feistel. A revised version of the algorithm was adopted as a U.S. government Federal Information Processing Standard: FIPS PUB 46 Data Encryption Standard (DES). It was chosen by the U.S. National Bureau of Standards (NBS) after a public invitation for submissions and some internal changes by NBS (and, potentially, the NSA). DES was publicly released in 1976 and has been widely used.

DES was designed to, among other things, resist a certain cryptanalytic attack known to the NSA and rediscovered by IBM, though unknown publicly until rediscovered again and published by Eli Biham and Adi Shamir in the late 1980s. The technique is called differential cryptanalysis and remains one of the few general attacks against block ciphers; linear cryptanalysis is another, but may have been unknown even to the NSA, prior to its publication by Mitsuru Matsui. DES prompted a large amount of other work and publications in cryptography and cryptanalysis in the open community and it inspired many new cipher designs.

DES has a block size of 64 bits and a key size of 56 bits. 64-bit blocks became common in block cipher designs after DES. Key length depended on several factors, including government regulation. Many observers[who?] in the 1970s commented that the 56-bit key length used for DES was too short. As time went on, its inadequacy became apparent, especially after a special purpose machine designed to break DES was demonstrated in 1998 by the Electronic Frontier Foundation. An extension to DES, Triple DES, triple-encrypts each block with either two independent keys (112-bit key and 80-bit security) or three independent keys (168-bit key and 112-bit security). It was widely adopted as a replacement. As of 2011, the three-key version is still considered secure, though the National Institute of Standards and Technology (NIST) standards no longer permit the use of the two-key version in new applications, due to its 80-bit security level.

IDEA

The *International Data Encryption Algorithm (IDEA)* is a block cipher designed by James Massey of ETH Zurich and Xuejia Lai; it was first described in 1991, as an intended replacement for DES.

IDEA operates on 64-bit blocks using a 128-bit key, and consists of a series of eight identical transformations (a *round*) and an output transformation (the *half-round*). The processes for encryption and decryption are similar. IDEA derives much of its security by interleaving operations from different groups — modular addition and multiplication, and bitwise *exclusive or* (XOR) — which are algebraically "incompatible" in some sense.

The designers analysed IDEA to measure its strength against differential cryptanalysis and concluded that it is immune under certain assumptions. No successful linear or algebraic weaknesses have been reported. As of 2012 the best attack which applies to all keys can break full 8.5 round IDEA using a narrow-bicliques attack about four times faster than brute force.

RC5

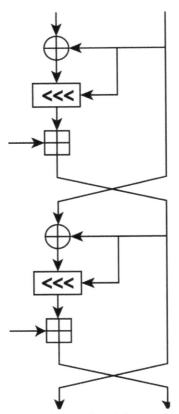

One round (two half-rounds) of the RC5 block cipher

RC5 is a block cipher designed by Ronald Rivest in 1994 which, unlike many other ciphers, has a variable block size (32, 64 or 128 bits), key size (0 to 2040 bits) and number of rounds (0 to 255). The original suggested choice of parameters were a block size of 64 bits, a 128-bit key and 12 rounds.

A key feature of RC5 is the use of data-dependent rotations; one of the goals of RC5 was to prompt the study and evaluation of such operations as a cryptographic primitive. RC5 also consists of a number of modular additions and XORs. The general structure of the algorithm is a Feistel-like network. The encryption and decryption routines can be specified in a few lines of code. The key schedule, however, is more complex, expanding the key using an essentially one-way function with the binary expansions of both e and the golden ratio as sources of "nothing up my sleeve numbers". The tantalising simplicity of the algorithm together with the novelty of the data-dependent rotations has made RC5 an attractive object of study for cryptanalysts.

12-round RC5 (with 64-bit blocks) is susceptible to a differential attack using 2^{44} chosen plaintexts. 18–20 rounds are suggested as sufficient protection.

Rijndael / AES

DES has been superseded as a United States Federal Standard by the AES, adopted by NIST in 2001 after a 5-year public competition. The cipher was developed by two Belgian cryptographers, Joan Daemen and Vincent Rijmen, and submitted under the name *Rijndael*.

AES has a fixed block size of 128 bits and a key size of 128, 192, or 256 bits, whereas Rijndael can be specified with block and key sizes in any multiple of 32 bits, with a minimum of 128 bits. The blocksize has a maximum of 256 bits, but the keysize has no theoretical maximum. AES operates on a 4×4 column-major order matrix of bytes, termed the *state* (versions of Rijndael with a larger block size have additional columns in the state).

Blowfish

Blowfish is a block cipher, designed in 1993 by Bruce Schneier and included in a large number of cipher suites and encryption products. Blowfish has a 64-bit block size and a variable key length from 1 bit up to 448 bits. It is a 16-round Feistel cipher and uses large key-dependent S-boxes. Notable features of the design include the key-dependent S-boxes and a highly complex key schedule.

Schneier designed Blowfish as a general-purpose algorithm, intended as an alternative to the ageing DES and free of the problems and constraints associated with other algorithms. At the time Blowfish was released, many other designs were proprietary, encumbered by patents or were commercial/government secrets. Schneier has stated that, "Blowfish is unpatented, and will remain so in all countries. The algorithm is hereby placed in the public domain, and can be freely used by anyone." Blowfish provides a good encryption rate in software and no effective cryptanalysis of the full-round version has been found to date.

Generalizations

Tweakable Block Ciphers

M. Liskov, R. Rivest, and D. Wagner have described a generalized version of block ciphers called "tweakable" block ciphers. A tweakable block cipher accepts a second input called the *tweak* along with its usual plaintext or ciphertext input. The tweak, along with the key, selects the permutation computed by the cipher. If changing tweaks is sufficiently lightweight (compared with a usually fairly expensive key setup operation), then some interesting new operation modes become possible. The disk encryption theory article describes some of these modes.

Format-preserving Encryption

Block ciphers traditionally work over a binary alphabet. That is, both the input and the output are binary strings, consisting of n zeroes and ones. In some situations, however, one may wish to have a block cipher that works over some other alphabet; for example, encrypting 16-digit credit card numbers in such a way that the ciphertext is also a 16-digit number might facilitate adding an encryption layer to legacy software. This is an example of *format-preserving encryption*. More generally, format-preserving encryption requires a keyed permutation on some finite language. This makes format-preserving encryption schemes a natural generalization of (tweakable) block ciphers. In contrast, traditional encryption schemes, such as CBC, are not permutations because the same plaintext can encrypt to multiple different ciphertexts, even when using a fixed key.

Relation to other Cryptographic Primitives

Block ciphers can be used to build other cryptographic primitives, such as those below. For these other primitives to be cryptographically secure, care has to be taken to build them the right way.

- Stream ciphers can be built using block ciphers. OFB-mode and CTR mode are block modes that turn a block cipher into a stream cipher.

- Cryptographic hash functions can be built using block ciphers. The methods resemble the block cipher modes of operation usually used for encryption.

- Cryptographically secure pseudorandom number generators (CSPRNGs) can be built using block ciphers.

- Secure pseudorandom permutations of arbitrarily sized finite sets can be constructed with block ciphers.

- Message authentication codes (MACs) are often built from block ciphers. CBC-MAC, OMAC and PMAC are such MACs.

- Authenticated encryption is also built from block ciphers. It means to both encrypt and MAC at the same time. That is to both provide confidentiality and authentication. CCM, EAX, GCM and OCB are such authenticated encryption modes.

Just as block ciphers can be used to build hash functions, hash functions can be used to build block ciphers. Examples of such block ciphers are SHACAL, BEAR and LION.

Product Cipher

In cryptography, a product cipher combines two or more transformations in a manner intending that the resulting cipher is more secure than the individual components to make it resistant to cryptanalysis. The product cipher combines a sequence of simple transformations such as substitution (S-box), permutation (P-box), and modular arithmetic. The concept of product ciphers is due to Claude Shannon, who presented the idea in his foundational paper, *Communication Theory of Secrecy Systems*.

For transformation involving reasonable number of n message symbols, both of the foregoing cipher systems (the S-box and P-box) are by themselves wanting. Shannon suggested using a combination of S-box and P-box transformation—a product cipher. The combination could yield a cipher system more powerful than either one alone. This approach of alternatively applying substitution and permutation transformation has been used by IBM in the Lucifer cipher system, and has become the standard for national data encryption standards such as the Data Encryption Standard and the Advanced Encryption Standard. A product cipher that uses only substitutions and permutations is called a SP-network. Feistel ciphers are an important class of product ciphers.

Feistel Cipher

In cryptography, a Feistel cipher is a symmetric structure used in the construction of block ciphers, named after the German-born physicist and cryptographer Horst Feistel who did pioneering research while working for IBM (USA); it is also commonly known as a Feistel network. A large proportion of block ciphers use the scheme, including the Data Encryption Standard (DES). The Feistel structure has the advantage that encryption and decryption operations are very similar, even identical in some cases, requiring only a reversal of the key schedule. Therefore, the size of the code or circuitry required to implement such a cipher is nearly halved.

A Feistel network is an iterated cipher with an internal function called a round function.

Historical

Feistel networks were first seen commercially in IBM's Lucifer cipher, designed by Horst Feistel and Don Coppersmith in 1973. Feistel networks gained respectability when the U.S. Federal Government adopted the DES (a cipher based on Lucifer, with changes made by the NSA). Like other components of the DES, the iterative nature of the Feistel construction makes implementing the cryptosystem in hardware easier (particularly on the hardware available at the time of DES's design).

Theoretical Work

Many modern and also some old symmetric block ciphers are based on Feistel networks (e.g. GOST 28147-89 block cipher), and the structure and properties of Feistel ciphers have been extensively explored by cryptographers. Specifically, Michael Luby and Charles Rackoff analyzed the Feistel cipher construction, and proved that if the round function is a cryptographically secure pseudorandom function, with K_i used as the seed, then 3 rounds are sufficient to make the block cipher a pseudorandom permutation, while 4 rounds are sufficient to make it a "strong" pseudorandom permutation (which means that it remains pseudorandom even to an adversary who gets oracle access to its inverse permutation).

Because of this very important result of Luby and Rackoff, Feistel ciphers are sometimes called Luby–Rackoff block ciphers. Further theoretical work has generalized the construction somewhat, and given more precise bounds for security.

Construction Details

Let F be the round function and let $K_0, K_1, \ldots, K_n$ be the sub-keys for the rounds $0, 1, \ldots, n$ respectively.

Then the basic operation is as follows:

Split the plaintext block into two equal pieces, (L_0, R_0)

For each round $i = 0, 1, \ldots, n$, compute

$$L_{i+1} = R_i$$

$$R_{i+1} = L_i \oplus F(R_i, K_i).$$

Then the ciphertext is (R_{n+1}, L_{n+1}).

Decryption of a ciphertext (R_{n+1}, L_{n+1}) is accomplished by computing for

$$i = n, n-1, \ldots, 0$$

$$R_i = L_{i+1}$$

$$L_i = R_{i+1} \oplus F(L_{i+1}, K_i).$$

Then (L_0, R_0) is the plaintext again.

One advantage of the Feistel model compared to a substitution-permutation network is that the round function F does not have to be invertible.

The diagram illustrates both encryption and decryption. Note the reversal of the subkey order for decryption; this is the only difference between encryption and decryption.

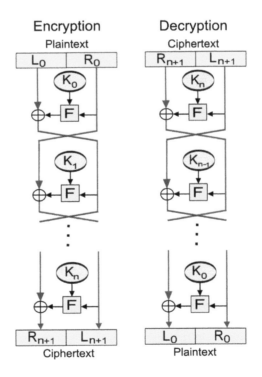

Unbalanced Feistel Cipher

Unbalanced Feistel ciphers use a modified structure where L_0 and R_0 are not of equal lengths. The

Skipjack cipher is an example of such a cipher. The Texas Instruments Digital Signature Transponder uses a proprietary unbalanced Feistel cipher to perform challenge-response authentication.

The Thorp shuffle is an extreme case of an unbalanced Feistel cipher in which one side is a single bit. This has better provable security than a balanced Feistel cipher but requires more rounds.

Other uses

The Feistel construction is also used in cryptographic algorithms other than block ciphers. For example, the optimal asymmetric encryption padding (OAEP) scheme uses a simple Feistel network to randomize ciphertexts in certain asymmetric key encryption schemes.

A generalized Feistel algorithm can be used to create strong permutations on small domains of size not a power of two.

Feistel Networks as a Design Component

Whether the entire cipher is a Feistel cipher or not, Feistel-like networks can be used as a component of a cipher's design. For example, MISTY1 is a Feistel cipher using a three-round Feistel network in its round function, Skipjack is a modified Feistel cipher using a Feistel network in its G permutation, and Threefish (part of Skein) is a non-Feistel block cipher that uses a Feistel-like MIX function.

List of Feistel Ciphers

Feistel or modified Feistel:

• Blowfish	• KASUMI	• RC5
• Camellia	• LOKI97	• Simon
• CAST-128	• Lucifer	• TEA
• DES	• MARS	• Triple DES
• FEAL	• MAGENTA	• Twofish
• GOST 28147-89	• MISTY1	• XTEA
• ICE		

Generalised Feistel:

• CAST-256	• RC6
• CLEFIA	• Skipjack
• MacGuffin	• SMS4
• RC2	

Stream Cipher

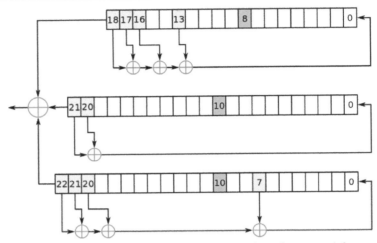

The operation of the keystream generator in A5/1, an LFSR-based stream cipher used to encrypt mobile phone conversations.

A stream cipher is a symmetric key cipher where plaintext digits are combined with a pseudorandom cipher digit stream (keystream). In a stream cipher each plaintext digit is encrypted one at a time with the corresponding digit of the keystream, to give a digit of the ciphertext stream. Since encryption of each digit is dependent on the current state of the cipher, it is also known as *state cipher*. In practice, a digit is typically a bit and the combining operation an exclusive-or (XOR).

The pseudorandom keystream is typically generated serially from a random seed value using digital shift registers. The seed value serves as the cryptographic key for decrypting the ciphertext stream. Stream ciphers represent a different approach to symmetric encryption from block ciphers. Block ciphers operate on large blocks of digits with a fixed, unvarying transformation. This distinction is not always clear-cut: in some modes of operation, a block cipher primitive is used in such a way that it acts effectively as a stream cipher. Stream ciphers typically execute at a higher speed than block ciphers and have lower hardware complexity. However, stream ciphers can be susceptible to serious security problems if used incorrectly in particular, the same starting state (seed) must never be used twice.

Loose Inspiration from the One-time Pad

Stream ciphers can be viewed as approximating the action of a proven unbreakable cipher, the one-time pad (OTP), sometimes known as the Vernam cipher. A one-time pad uses a keystream of completely random digits. The keystream is combined with the plaintext digits one at a time to form the ciphertext. This system was proved to be secure by Claude E. Shannon in 1949. However, the keystream must be generated completely at random with at least the same length as the plaintext and cannot be used more than once. This makes the system very cumbersome to implement in practice, and as a result the one-time pad has not been widely used, except for the most critical applications

A stream cipher makes use of a much smaller and more convenient key such as 128 bits. Based on this key, it generates a pseudorandom keystream which can be combined with the plaintext digits in a similar fashion to the one-time pad. However, this comes at a cost. The keystream is now pseudorandom and so is not truly random. The proof of security associated with the one-time pad no longer holds. It is quite possible for a stream cipher to be completely insecure.

Types of Stream Ciphers

A stream cipher generates successive elements of the keystream based on an internal state. This state is updated in essentially two ways: if the state changes independently of the plaintext or ciphertext messages, the cipher is classified as a *synchronous* stream cipher. By contrast, *self-synchronising* stream ciphers update their state based on previous ciphertext digits.

Synchronous Stream Ciphers

In a synchronous stream cipher a stream of pseudo-random digits is generated independently of the plaintext and ciphertext messages, and then combined with the plaintext (to encrypt) or the ciphertext (to decrypt). In the most common form, binary digits are used (bits), and the keystream is combined with the plaintext using the exclusive or operation (XOR). This is termed a binary additive stream cipher.

In a synchronous stream cipher, the sender and receiver must be exactly in step for decryption to be successful. If digits are added or removed from the message during transmission, synchronisation is lost. To restore synchronisation, various offsets can be tried systematically to obtain the correct decryption. Another approach is to tag the ciphertext with markers at regular points in the output.

If, however, a digit is corrupted in transmission, rather than added or lost, only a single digit in the plaintext is affected and the error does not propagate to other parts of the message. This property is useful when the transmission error rate is high; however, it makes it less likely the error would be detected without further mechanisms. Moreover, because of this property, synchronous stream ciphers are very susceptible to active attacks: if an attacker can change a digit in the ciphertext, he might be able to make predictable changes to the corresponding plaintext bit; for example, flipping a bit in the ciphertext causes the same bit to be flipped in the plaintext.

Self-synchronizing Stream Ciphers

Another approach uses several of the previous N ciphertext digits to compute the keystream. Such schemes are known as self-synchronizing stream ciphers, asynchronous stream ciphers or ciphertext autokey (CTAK). The idea of self-synchronization was patented in 1946, and has the advantage that the receiver will automatically synchronise with the keystream generator after receiving N ciphertext digits, making it easier to recover if digits are dropped or added to the message stream. Single-digit errors are limited in their effect, affecting only up to N plaintext digits.

An example of a self-synchronising stream cipher is a block cipher in cipher feedback (CFB) mode.

Linear Feedback Shift Register-based Stream Ciphers

Binary stream ciphers are often constructed using linear feedback shift registers (LFSRs) because they can be easily implemented in hardware and can be readily analysed mathematically. The use of LFSRs on their own, however, is insufficient to provide good security. Various schemes have been proposed to increase the security of LFSRs.

Non-linear Combining Functions

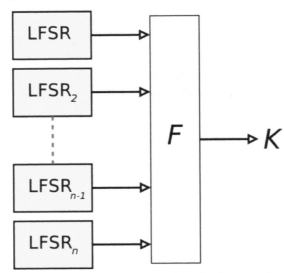

One approach is to use n LFSRs in parallel, their outputs combined using an n-input binary Boolean function (F).

Because LFSRs are inherently linear, one technique for removing the linearity is to feed the outputs of several parallel LFSRs into a non-linear Boolean function to form a *combination generator*. Various properties of such a *combining function* are critical for ensuring the security of the resultant scheme, for example, in order to avoid correlation attacks.

Clock-controlled Generators

Normally LFSRs are stepped regularly. One approach to introducing non-linearity is to have the LFSR clocked irregularly, controlled by the output of a second LFSR. Such generators include the stop-and-go generator, the alternating step generator and the shrinking generator.

An alternating step generator comprises three linear feedback shift registers, which we will call LFSR0, LFSR1 and LFSR2 for convenience. The output of one of the registers decides which of the other two is to be used; for instance if LFSR2 outputs a 0, LFSR0 is clocked, and if it outputs a 1, LFSR1 is clocked instead. The output is the exclusive OR of the last bit produced by LFSR0 and LFSR1. The initial state of the three LFSRs is the key.

The stop-and-go generator (Beth and Piper, 1984) consists of two LFSRs. One LFSR is clocked if the output of a second is a "1", otherwise it repeats its previous output. This output is then (in some versions) combined with the output of a third LFSR clocked at a regular rate.

The shrinking generator takes a different approach. Two LFSRs are used, both clocked regularly. If the output of the first LFSR is "1", the output of the second LFSR becomes the output of the generator. If the first LFSR outputs "0", however, the output of the second is discarded, and no bit is output by the generator. This mechanism suffers from timing attacks on the second generator, since the speed of the output is variable in a manner that depends on the second generator's state. This can be alleviated by buffering the output.

Filter Generator

Another approach to improving the security of an LFSR is to pass the entire state of a single LFSR into a non-linear *filtering function*.

Other Designs

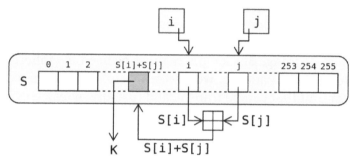

RC4 is one of the most widely used stream cipher designs.

Instead of a linear driving device, one may use a nonlinear update function. For example, Klimov and Shamir proposed triangular functions (T-functions) with a single cycle on n bit words.

Security

For a stream cipher to be secure, its keystream must have a large period and it must be impossible to *recover the cipher's key* or internal state from the keystream. Cryptographers also demand that the keystream be free of even subtle biases that would let attackers *distinguish* a stream from random noise, and free of detectable relationships between keystreams that correspond to *related keys* or related cryptographic nonces. This should be true for all keys (there should be no *weak keys*), and true even if the attacker can *know* or *choose* some *plaintext* or *ciphertext*.

As with other attacks in cryptography, stream cipher attacks can be *certificational*, meaning they are not necessarily practical ways to break the cipher but indicate that the cipher might have other weaknesses.

Securely using a secure synchronous stream cipher requires that one never reuse the same keystream twice; that generally means a different nonce or key must be supplied to each invocation of the cipher. Application designers must also recognize that most stream ciphers don't provide *authenticity*, only *privacy*: encrypted messages may still have been modified in transit.

Short periods for stream ciphers have been a practical concern. For example, 64-bit block ciphers like DES can be used to generate a keystream in output feedback (OFB) mode. However, when not using full feedback, the resulting stream has a period of around 2^{32} blocks on average; for many applications, this period is far too low. For example, if encryption is being performed at a rate of 8 megabytes per second, a stream of period 2^{32} blocks will repeat after about a half an hour.

Some applications using the stream cipher RC4 are attackable because of weaknesses in RC4's key setup routine; new applications should either avoid RC4 or make sure all keys are unique and ideally unrelated (such as generated by a well-seeded CSPRNG or a cryptographic hash function) and that the first bytes of the keystream are discarded.

Usage

Stream ciphers are often used for their speed and simplicity of implementation in hardware, and in applications where plaintext comes in quantities of unknowable length like a secure wireless connection. If a block cipher (not operating in a stream cipher mode) were to be used in this type of application, the designer would need to choose either transmission efficiency or implementation complexity, since block ciphers cannot directly work on blocks shorter than their block size. For example, if a 128-bit block cipher received separate 32-bit bursts of plaintext, three quarters of the data transmitted would be padding. Block ciphers must be used in ciphertext stealing or residual block termination mode to avoid padding, while stream ciphers eliminate this issue by naturally operating on the smallest unit that can be transmitted (usually bytes).

Another advantage of stream ciphers in military cryptography is that the cipher stream can be generated in a separate box that is subject to strict security measures and fed to other devices such as a radio set, which will perform the xor operation as part of their function. The latter device can then be designed and used in less stringent environments.

RC4 is the most widely used stream cipher in software; others include: A5/1, A5/2, Chameleon, FISH, Helix, ISAAC, MUGI, Panama, Phelix, Pike, SEAL, SOBER, SOBER-128 and WAKE.

Comparison Of Stream Ciphers

Stream Cipher	Cre-ation Date	Speed (cycles per byte)	(bits)			Attack	
			Effective Key-Length	Initialization vector	Internal State	Best Known	Computational Complexity
A5/1	1989	Voice (W_{phone})	54 or 64 (in 2G)	22 (in 2G)	64	Active KPA OR KPA Time-Memory Tradeoff	~2 seconds OR $2^{39.91}$
A5/2	1989	Voice (W_{phone})	54	114	64?	Active	4.6 milliseconds
Achter-bahn-128/80	2006	1 (hard-ware)	80/128	80/128	297/351	Brute force for frame lengths L $\leq 2^{44}$. Correlation attack for L $\geq 2^{48}$.	2^{80} resp. 2^{128} for $L \leq 2^{44}$.
CryptMT	2005	?	Variable	up to 19968	19968	N/A (2008)	N/A (2008)
FISH	1993	?	Variable	?	?	Known-plaintext attack	2^{11}
Grain	Pre-2004	?	80	64	160	Key-Derivation	2^{43}
HC-256	Pre-2004	4 (W_{P4})	256	256	65536	?	?

Stream Cipher	Creation Date	Speed (cycles per byte)	(bits)			Attack	
			Effective Key-Length	Initialization vector	Internal State	Best Known	Computational Complexity
ISAAC	1996	$2.375 (W_{64\text{-}bit}) - 4.6875 (W_{32\text{-}bit})$	8-8288 usually 40-256	N/A	8288	(2006) First-round Weak-Internal-State-Derivation	4.67×10^{1240} (2001)
MUGI	1998–2002	?	128	128	1216	N/A (2002)	$\sim 2^{82}$
PANAMA	1998	2	256	128?	1216?	Hash Collisions (2001)	2^{82}
Phelix	Pre-2004	up to 8 (W_{x86})	256 + a 128-bit Nonce	128?	?	Differential (2006)	2^{37}
Pike	1994	?	Variable	?	?	N/A (2004)	N/A (2004)
Py	Pre-2004	2.6	8-2048? usually 40-256?	64	8320	Cryptanalytic Theory (2006)	2^{75}
Rabbit	2003-Feb	$3.7(W_{P3})-9.7(W_{ARM7})$	128	64	512	N/A (2006)	N/A (2006)
RC4	1987	$7 W_{P5}$	8-2048 usually 40-256	RC4 does not take an IV. If one desires an IV, it must be mixed into the key somehow.	2064	Shamir Initial-Bytes Key-Derivation OR KPA	2^{13} OR 2^{33}
Salsa20	Pre-2004	$4.24 (W_{G4}) - 11.84 (W_{P4})$	256	a 64-bit Nonce + a 64-bit stream position	512	Probabilistic neutral bits method	2^{251} for 8 rounds (2007)
Scream	2002	$4 - 5 (W_{soft})$	128 + a 128-bit Nonce	32?	64-bit round function	?	?
SEAL	1997	?	?	32?	?	?	?
SNOW	Pre-2003	?	128 OR 256	32	?	?	?
SOBER-128	2003	?	up to 128	?	?	Message Forge	2^{-6}
SOSEMA-NUK	Pre-2004	?	128	128	?	?	?
Trivium	Pre-2004	$4 (W_{x86}) - 8 (W_{LG})$	80	80	288	Brute force attack (2006)	2^{135}
Turing	2000–2003	$5.5 (W_{x86})$	?	160	?	?	?
VEST	2005	$42 (W_{ASIC}) - 64 (W_{FPGA})$	Variable usually 80-256	Variable usually 80-256	256 - 800	N/A (2006)	N/A (2006)
WAKE	1993	?	?	?	8192	CPA & CCA	Vulnerable

Trivia

- United States National Security Agency documents sometimes use the term combiner-type algorithms, referring to algorithms that use some function to combine a pseudorandom number generator (PRNG) with a plaintext stream.

Ciphertext

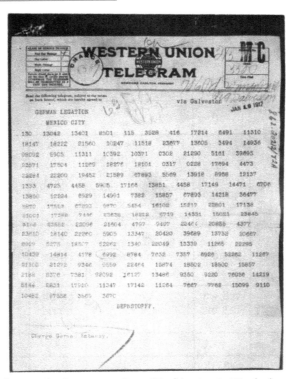

The Zimmermann Telegram (as it was sent from Washington to Mexico) encrypted as ciphertext.

KGB ciphertext found in a hollow nickel in Brooklyn in 1953

In cryptography, ciphertext or cyphertext is the result of encryption performed on plaintext using an algorithm, called a cipher. Ciphertext is also known as encrypted or encoded information because it contains a form of the original plaintext that is unreadable by a human or computer without the proper cipher to decrypt it. Decryption, the inverse of encryption, is the process of turning ciphertext into readable plaintext.

Symmetric Key Example

Let E_K be the plaintext message that Alice wants to secretly transmit to Bob and let k be the encryption cipher, where c, is a secret key. Alice must first transform the plaintext into ciphertext, , in order to securely send the message to Bob.

$$c = E_k(m)$$

Both Alice and Bob must know the choice of key, k, or else the ciphertext is useless. Once the message is encrypted as ciphertext, Alice can safely transmit it to Bob (assuming no one else knows the key). In order to read Alice's message, Bob must decrypt the ciphertext using E_k^{-1} which is known as the decryption cipher, D_k.

$$D_k(c) = D_k(E_k(m)) = m \quad D_k(c) = D_k(E_k(m)) = m$$

Types of Ciphers

The history of cryptography began thousands of years ago. Cryptography uses a variety of different types of encryption. Earlier algorithms were performed by hand and are substantially different from modern algorithms, which are generally executed by a machine.

Historical Ciphers

Historical pen and paper ciphers used in the past are sometimes known as classical ciphers. They include:

- Substitution cipher: the units of plaintext are replaced with ciphertext (Caesar cipher and One-time pad)

- Transposition cipher: the ciphertext is a permutation of the plaintext (Rail fence cipher)

- Polyalphabetic substitution cipher: a substitution cipher using multiple substitution alphabets (Vigenère cipher and Enigma machine)

- Permutation cipher: a transposition cipher in which the key is a permutation

Historical ciphers are not generally used as a standalone encryption solution because they are quite easy to crack. Many of the classical ciphers can be cracked using brute force or by analyzing only ciphertext with the exception of the one-time pad.

Modern Ciphers

Modern ciphers are more secure than classical ciphers and are designed to withstand a wide range of attacks. An attacker should not be able to find the key used in a modern cipher, even if he knows any amount of plaintext and corresponding ciphertext. Modern encryption methods can be divided into the following categories:

- Private-key cryptography (symmetric key algorithm): the same key is used for encryption and decryption

- Public-key cryptography (asymmetric key algorithm): two different keys are used for encryption and decryption

In a symmetric key algorithm (e.g., DES and AES), the sender and receiver must have a shared key set up in advance and kept secret from all other parties; the sender uses this key for encryption, and the receiver uses the same key for decryption. In an asymmetric key algorithm (e.g., RSA), there are two separate keys: a *public key* is published and enables any sender to perform encryption, while a *private key* is kept secret by the receiver and enables only him to perform correct decryption.

Symmetric key ciphers can be divided into block ciphers and stream ciphers. Block ciphers operate on fixed-length groups of bits, called blocks, with an unvarying transformation. Stream ciphers encrypt plaintext digits one at a time on a continuous stream of data and the transformation of successive digits varies during the encryption process.

Cryptanalysis

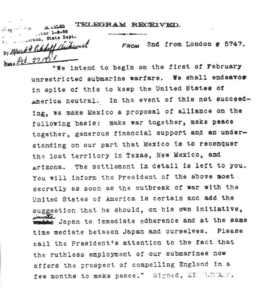

The Zimmermann Telegram decrypted into plaintext (and translated into English).

Cryptanalysis is the study of methods for obtaining the meaning of encrypted information, without access to the secret information that is normally required to do so. Typically, this involves knowing how the system works and finding a secret key. Cryptanalysis is also referred to as codebreaking or cracking the code. Ciphertext is generally the easiest part of a cryptosystem to obtain and therefore is an important part of cryptanalysis. Depending on what information is available and what type of cipher is being analyzed, crypanalysts can follow one or more attack models to crack a cipher.

Attack Models

- Ciphertext-only: the cryptanalyst has access only to a collection of ciphertexts or codetexts

- Known-plaintext: the attacker has a set of ciphertexts to which he knows the corresponding plaintext

- Chosen-plaintext attack: the attacker can obtain the ciphertexts corresponding to an arbitrary set of plaintexts of his own choosing

    o Batch chosen-plaintext attack: where the cryptanalyst chooses all plaintexts before any of them are encrypted. This is often the meaning of an unqualified use of "chosen-plaintext attack".

    o Adaptive chosen-plaintext attack: where the cryptanalyst makes a series of interactive queries, choosing subsequent plaintexts based on the information from the previous encryptions.

- Chosen-ciphertext attack: the attacker can obtain the plaintexts corresponding to an arbitrary set of ciphertexts of his own choosing

    o Adaptive chosen-ciphertext attack

    o Indifferent chosen-ciphertext attack

- Related-key attack: like a chosen-plaintext attack, except the attacker can obtain ciphertexts encrypted under two different keys. The keys are unknown, but the relationship between them is known; for example, two keys that differ in the one bit.

The ciphertext-only attack model is the weakest because it implies that the cryptanalyst has nothing but ciphertext. Modern ciphers rarely fail under this attack.

Famous Ciphertexts

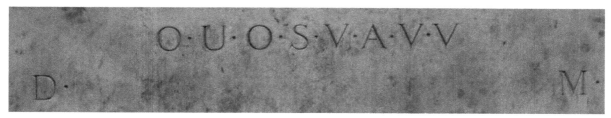

The Shugborough inscription, England

- The Babington Plot ciphers

- The Shugborough inscription

- The Zimmermann Telegram

- The Magic Words are Squeamish Ossifrage

- The cryptogram in "The Gold-Bug"

- Beale ciphers

- Kryptos

- Zodiac Killer ciphers

Substitution Cipher

In cryptography, a substitution cipher is a method of encoding by which units of plaintext are replaced with ciphertext, according to a fixed system; the "units" may be single letters (the most common), pairs of letters, triplets of letters, mixtures of the above, and so forth. The receiver deciphers the text by performing the inverse substitution.

Substitution ciphers can be compared with transposition ciphers. In a transposition cipher, the units of the plaintext are rearranged in a different and usually quite complex order, but the units themselves are left unchanged. By contrast, in a substitution cipher, the units of the plaintext are retained in the same sequence in the ciphertext, but the units themselves are altered.

There are a number of different types of substitution cipher. If the cipher operates on single letters, it is termed a simple substitution cipher; a cipher that operates on larger groups of letters is termed polygraphic. A monoalphabetic cipher uses fixed substitution over the entire message, whereas a polyalphabetic cipher uses a number of substitutions at different positions in the message, where a unit from the plaintext is mapped to one of several possibilities in the ciphertext and vice versa.

Simple Substitution

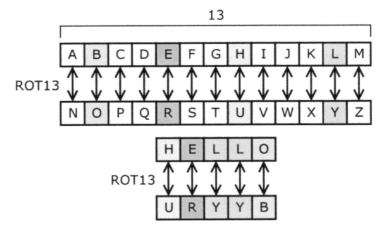

ROT13 is a Caesar cipher, a type of substitution cipher. In ROT13, the alphabet is rotated 13 steps.

Substitution of single letters separately—simple substitution—can be demonstrated by writing out the alphabet in some order to represent the substitution. This is termed a substitution alphabet. The cipher alphabet may be shifted or reversed (creating the Caesar and Atbash ciphers, respectively) or scrambled in a more complex fashion, in which case it is called a *mixed alphabet* or *deranged alphabet*. Traditionally, mixed alphabets may be created by first writing out a keyword, removing repeated letters in it, then writing all the remaining letters in the alphabet in the usual order.

Using this system, the keyword "zebras" gives us the following alphabets:

Plaintext alphabet:	ABCDEFGHIJKLMNOPQRSTUVWXYZ
Ciphertext alphabet:	ZEBRASCDFGHIJKLMNOPQTUVWXY

A message of

> flee at once. we are discovered!

enciphers to

> SIAA ZQ LKBA. VA ZOA RFPBLUAOAR!

Traditionally, the ciphertext is written out in blocks of fixed length, omitting punctuation and spaces; this is done to help avoid transmission errors and to disguise word boundaries from the plaintext. These blocks are called "groups", and sometimes a "group count" (i.e., the number of groups) is given as an additional check. Five letter groups are traditional, dating from when messages used to be transmitted by telegraph:

> SIAAZ QLKBA VAZOA RFPBL UAOAR

If the length of the message happens not to be divisible by five, it may be padded at the end with "nulls". These can be any characters that decrypt to obvious nonsense, so the receiver can easily spot them and discard them.

The ciphertext alphabet is sometimes different from the plaintext alphabet; for example, in the pigpen cipher, the ciphertext consists of a set of symbols derived from a grid. For example:

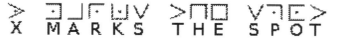
X MARKS THE SPOT

Such features make little difference to the security of a scheme, however – at the very least, any set of strange symbols can be transcribed back into an A-Z alphabet and dealt with as normal.

In lists and catalogues for salespeople, a very simple encryption is sometimes used to replace numeric digits by letters.

Plaintext digits:	1234567890
Ciphertext alphabets:	MAKEPROFIT

Example: MAT would be used to represent 120.

Security for Simple Substitution Ciphers

A disadvantage of this method of derangement is that the last letters of the alphabet (which are mostly low frequency) tend to stay at the end. A stronger way of constructing a mixed alphabet is to perform a columnar transposition on the ordinary alphabet using the keyword, but this is not often done.

Although the number of possible keys is very large ($26! \approx 2^{88.4}$, or about 88 bits), this cipher is not very strong, and is easily broken. Provided the message is of reasonable length, the cryptanalyst can deduce the probable meaning of the most common symbols by analyzing the frequency distribution of the ciphertext—frequency analysis. This allows formation of partial words, which can be tentatively filled in, progressively expanding the (partial) solution. In some cases, underlying words can also be determined from the pattern of their letters; for example, *attract*, *osseous*, and words with those two as the root are the only common English words with the pattern *ABBCADB*. Many people solve such ciphers for recreation, as with cryptogram puzzles in the newspaper.

According to the unicity distance of English, 27.6 letters of ciphertext are required to crack a mixed alphabet simple substitution. In practice, typically about 50 letters are needed, although some messages can be broken with fewer if unusual patterns are found. In other cases, the plaintext can be contrived to have a nearly flat frequency distribution, and much longer plaintexts will then be required by the user.

Homophonic Substitution

An early attempt to increase the difficulty of frequency analysis attacks on substitution ciphers was to disguise plaintext letter frequencies by homophony. In these ciphers, plaintext letters map to more than one ciphertext symbol. Usually, the highest-frequency plaintext symbols are given more equivalents than lower frequency letters. In this way, the frequency distribution is flattened, making analysis more difficult.

The forged nomenclator message used in the Babington Plot

Since more than 26 characters will be required in the ciphertext alphabet, various solutions are employed to invent larger alphabets. Perhaps the simplest is to use a numeric substitution 'alphabet'. Another method consists of simple variations on the existing alphabet; uppercase, lowercase, upside down, etc. More artistically, though not necessarily more securely, some homophonic ciphers employed wholly invented alphabets of fanciful symbols.

One variant is the nomenclator. Named after the public official who announced the titles of visiting dignitaries, this cipher combines a small codebook with large homophonic substitution tables. Originally the code was restricted to the names of important people, hence the name of the cipher; in later years it covered many common words and place names as well. The symbols for whole words (*codewords* in modern parlance) and letters (*cipher* in modern parlance) were not distinguished in the ciphertext. The Rossignols' Great Cipher used by Louis XIV of France was one; after it went out of use, messages in French archives were unbroken for several hundred years.

Nomenclators were the standard fare of diplomatic correspondence, espionage, and advanced political conspiracy from the early fifteenth century to the late eighteenth century; most conspirators were and have remained less cryptographically sophisticated. Although government intelligence cryptanalysts were systematically breaking nomenclators by the mid-sixteenth century, and superior systems had been available since 1467, the usual response to cryptanalysis was simply to make the tables larger. By the late eighteenth century, when the system was beginning to die out, some nomenclators had 50,000 symbols.

Nevertheless, not all nomenclators were broken; today, cryptanalysis of archived ciphertexts remains a fruitful area of historical research.

The Beale ciphers are another example of a homophonic cipher. This is a story of buried treasure that was described in 1819–21 by use of a ciphered text that was keyed to the Declaration of Independence. Here each ciphertext character was represented by a number. The number was determined by taking the plaintext character and finding a word in the Declaration of Independence that started with that character and using the numerical position of that word in the Declaration of Independence as the encrypted form of that letter. Since many words in the Declaration of Independence start with the same letter, the encryption of that character could be any of the numbers associated with the words in the Declaration of Independence that start with that letter. Deciphering the encrypted text character X (which is a number) is as simple as looking up the Xth word of the Declaration of Independence and using the first letter of that word as the decrypted character.

Another homophonic cipher was described by Stahl and was one of the first attempts to provide for computer security of data systems in computers through encryption. Stahl constructed the cipher in such a way that the number of homophones for a given character was in proportion to the frequency of the character, thus making frequency analysis much more difficult.

The book cipher and straddling checkerboard are types of homophonic cipher.

Francesco I Gonzaga, Duke of Mantua, is the one who use the earliest example of Homophonic Substitution cipher in 1401 for correspondence with one Simone de Crema.

Polyalphabetic Substitution

Polyalphabetic substitution ciphers were first described in 1467 by Leone Battista Alberti in the form of disks. Johannes Trithemius, in his book *Steganographia* (Ancient Greek for "hidden writing") introduced the now more standard form of a *tableau*. A more sophisticated version using mixed alphabets was described in 1563 by Giovanni Battista della Porta in his book, *De Furtivis Literarum Notis* (Latin for "On concealed characters in writing").

In a polyalphabetic cipher, multiple cipher alphabets are used. To facilitate encryption, all the alpha-bets are usually written out in a large table, traditionally called a *tableau*. The tableau is usually 26×26, so that 26 full ciphertext alphabets are available. The method of filling the tableau, and of choosing which alphabet to use next, defines the particular polyalphabetic cipher. All such ciphers are easier to break than once believed, as substitution alphabets are repeated for sufficiently large plaintexts.

One of the most popular was that of Blaise de Vigenère. First published in 1585, it was considered unbreakable until 1863, and indeed was commonly called *le chiffre indéchiffrable* (French for "indecipherable cipher").

In the Vigenère cipher, the first row of the tableau is filled out with a copy of the plaintext alphabet, and successive rows are simply shifted one place to the left. (Such a simple tableau is called a *tabula recta*, and mathematically corresponds to adding the plaintext and key letters, modulo 26.) A keyword is then used to choose which ciphertext alphabet to use. Each letter of the keyword is used in turn, and then they are repeated again from the beginning. So if the keyword is 'CAT', the first letter of plaintext is enciphered under alphabet 'C', the second under 'A', the third under 'T', the fourth under 'C' again, and so on. In practice, Vigenère keys were often phrases several words long.

In 1863, Friedrich Kasiski published a method (probably discovered secretly and independently before the Crimean War by Charles Babbage) which enabled the calculation of the length of the keyword in a Vigenère ciphered message. Once this was done, ciphertext letters that had been enciphered under the same alphabet could be picked out and attacked separately as a number of semi-independent simple substitutions - complicated by the fact that within one alphabet letters were separated and did not form complete words, but simplified by the fact that usually a *tabula recta* had been employed.

As such, even today a Vigenère type cipher should theoretically be difficult to break if mixed alphabets are used in the tableau, if the keyword is random, and if the total length of ciphertext is less than 27.6 times the length of the keyword. These requirements are rarely understood in practice, and so Vigenère enciphered message security is usually less than might have been.

Other notable polyalphabetics include:

- The Gronsfeld cipher. This is identical to the Vigenère except that only 10 alphabets are used, and so the "keyword" is numerical.

- The Beaufort cipher. This is practically the same as the Vigenère, except the *tabula recta* is replaced by a backwards one, mathematically equivalent to ciphertext = key - plaintext.

This operation is *self-inverse*, whereby the same table is used for both encryption and decryption.

- The autokey cipher, which mixes plaintext with a key to avoid periodicity.

- The running key cipher, where the key is made very long by using a passage from a book or similar text.

Modern stream ciphers can also be seen, from a sufficiently abstract perspective, to be a form of polyalphabetic cipher in which all the effort has gone into making the keystream as long and unpredictable as possible.

Polygraphic Substitution

In a polygraphic substitution cipher, plaintext letters are substituted in larger groups, instead of substituting letters individually. The first advantage is that the frequency distribution is much flatter than that of individual letters (though not actually flat in real languages; for example, 'TH' is much more common than 'XQ' in English). Second, the larger number of symbols requires correspondingly more ciphertext to productively analyze letter frequencies.

To substitute *pairs* of letters would take a substitution alphabet 676 symbols long ($26^2 = 676$). In the same *De Furtivis Literarum Notis* mentioned above, della Porta actually proposed such a system, with a 20 x 20 tableau (for the 20 letters of the Italian/Latin alphabet he was using) filled with 400 unique glyphs. However the system was impractical and probably never actually used.

The earliest practical digraphic cipher (pairwise substitution), was the so-called Playfair cipher, invented by Sir Charles Wheatstone in 1854. In this cipher, a 5 x 5 grid is filled with the letters of a mixed alphabet (two letters, usually I and J, are combined). A digraphic substitution is then simulated by taking pairs of letters as two corners of a rectangle, and using the other two corners as the ciphertext. Special rules handle double letters and pairs falling in the same row or column. Playfair was in military use from the Boer War through World War II.

Several other practical polygraphics were introduced in 1901 by Felix Delastelle, including the bifid and four-square ciphers (both digraphic) and the trifid cipher (probably the first practical trigraphic).

The Hill cipher, invented in 1929 by Lester S. Hill, is a polygraphic substitution which can combine much larger groups of letters simultaneously using linear algebra. Each letter is treated as a digit in base 26: A = 0, B =1, and so on. (In a variation, 3 extra symbols are added to make the basis prime.) A block of n letters is then considered as a vector of n dimensions, and multiplied by a n x n matrix, modulo 26. The components of the matrix are the key, and should be random provided that the matrix is invertible in $26^2 = 676$ (to ensure decryption is possible). A mechanical version of the Hill cipher of dimension 6 was patented in 1929.

The Hill cipher is vulnerable to a known-plaintext attack because it is completely linear, so it must be combined with some non-linear step to defeat this attack. The combination of wider and wider weak, linear diffusive steps like a Hill cipher, with non-linear substitution steps, ultimately leads to a substitution-permutation network (e.g. a Feistel cipher), so it is possible – from this extreme perspective – to consider modern block ciphers as a type of polygraphic substitution.

Mechanical Substitution Ciphers

Between circa World War I and the widespread availability of computers (for some governments this was approximately the 1950s or 1960s; for other organizations it was a decade or more later; for individuals it was no earlier than 1975), mechanical implementations of polyalphabetic substitution ciphers were widely used. Several inventors had similar ideas about the same time, and rotor cipher machines were patented four times in 1919. The most important of the resulting machines was the Enigma, especially in the versions used by the German military from approximately 1930. The Allies also developed and used rotor machines (e.g., SIGABA and Typex).

All of these were similar in that the substituted letter was chosen electrically from amongst the huge number of possible combinations resulting from the rotation of several letter disks. Since one or more of the disks rotated mechanically with each plaintext letter enciphered, the number of alphabets used was substantially more than astronomical. Early versions of these machine were, nevertheless, breakable. William F. Friedman of the US Army's SIS early found vulnerabilities in Hebern's rotor machine, and GC&CS's Dillwyn Knox solved versions of the Enigma machine (those without the "plugboard") well before WWII began. Traffic protected by essentially all of the German military Enigmas was broken by Allied cryptanalysts, most notably those at Bletchley Park, beginning with the German Army variant used in the early 1930s. This version was broken by inspired mathematical insight by Marian Rejewski in Poland.

No messages protected by the SIGABA and Typex machines were ever, so far as is publicly known, broken.

The One-time Pad

One type of substitution cipher, the one-time pad, is quite special. It was invented near the end of WWI by Gilbert Vernam and Joseph Mauborgne in the US. It was mathematically proven unbreakable by Claude Shannon, probably during WWII; his work was first published in the late 1940s. In its most common implementation, the one-time pad can be called a substitution cipher only from an unusual perspective; typically, the plaintext letter is combined (not substituted) in some manner (e.g., XOR) with the key material character at that position.

The one-time pad is, in most cases, impractical as it requires that the key material be as long as the plaintext, *actually* random, used once and *only* once, and kept entirely secret from all except the sender and intended receiver. When these conditions are violated, even marginally, the one-time pad is no longer unbreakable. Soviet one-time pad messages sent from the US for a brief time during WWII used non-random key material. US cryptanalysts, beginning in the late 40s, were able to, entirely or partially, break a few thousand messages out of several hundred thousand.

In a mechanical implementation, rather like the Rockex equipment, the one-time pad was used for messages sent on the Moscow-Washington *hot line* established after the Cuban missile crisis.

Substitution in Modern Cryptography

Substitution ciphers as discussed above, especially the older pencil-and-paper hand ciphers, are no longer in serious use. However, the cryptographic concept of substitution carries on even today. From a sufficiently abstract perspective, modern bit-oriented block ciphers (e.g., DES, or AES) can be viewed as substitution ciphers on an enormously large binary alphabet. In addition, block ciphers often include smaller substitution tables called S-boxes.

Substitution Ciphers in Popular Culture

- Sherlock Holmes breaks a substitution cipher in "The Adventure of the Dancing Men". There, the cipher remained undeciphered for years if not decades; not due to its difficulty, but because no one suspected it to be a code, instead considering it childish scribblings.

- The Al Bhed language in *Final Fantasy X* is actually a substitution cipher, although it is pronounced phonetically (i.e. "you" in English is translated to "oui" in Al Bhed, but is pronounced the same way that "oui" is pronounced in French).

- The Minbari's alphabet from the *Babylon 5* series is a substitution cipher from English.

- The language in *Starfox Adventures*: Dinosaur Planet spoken by native Saurians and Krystal is also a substitution cipher of the English alphabet.

- The television program *Futurama* contained a substitution cipher in which all 26 letters were replaced by symbols and called "Alien Language". This was deciphered rather quickly by the die hard viewers by showing a "Slurm" ad with the word "Drink" in both plain English and the Alien language thus giving the key. Later, the producers created a second alien language that used a combination of replacement and mathematical Ciphers. Once the English letter of the alien language is deciphered, then the numerical value of that letter (0 for "A" through 25 for "Z" respectively) is then added (modulo 26) to the value of the previous letter showing the actual intended letter. These messages can be seen throughout every episode of the series and the subsequent movies.

- At the end of every season 1 episode of the cartoon series *Gravity Falls*, during the credit roll, there is one of three simple substitution ciphers: A -3 Caesar cipher (hinted by "3 letters back" at the end of the opening sequence), an Atbash cipher, or a letter-to-number simple substitution cipher. The season 1 finale encodes a message with all three. In the second season, Vigenère ciphers are used in place of the various monoalphabetic ciphers, each using a key hidden within the its episode.

- In the Artemis Fowl series by Eoin Colfer there are three substitution ciphers; Gnommish, Centaurean and Eternean, which run along the bottom of the pages or are somewhere else within the books.

- In *Bitterblue*, the third novel by Kristin Cashore, substitution ciphers serve as an important form of coded communication.

- In the 2013 video game *BioShock Infinite*, there are substitution ciphers hidden throughout the game in which the player must find code books to help decipher them and gain access to a surplus of supplies.

References

- David A. King, The ciphers of the monks - A forgotten number notation of the Middle Ages, Stuttgart: Franz Steiner, 2001 (ISBN 3-515-07640-9)

- Abraham Sinkov, Elementary Cryptanalysis: A Mathematical Approach, Mathematical Association of America, 1966. ISBN 0-88385-622-0

- van Tilborg, Henk C. A.; Jajodia, Sushil, eds. (2011). Encyclopedia of Cryptography and Security. Springer. ISBN 978-1-4419-5905-8. , p. 455.

- Cusick, Thomas W. & Stanica, Pantelimon (2009). Cryptographic Boolean functions and applications. Academic Press. pp. 158–159. ISBN 9780123748904.

- Menezes, Alfred J.; van Oorschot, Paul C.; Vanstone, Scott A. (1996). "Chapter 7: Block Ciphers". Handbook of Applied Cryptography. CRC Press. ISBN 0-8493-8523-7.

- Junod, Pascal & Canteaut, Anne (2011). Advanced Linear Cryptanalysis of Block and Stream Ciphers. IOS Press. p. 2. ISBN 9781607508441.

- Baigneres, Thomas & Finiasz, Matthieu (2007). "Dial 'C' for Cipher". In Biham, Eli & Yousseff, Amr. Selected areas in cryptography: 13th international workshop, SAC 2006, Montreal, Canada, August 17-18, 2006 : revised selected papers. Springer. p. 77. ISBN 9783540744610.

- Cusick, Thomas W. & Stanica, Pantelimon (2009). Cryptographic Boolean functions and applications. Academic Press. p. 164. ISBN 9780123748904.

- Martin, Keith M. (2012). Everyday Cryptography: Fundamental Principles and Applications. Oxford University Press. p. 114. ISBN 9780199695591.

- Paar, Cristof et al. (2010). Understanding Cryptography: A Textbook for Students and Practitioners. Springer. p. 30. ISBN 9783642041006.

- Menezes, Alfred J.; Oorschot, Paul C. van; Vanstone, Scott A. (2001). Handbook of Applied Cryptography (Fifth ed.). p. 251. ISBN 0849385237.

- Chakraborty, D. & Rodriguez-Henriquez F. (2008). "Block Cipher Modes of Operation from a Hardware Implementation Perspective". In Koç, Çetin K. Cryptographic Engineering. Springer. p. 321. ISBN 9780387718163.

7

Cryptographic Key: An Integrated Study

Key exchange, key size, key whitening and key agreement protocol are some of the topics illustrated in this chapter. It strategically encompasses and incorporates the major components and concepts of cryptography, contributing to the readers understanding on cryptography key.

Key (Cryptography)

In cryptography, a key is a piece of information (a parameter) that determines the functional output of a cryptographic algorithm. For encryption algorithms, a key specifies the transformation of plaintext into ciphertext, and vice versa for decryption algorithms. Keys also specify transformations in other cryptographic algorithms, such as digital signature schemes and message authentication codes.

Need for Secrecy

In designing security systems, it is wise to assume that the details of the cryptographic algorithm are already available to the attacker. This is known as Kerckhoffs' principle — "*only secrecy of the key provides security*", or, reformulated as Shannon's maxim, "*the enemy knows the system*". The history of cryptography provides evidence that it can be difficult to keep the details of a widely used algorithm secret. A key is often easier to protect (it's typically a small piece of information) than an encryption algorithm, and easier to change if compromised. Thus, the security of an encryption system in most cases relies on some key being kept secret.

Trying to keep keys secret is one of the most difficult problems in practical cryptography. An attacker who obtains the key (by, for example, theft, extortion, dumpster diving, assault, torture, or social engineering) can recover the original message from the encrypted data, and issue signatures.

Key Scope

Keys are generated to be used with a given *suite of algorithms*, called a cryptosystem. Encryption algorithms which use the same key for both encryption and decryption are known as symmetric key algorithms. A newer class of "public key" cryptographic algorithms was invented in the 1970s. These asymmetric key algorithms use a pair of keys —or *keypair*— a public key and a private one. Public keys are used for encryption or signature verification; private ones decrypt and sign. The design is such that finding out the private key is extremely difficult, even if the corresponding public key is known. As that design involves lengthy computations, a keypair is often used to exchange an on-the-fly symmetric key, which will only be used for the current session.

RSA and DSA are two popular public-key cryptosystems; DSA keys can only be used for signing and verifying, not for encryption.

Ownership and Revocation

Part of the security brought about by cryptography concerns confidence about who signed a given document, or who replies at the other side of a connection. Assuming that keys are not compromised, that question consists of determining the owner of the relevant public key. To be able to tell a key's owner, public keys are often enriched with attributes such as names, addresses, and similar identifiers. The packed collection of a public key and its attributes can be digitally signed by one or more supporters. In the PKI model, the resulting object is called a certificate and is signed by a certificate authority (CA). In the PGP model, it is still called a "key", and is signed by various people who personally verified that the attributes match the subject.

In both PKI and PGP models, compromised keys can be revoked. Revocation has the side effect of disrupting the relationship between a key's attributes and the subject, which may still be valid. In order to have a possibility to recover from such disruption, signers often use different keys for everyday tasks: Signing with an *intermediate certificate* (for PKI) or a *subkey* (for PGP) facilitates keeping the principal private key in an offline safe.

Key Sizes

For the one-time pad system the key must be at least as long as the message. In encryption systems that use a cipher algorithm, messages can be much longer than the key. The key must, however, be long enough so that an attacker cannot try all possible combinations.

A key length of 80 bits is generally considered the minimum for strong security with symmetric encryption algorithms. 128-bit keys are commonly used and considered very strong.

The keys used in public key cryptography have some mathematical structure. For example, public keys used in the RSA system are the product of two prime numbers. Thus public key systems require longer key lengths than symmetric systems for an equivalent level of security. 3072 bits is the suggested key length for systems based on factoring and integer discrete logarithms which aim to have security equivalent to a 128 bit symmetric cipher. Elliptic curve cryptography may allow smaller-size keys for equivalent security, but these algorithms have only been known for a relatively short time and current estimates of the difficulty of searching for their keys may not survive. As of 2004, a message encrypted using a 109-bit key elliptic curve algorithm had been broken by brute force. The current rule of thumb is to use an ECC key twice as long as the symmetric key security level desired. Except for the random one-time pad, the security of these systems has not been proven mathematically, so a theoretical breakthrough could make everything one has encrypted an open book. This is another reason to err on the side of choosing longer keys.

Key Choice

To prevent a key from being guessed, keys need to be generated truly randomly and contain sufficient entropy. The problem of how to safely generate truly random keys is difficult, and has been addressed in many ways by various cryptographic systems. There is a RFC on generating randomness (RFC 4086, *Randomness Requirements for Security*). Some operating systems include tools for "collecting" entropy from the timing of unpredictable operations such as disk drive head movements. For the production of small amounts of keying material, ordinary dice provide a good source of high quality randomness.

Key vs Password

For most computer security purposes and for most users, "key" is not synonymous with "password" (or "passphrase"), although a password can in fact be used as a key. The primary practical difference between keys and passwords is that the latter are intended to be generated, read, remembered, and reproduced by a human user (although nowadays the user may delegate those tasks to password management software). A key, by contrast, is intended for use by the software that is implementing the cryptographic algorithm, and so human readability etc. is not required. In fact, most users will, in most cases, be unaware of even the existence of the keys being used on their behalf by the security components of their everyday software applications.

If a password *is* used as an encryption key, then in a well-designed crypto system it would not be used as such on its own. This is because the very fact that passwords do tend to be human-readable means they may not be particularly secure. To compensate, a good crypto system will use the *password-acting-as-key* not to perform the primary encryption task itself, but rather to act as an input to a key derivation function. That KDF uses the password as a starting point from which it will then generate the actual secure encryption key itself, using various methods such as adding a salt and key stretching.

Key Exchange

Key exchange (also known as "key establishment") is any method in cryptography by which cryptographic keys are exchanged between two parties, allowing use of a cryptographic algorithm.

If sender and receiver wish to exchange encrypted messages, each must be equipped to encrypt messages to be sent and decrypt messages received. The nature of the equipping they require depends on the encryption technique they might use. If they use a code, both will require a copy of the same codebook. If they use a cipher, they will need appropriate keys. If the cipher is a symmetric key cipher, both will need a copy of the same key. If an asymmetric key cipher with the public/private key property, both will need the other's public key.

The Key Exchange Problem

The key exchange problem is how to exchange whatever keys or other information are needed so that no one else can obtain a copy. Historically, this required trusted couriers, diplomatic bags, or some other secure channel. With the advent of public key and private key cipher algorithms, the encrypting key (aka public key) could be made public, since (at least for high quality algorithms) no one without the decrypting key (aka, the private key) could decrypt the message.

Identification

In principle, the only remaining problem was to be sure (or at least confident) that a public key actually belonged to its supposed owner. Because it is possible to 'spoof' another's identity in any of several ways, this is not a trivial or easily solved problem, particularly when the two users involved have never met and know nothing about each other.

Diffie–hellman Key Exchange

In 1976, Whitfield Diffie and Martin Hellman published a cryptographic protocol called the Diffie–Hellman key exchange (D–H) based on concepts developed by Hellman's PhD student Ralph Merkle. The protocol enables users to securely exchange secret keys even if an opponent is monitoring that communication channel. The D–H key exchange protocol, however, does not by itself address authentication (i.e. the problem of being sure of the actual identity of the person or 'entity' at the other end of the communication channel). Authentication is crucial when an opponent can both monitor *and alter* messages within the communication channel (aka man-in-the-middle or MITM attacks) and was addressed in the fourth section of the paper.

Public Key Infrastructure

Public key infrastructures (PKIs) have been proposed as a way around this problem of identity authentication. In their most usual implementation, each user applies to a 'certificate authority' for a digital certificate which serves for other users as a non-tamperable authentication of identity, at the risk of compromising every user in case the CA itself is compromised.

Several countries and other jurisdictions have passed legislation or issued regulations encouraging PKIs by giving (more or less) legal effect to these digital certificates. Several commercial firms, and a few government departments, have established such certificate authorities. VeriSign is the most prominent commercial firm.

This does nothing to solve the problem though, as the trustworthiness of the CA itself is still not guaranteed from an individual's standpoint. It is a form of argument from authority fallacy. For actual trustworthiness, personal verification that the certificate belongs to the CA and establishment of trust in the CA are required. This is usually not possible.

For those new to such things, these arrangements are best thought of as electronic notary endorsements that "this public key belongs to this user". As with notary endorsements, there can be mistakes or misunderstandings in such vouchings. Additionally, the notary itself can be untrusted. There have been several high profile public failures by assorted certificate authorities.

Web of Trust

At the other end of the conceptual range is the web of trust system, which avoids central Certificate Authorities entirely. Each user is responsible for getting any certificate from another before using that certificate to communicate with, vet digital signatures from, ... the user claimed to be associated with the particular public key in a certificate. PGP (and GPG, an implementation of the OpenPGP Internet Standard) employ just such a web of trust mechanism. Together they are the most widely used high quality cryptographic system in the world.

Password-authenticated Key Agreement

Password-authenticated key agreement algorithms can perform a cryptographic key exchange utilizing knowledge of a user's password.

Quantum Key Exchange

The BB84 key exchange protocol—like any quantum key exchange protocol—exploits certain properties of quantum physics to ensure its security. Since quantum mechanics ensures physical traces as a result of mere observation, it provides protection against man-in-the-middle attacks that cannot, as a matter of physical principle, be circumvented.

Key Size

In cryptography, key size or key length is the number of bits in a key used by a cryptographic algorithm (such as a cipher).

Key length defines the upper-bound on an algorithm's security (i.e., a logarithmic measure of the fastest known attack against an algorithm, relative to the key length), since the security of all algorithms can be violated by brute force attacks. Ideally, key length would coincide with the lower-bound on an algorithm's security. Indeed, most symmetric-key algorithms are designed to have security equal to their key length. However, after design, a new attack might be discovered. For instance, Triple DES was designed to have a 168 bit key, but an attack of complexity 2^{112} is now known (i.e., Triple DES has 112 bits of security). Nevertheless, as long as the relation between key length and security is sufficient for a particular application, then it doesn't matter if key length and security coincide. This is important for asymmetric-key algorithms, because no such algorithm is known to satisfy this property; elliptic curve cryptography comes the closest with an effective security of roughly half its key length.

Significance

Keys are used to control the operation of a cipher so that only the correct key can convert encrypted text (ciphertext) to plaintext. Many ciphers are actually based on publicly known algorithms or are open source and so it is only the difficulty of obtaining the key that determines security of the system, provided that there is no analytic attack (i.e., a 'structural weakness' in the algorithms or protocols used), and assuming that the key is not otherwise available (such as via theft, extortion, or compromise of computer systems). The widely accepted notion that the security of the system should depend on the key alone has been explicitly formulated by Auguste Kerckhoffs (in the 1880s) and Claude Shannon (in the 1940s); the statements are known as Kerckhoffs' principle and Shannon's Maxim respectively.

A key should therefore be large enough that a brute force attack (possible against any encryption algorithm) is infeasible – i.e., would take too long to execute. Shannon's work on information theory showed that to achieve so called *perfect secrecy*, the key length must be at least as large as the message and only used once (this algorithm is called the One-time pad). In light of this, and the practical difficulty of managing such long keys, modern cryptographic practice has discarded the notion of perfect secrecy as a requirement for encryption, and instead focuses on *computational security*, under which the computational requirements of breaking an encrypted text must be infeasible for an attacker.

Key Size and Encryption System

Encryption systems are often grouped into families. Common families include symmetric systems (e.g. AES) and asymmetric systems (e.g. RSA); they may alternatively be grouped according to the central algorithm used (e.g. elliptic curve cryptography).

As each of these is of a different level of cryptographic complexity, it is usual to have different key sizes for the same level of security, depending upon the algorithm used. For example, the security available with a 1024-bit key using asymmetric RSA is considered approximately equal in security to an 80-bit key in a symmetric algorithm.

The actual degree of security achieved over time varies, as more computational power and more powerful mathematical analytic methods become available. For this reason cryptologists tend to look at indicators that an algorithm or key length shows signs of potential vulnerability, to move to longer key sizes or more difficult algorithms. A 1039 bit integer was factored with the special number field sieve using 400 computers over 11 months. The factored number was of a special form; the special number field sieve cannot be used on RSA keys. The computation is roughly equivalent to breaking a 700 bit RSA key. However, this might be an advance warning that 1024 bit RSA used in secure online commerce should be deprecated, since they may become breakable in the near future. Cryptography professor Arjen Lenstra observed that "Last time, it took nine years for us to generalize from a special to a nonspecial, hard-to-factor number" and when asked whether 1024-bit RSA keys are dead, said: "The answer to that question is an unqualified yes."

The 2015 Logjam attack revealed additional dangers in using Diffie-Helman key exchange when only one or a few common 1024-bit or smaller prime moduli are in use. This common practice allows large amounts of communications to be compromised at the expense of attacking a small number of primes.

Brute Force Attack

Even if a symmetric cipher is currently unbreakable by exploiting structural weaknesses in its algorithm, it is possible to run through the entire space of keys in what is known as a *brute force attack*. Since longer symmetric keys require exponentially more work to brute force search, a sufficiently long symmetric key makes this line of attack impractical.

With a key of length n bits, there are 2^n possible keys. This number grows very rapidly as n increases. The large number of operations (2^{128}) required to try all possible 128-bit keys is widely considered out of reach for conventional digital computing techniques for the foreseeable future. However, experts anticipate alternative computing technologies that may have processing power superior to current computer technology. If a suitably sized quantum computer capable of running Grover's algorithm reliably becomes available, it would reduce a 128-bit key down to 64-bit security, roughly a DES equivalent. This is one of the reasons why AES supports a 256-bit key length.

Symmetric Algorithm Key Lengths

US Government export policy has long restricted the 'strength' of cryptography that can be sent out of the country. For many years the limit was 40 bits. Today, a key length of 40 bits offers little protection against even a casual attacker with a single PC, a predictable and inevitable consequence of governmental restrictions limiting key length. In response, by the year 2000, most of the major US restrictions on the use of strong encryption were relaxed. However, not all regulations have been removed, and encryption registration with the U.S. Bureau of Industry and Security is still required to export "mass market encryption commodities, software and components with encryption exceeding 64 bits" (75 FR 36494).

IBM's Lucifer cipher was selected in 1974 as the base for what would become the Data Encryption Standard. Lucifer's key length was reduced from 128-bits to 56 bits, which the NSA and NIST argued was sufficient. The NSA has major computing resources and a large budget; some cryptographers including Whitfield Diffie and Martin Hellman complained that this made the cipher so weak that NSA computers would be able to break a DES key in a day through brute force parallel computing. The NSA disputed this, claiming brute forcing DES would take them something like 91 years. However, by the late 90s, it became clear that DES could be cracked in a few days' time-frame with custom-built hardware such as could be purchased by a large corporation or government. The book *Cracking DES* (O'Reilly and Associates) tells of the successful attempt in 1998 to break 56-bit DES by a brute force attack mounted by a cyber civil rights group with limited resources. Even before that demonstration, 56 bits was considered insufficient length for symmetric algorithm keys. In 2002, Distributed.net and its volunteers broke a 64-bit RC5 key after several years effort, using about seventy thousand (mostly home) computers.

The NSA's Skipjack algorithm used in its Fortezza program employs 80-bit keys.

DES has been replaced in many applications by Triple DES, which has 112 bits of security when used 168-bit keys (triple key)

The Advanced Encryption Standard published in 2001 uses a key sizes of 128 bits, 192 or 256 bits. Many observers consider 128 bits sufficient for the foreseeable future for symmetric algorithms of AES's quality until quantum computers become available. However, as of 2015, the U.S. National Security Agency has issued guidance that it plans to switch to quantum computing resistant algorithms and now requires 256-bit AES keys for data classified up to Top Secret.

In 2003, the U.S. National Institute for Standards and Technology, NIST proposed phasing out 80-bit keys by 2015. As of 2005, 80-bit keys were allowed only until 2010.

As of 2015, NIST guidance says that "the use of keys that provide less than 112 bits of security strength for key agreement is now disallowed." NIST approved symmetric encryption algorithms include three-key Triple DES, and AES. Approvals for two-key Triple DES and Skipjack have been withdrawn as of 2015.

Asymmetric Algorithm Key Lengths

The effectiveness of public key cryptosystems depends on the intractability (computational and theoretical) of certain mathematical problems such as integer factorization. These problems are time consuming to solve, but usually faster than trying all possible keys by brute force. Thus, asymmetric algorithm keys must be longer for equivalent resistance to attack than symmetric algorithm keys. As of 2002, an asymmetric key length of 1024 bits was generally considered by cryptology experts to be the minimum necessary for the RSA encryption algorithm.

As of 2003 RSA Security claims that 1024-bit RSA keys are equivalent in strength to 80-bit symmetric keys, 2048-bit RSA keys to 112-bit symmetric keys and 3072-bit RSA keys to 128-bit symmetric keys. RSA claims that 1024-bit keys are likely to become crackable some time between 2006 and 2010 and that 2048-bit keys are sufficient until 2030. An RSA key length of 3072 bits should be used if security is required beyond 2030. NIST key management guidelines further suggest that 15360-bit RSA keys are equivalent in strength to 256-bit symmetric keys.

The Finite Field Diffie-Hellman algorithm has roughly the same key strength as RSA for the same key sizes. The work factor for breaking Diffie-Hellman is based on the discrete logarithm problem, which is related to the integer factorization problem on which RSA's strength is based. Thus, a 3072-bit Diffie-Hellman key has about the same strength as a 3072-bit RSA key.

One of the asymmetric algorithm types, elliptic curve cryptography, or ECC, appears to be secure with shorter keys than other asymmetric key algorithms require. NIST guidelines state that ECC keys should be twice the length of equivalent strength symmetric key algorithms. So, for example, a 224-bit ECC key would have roughly the same strength as a 112-bit symmetric key. These estimates assume no major breakthroughs in solving the underlying mathematical problems that ECC is based on. A message encrypted with an elliptic key algorithm using a 109-bit long key has been broken by brute force.

The NSA previously specified that "Elliptic Curve Public Key Cryptography using the 256-bit prime modulus elliptic curve as specified in FIPS-186-2 and SHA-256 are appropriate for protecting classified information up to the SECRET level. Use of the 384-bit prime modulus elliptic curve and SHA-384 are necessary for the protection of TOP SECRET information." In 2015 the NSA announced that it plans to transition from Elliptic Curve Cryptography to new algorithms that are resistant to attack by future quantum computers. In the interim it recommends the larger 384-bit curve for all classified information.

Effect of Quantum Computing Attacks on Key Strength

The two best known quantum computing attacks are based on Shor's algorithm and Grover's algorithm. Of the two, Shor's offers the greater risk to current security systems.

Derivatives of Shor's algorithm are widely conjectured to be effective against all mainstream public-key algorithms including RSA, Diffie-Hellman and elliptic curve cryptography. According to Professor Gilles Brassard, an expert in quantum computing: "The time needed to factor an RSA integer is the same order as the time needed to use that same integer as modulus for a single RSA encryption. In other words, it takes no more time to break RSA on a quantum computer (up to a multiplicative constant) than to use it legitimately on a classical computer." The general consensus is that these public key algorithms are insecure at any key size if sufficiently large quantum computers capable of running Shor's algorithm become available. The implication of this attack is that all data encrypted using current standards based security systems such as the ubiquitous SSL used to protect e-commerce and Internet banking and SSH used to protect access to sensitive computing systems is at risk. Encrypted data protected using public-key algorithms can be archived and may be broken at a later time.

Mainstream symmetric ciphers (such as AES or Twofish) and collision resistant hash functions (such as SHA) are widely conjectured to offer greater security against known quantum computing attacks. They are widely thought most vulnerable to Grover's algorithm. Bennett, Bernstein, Brassard, and Vazirani proved in 1996 that a brute-force key search on a quantum computer cannot be faster than roughly $2^{n/2}$ invocations of the underlying cryptographic algorithm, compared with roughly 2^n in the classical case. Thus in the presence of large quantum computers an n-bit key can provide at least $n/2$ bits of security. Quantum brute force is easily defeated by doubling the key length, which has little extra computational cost in ordinary use. This implies that at least a 256-bit symmetric key is required to achieve 128-bit security rating against a quantum computer. As mentioned above, the NSA announced in 2015 that it plans to transition to quantum-resistant algorithms.

According to NSA "A sufficiently large quantum computer, if built, would be capable of undermining all widely-deployed public key algorithms used for key establishment and digital signatures. ... It is generally accepted that quantum computing techniques are much less effective against symmetric algorithms than against current widely used public key algorithms. While public key cryptography requires changes in the fundamental design to protect against a potential future quantum computer, symmetric key algorithms are believed to be secure provided a sufficiently large key size is used. ... In the longer term, NSA looks to NIST to identify a broadly accepted, standardized suite of commercial public key algorithms that are not vulnerable to quantum attacks.

As of 2016 NSA's The Commercial National Security Algorithm Suite includes:

Algorithm	Usage
RSA 3072-bit or larger	Key Establishment, Digital Signature
Diffie-Hellman (DH) 3072-bit or larger	Key Establishment
ECDH with NIST P-384	Key Establishment
ECDSA with NIST P-384	Digital Signature
SHA-384	Integrity
AES-256	Confidentiality

Key Whitening

In cryptography, key whitening is a technique intended to increase the security of an iterated block cipher. It consists of steps that combine the data with portions of the key.

The most common form of key whitening is xor-encrypt-xor -- using a simple XOR before the first round and after the last round of encryption.

The first block cipher to use a form of key whitening is DES-X, which simply uses two extra 64-bit keys for whitening, beyond the normal 56-bit key of DES. This is intended to increase the complexity of a brute force attack, increasing the effective size of the key without major changes in the algorithm. DES-X's inventor, Ron Rivest, named the technique *whitening*.

The cipher FEAL (followed by Khufu and Khafre) introduced the practice of key whitening using portions of the same key used in the rest of the cipher. Obviously this offers no additional protection from brute force attacks, but it can make other attacks more difficult. In a Feistel cipher or similar algorithm, key whitening can increase security by concealing the specific inputs to the first and last round functions. In particular, it is not susceptible to a meet-in-the-middle attack. This form of key whitening has been adopted as a feature of many later block ciphers, including AES, MARS, RC6, and Twofish.

Key-agreement Protocol

In cryptography, a key-agreement protocol is a protocol whereby two or more parties can agree on a key in such a way that both influence the outcome. If properly done, this precludes undesired third parties from forcing a key choice on the agreeing parties. Protocols that are useful in practice also do not reveal to any eavesdropping party what key has been agreed upon.

Many key exchange systems have one party generate the key, and simply send that key to the other party -- the other party has no influence on the key. Using a key-agreement protocol avoids some of the key distribution problems associated with such systems.

Protocols where both parties influence the final derived key are the only way to implement perfect forward secrecy.

Exponential Key Exchange

The first publicly known public-key agreement protocol that meets the above criteria was the Diffie–Hellman key exchange, in which two parties jointly exponentiate a generator with random numbers, in such a way that an eavesdropper cannot feasibly determine what the resultant value used to produce a shared key is.

Exponential key exchange in and of itself does not specify any prior agreement or subsequent authentication between the participants. It has thus been described as an anonymous key agreement protocol.

Authentication

Anonymous key exchange, like Diffie–Hellman, does not provide authentication of the parties, and is thus vulnerable to man-in-the-middle attacks.

A wide variety of cryptographic authentication schemes and protocols have been developed to provide authenticated key agreement to prevent man-in-the-middle and related attacks. These methods generally mathematically bind the agreed key to other agreed-upon data, such as the following:

- Public/private key pairs

- Shared secret keys

- Passwords

Public Keys

A widely used mechanism for defeating such attacks is the use of digitally signed keys that must be integrity-assured: if Bob's key is signed by a trusted third party vouching for his identity, Alice can have considerable confidence that a signed key she receives is not an attempt to intercept by Eve. When Alice and Bob have a public-key infrastructure, they may digitally sign an agreed Diffie-Hellman agreed key, or exchanged Diffie-Hellman public keys. Such signed keys, sometimes signed by a certificate authority, are one of the primary mechanisms used for secure web traffic (including HTTPS, SSL or Transport Layer Security protocols). Other specific examples are MQV, YAK and the ISAKMP component of the IPsec protocol suite for securing Internet Protocol communications. However, these systems require care in endorsing the match between identity information and public keys by certificate authorities in order to work properly.

Hybrid Systems

Hybrid systems use public-key cryptography to exchange secret keys, which are then used in a symmetric-key cryptography systems. Most practical applications of cryptography use a combination of cryptographic functions to implement an overall system that provides all of the four desirable features of secure communications (Confidentiality, Integrity, Authentication, and Non-repudiation).

Passwords

Password-authenticated key agreement protocols require the separate establishment of a password (which may be smaller than a key) in a manner that is both private and integrity-assured. These are designed to resist MITM and other active attacks on the password and the established keys. For example, DH-EKE, SPEKE, and SRP are password-authenticated variations of Diffie-Hellman.

Other Tricks

If one has an integrity-assured way to verify a shared key over a public channel, one may engage in a Diffie–Hellman key exchange to derive a short-term shared key, and then subsequently authenticate that the keys match. One way is to use a voice-authenticated read-out of the key, as in PGPfone. Voice authentication, however, presumes that it is infeasible for a MITM to spoof one participant's voice to the other in real-time, which may be an undesirable assumption. Such protocols may be designed to work with even a small public value, such as a password. Variations on this theme have been proposed for Bluetooth pairing protocols.

In an attempt to avoid using any additional out-of-band authentication factors, Davies and Price proposed the use of the Interlock Protocol of Ron Rivest and Adi Shamir, which has been subject to both attack and subsequent refinement.

Shared Secret Keys

Secret-key (symmetric) cryptography requires the initial exchange of a shared key in a manner that is private and integrity-assured. When done right, MITM attack is prevented. However, without the use of public-key cryptography, one may be left with undesirable key-management problems.

References

- Menezes, Alfred; van Oorschot, Paul; Vanstone, Scott (1997). Handbook of Applied Cryptography Boca Raton, Florida: CRC Press. ISBN 0-8493-8523-7.

- Singh, Simon (1999) The Code Book: the evolution of secrecy from Mary Queen of Scots to quantum cryptography New York: Doubleday ISBN 0-385-49531-5

- Matthew Copeland; Joergen Grahn; David A. Wheeler (1999). Mike Ashley, ed. "The GNU Privacy Handbook". GnuPG. Retrieved 14 December 2013.

- Blaze, Matt; Diffie, Whitefield; Rivest, Ronald L.; Schneier, Bruce; Shimomura, Tsutomu; Thompson, Eric; Wiener, Michael (January 1996). "Minimal key lengths for symmetric ciphers to provide adequate commercial security". Fortify. Retrieved 14 October 2011.

8

Modern Applications of Cryptography

A word or string of characters used for security or to prove identity, which is to be kept a secret to secure confidential and sensitive information is called a password. This chapter elaborates on the applications of cryptography in today's times. Password- authenticated key agreement, trusted time stamping and digital signature are explained in detail for the reader's understanding.

Password

A password is a word or string of characters used for user authentication to prove identity or access approval to gain access to a resource (example: an access code is a type of password), which is to be kept secret from those not allowed access.

The use of passwords is known to be ancient. Sentries would challenge those wishing to enter an area or approaching it to supply a password or *watchword*, and would only allow a person or group to pass if they knew the password. In modern times, user names and passwords are commonly used by people during a log in process that controls access to protected computer operating systems, mobile phones, cable TV decoders, automated teller machines (ATMs), etc. A typical computer user has passwords for many purposes: logging into accounts, retrieving e-mail, accessing applications, databases, networks, web sites, and even reading the morning newspaper online.

Despite the name, there is no need for passwords to be actual words; indeed passwords which are not actual words may be harder to guess, a desirable property. Some passwords are formed from multiple words and may more accurately be called a passphrase. The terms passcode and passkey are sometimes used when the secret information is purely numeric, such as the personal identification number (PIN) commonly used for ATM access. Passwords are generally short enough to be easily memorized and typed.

Most organizations specify a password policy that sets requirements for the composition and usage of passwords, typically dictating minimum length, required categories (e.g. upper and lower case, numbers, and special characters), prohibited elements (e.g. own name, date of birth, address, telephone number). Some governments have national authentication frameworks that define requirements for user authentication to government services, including requirements for passwords.

Choosing a Secure and Memorable Password

The easier a password is for the owner to remember generally means it will be easier for an attacker to guess. However, passwords which are difficult to remember may also reduce the security of a system because (a) users might need to write down or electronically store the password, (b) users will need frequent password resets and (c) users are more likely to re-use the same password. Similarly, the more stringent requirements for password strength, e.g. "have a mix of uppercase and lowercase letters and digits" or "change it monthly", the greater the degree to which users will subvert the system. Others argue longer passwords provide more security (e.g., entropy) than shorter passwords with a wide variety of characters.

In *The Memorability and Security of Passwords*, Jeff Yan et al. examine the effect of advice given to users about a good choice of password. They found that passwords based on thinking of a phrase and taking the first letter of each word are just as memorable as naively selected passwords, and just as hard to crack as randomly generated passwords.

Combining two or more unrelated words is another good method, but a single dictionary word is not. Having a personally designed algorithm for generating obscure passwords is another good method

However, asking users to remember a password consisting of a "mix of uppercase and lowercase characters" is similar to asking them to remember a sequence of bits: hard to remember, and only a little bit harder to crack (e.g. only 128 times harder to crack for 7-letter passwords, less if the user simply capitalises one of the letters). Asking users to use "both letters and digits" will often lead to easy-to-guess substitutions such as 'E' → '3' and 'I' → '1', substitutions which are well known to attackers. Similarly typing the password one keyboard row higher is a common trick known to attackers.

In 2013, Google released a list of the most common password types, all of which are considered insecure because they are too easy to guess (especially after researching an individual on social media):

- The name of a pet, child, family member, or significant other
- Anniversary dates and birthdays
- Birthplace
- Name of a favorite holiday
- Something related to a favorite sports team
- The word "password"

Factors in the Security of a Password System

The security of a password-protected system depends on several factors. The overall system must, of course, be designed for sound security, with protection against computer viruses, man-in-the-middle attacks and the like. Physical security issues are also a concern, from deterring shoulder surfing to more sophisticated physical threats such as video cameras and keyboard sniffers. And, of course, passwords should be chosen so that they are hard for an attacker to guess and hard for an attacker to discover using any (and all) of the available automatic attack schemes.

Nowadays, it is a common practice for computer systems to hide passwords as they are typed. The purpose of this measure is to avoid bystanders reading the password. However, some argue that this practice may lead to mistakes and stress, encouraging users to choose weak passwords. As an alternative, users should have the option to show or hide passwords as they type them.

Effective access control provisions may force extreme measures on criminals seeking to acquire a password or biometric token. Less extreme measures include extortion, rubber hose cryptanalysis, and side channel attack.

Here are some specific password management issues that must be considered in thinking about, choosing, and handling, a password.

Rate at which an Attacker can Try Guessed Passwords

The rate at which an attacker can submit guessed passwords to the system is a key factor in determining system security. Some systems impose a time-out of several seconds after a small number (e.g., three) of failed password entry attempts. In the absence of other vulnerabilities, such systems can be effectively secure with relatively simple passwords, if they have been well chosen and are not easily guessed.

Many systems store a cryptographic hash of the password. If an attacker gets access to the file of hashed passwords guessing can be done off-line, rapidly testing candidate passwords against the true password's hash value. In the example of a web-server, an online attacker can guess only at the rate at which the server will respond, while an off-line attacker (who gains access to the file) can guess at a rate limited only by the hardware that is brought to bear.

Passwords that are used to generate cryptographic keys (e.g., for disk encryption or Wi-Fi security) can also be subjected to high rate guessing. Lists of common passwords are widely available and can make password attacks very efficient. Security in such situations depends on using passwords or passphrases of adequate complexity, making such an attack computationally infeasible for the attacker. Some systems, such as PGP and Wi-Fi WPA, apply a computation-intensive hash to the password to slow such attacks.

Limits on the Number of Password Guesses

An alternative to limiting the rate at which an attacker can make guesses on a password is to limit the total number of guesses that can be made. The password can be disabled, requiring a reset, after a small number of consecutive bad guesses (say 5); and the user may be required to change the password after a larger cumulative number of bad guesses (say 30), to prevent an attacker from making an arbitrarily large number of bad guesses by interspersing them between good guesses made by the legitimate password owner.

Form of Stored Passwords

Some computer systems store user passwords as plaintext, against which to compare user log on attempts. If an attacker gains access to such an internal password store, all passwords—and so all user accounts—will be compromised. If some users employ the same password for accounts on different systems, those will be compromised as well.

More secure systems store each password in a cryptographically protected form, so access to the actual password will still be difficult for a snooper who gains internal access to the system, while validation of user access attempts remains possible. The most secure don't store passwords at all, but a one-way derivation, such as a polynomial, modulus, or an advanced hash function. Roger Needham invented the now common approach of storing only a "hashed" form of the plaintext password.

When a user types in a password on such a system, the password handling software runs through a cryptographic hash algorithm, and if the hash value generated from the user's entry matches the hash stored in the password database, the user is permitted access. The hash value is created by applying a cryptographic hash function to a string consisting of the submitted password and, in many implementations, another value known as a salt. A salt prevents attackers from easily building a list of hash values for common passwords and prevents password cracking efforts from scaling across all users. MD5 and SHA1 are frequently used cryptographic hash functions but they are not recommended for password hashing unless they are used as part of a larger construction such as in PBKDF2.

The stored data—sometimes called the "password verifier" or the "password hash"—is often stored in Modular Crypt Format or RFC 2307 hash format, sometimes in the /etc/passwd file or the /etc/shadow file.

The main storage methods for passwords are plain text, hashed, hashed and salted, and reversibly encrypted. If an attacker gains access to the password file, then if it is stored as plain text, no cracking is necessary. If it is hashed but not salted then it is vulnerable to rainbow table attacks (which are more efficient than cracking). If it is reversibly encrypted then if the attacker gets the decryption key along with the file no cracking is necessary, while if he fails to get the key cracking is not possible. Thus, of the common storage formats for passwords only when passwords have been salted and hashed is cracking both necessary and possible.

If a cryptographic hash function is well designed, it is computationally infeasible to reverse the function to recover a plaintext password. An attacker can, however, use widely available tools to attempt to guess the passwords. These tools work by hashing possible passwords and comparing the result of each guess to the actual password hashes. If the attacker finds a match, they know that their guess is the actual password for the associated user. Password cracking tools can operate by brute force (i.e. trying every possible combination of characters) or by hashing every word from a list; large lists of possible passwords in many languages are widely available on the Internet. The existence of password cracking tools allows attackers to easily recover poorly chosen passwords. In particular, attackers can quickly recover passwords that are short, dictionary words, simple variations on dictionary words or that use easily guessable patterns. A modified version of the DES algorithm was used as the basis for the password hashing algorithm in early Unix systems. The crypt algorithm used a 12-bit salt value so that each user's hash was unique and iterated the DES algorithm 25 times in order to make the hash function slower, both measures intended to frustrate automated guessing attacks. The user's password was used as a key to encrypt a fixed value. More recent Unix or Unix like systems (e.g., Linux or the various BSD systems) use more secure password hashing algorithms such as PBKDF2, bcrypt, and scrypt which have large salts and an adjustable cost or number of iterations. A poorly designed hash function can make attacks feasible even if a strong password is chosen.

Methods of Verifying a Password Over a Network

Simple Transmission of the Password

Passwords are vulnerable to interception (i.e., "snooping") while being transmitted to the authenticating machine or person. If the password is carried as electrical signals on unsecured physical wiring between the user access point and the central system controlling the password database, it is subject to snooping by wiretapping methods. If it is carried as packeted data over the Internet, anyone able to watch the packets containing the logon information can snoop with a very low probability of detection.

Email is sometimes used to distribute passwords but this is generally an insecure method. Since most email is sent as plaintext, a message containing a password is readable without effort during transport by any eavesdropper. Further, the message will be stored as plaintext on at least two computers: the sender's and the recipient's. If it passes through intermediate systems during its travels, it will probably be stored on there as well, at least for some time, and may be copied to backup, cache or history files on any of these systems.

Using client-side encryption will only protect transmission from the mail handling system server to the client machine. Previous or subsequent relays of the email will not be protected and the email will probably be stored on multiple computers, certainly on the originating and receiving computers, most often in clear text.

Transmission Through Encrypted Channels

The risk of interception of passwords sent over the Internet can be reduced by, among other approaches, using cryptographic protection. The most widely used is the Transport Layer Security (TLS, previously called SSL) feature built into most current Internet browsers. Most browsers alert the user of a TLS/SSL protected exchange with a server by displaying a closed lock icon, or some other sign, when TLS is in use.

Hash-based Challenge-response Methods

Unfortunately, there is a conflict between stored hashed-passwords and hash-based challenge-response authentication; the latter requires a client to prove to a server that they know what the shared secret (i.e., password) is, and to do this, the server must be able to obtain the shared secret from its stored form. On many systems (including Unix-type systems) doing remote authentication, the shared secret usually becomes the hashed form and has the serious limitation of exposing passwords to offline guessing attacks. In addition, when the hash is used as a shared secret, an attacker does not need the original password to authenticate remotely; they only need the hash.

Zero-knowledge Password Proofs

Rather than transmitting a password, or transmitting the hash of the password, password-authenticated key agreement systems can perform a zero-knowledge password proof, which proves knowledge of the password without exposing it.

Moving a step further, augmented systems for password-authenticated key agreement (e.g., AMP, B-SPEKE, PAK-Z, SRP-6) avoid both the conflict and limitation of hash-based methods. An augmented system allows a client to prove knowledge of the password to a server, where the server knows only a (not exactly) hashed password, and where the unhashed password is required to gain access.

Procedures for Changing Passwords

Usually, a system must provide a way to change a password, either because a user believes the current password has been (or might have been) compromised, or as a precautionary measure. If a new password is passed to the system in unencrypted form, security can be lost (e.g., via wire-tapping) before the new password can even be installed in the password database. And, of course, if the new password is given to a compromised employee, little is gained. Some web sites include the user-selected password in an unencrypted confirmation e-mail message, with the obvious increased vulnerability.

Identity management systems are increasingly used to automate issuance of replacements for lost passwords, a feature called self service password reset. The user's identity is verified by asking questions and comparing the answers to ones previously stored (i.e., when the account was opened).

Some password reset questions ask for personal information that could be found on social media, such as mother's maiden name. As a result, some security experts recommend either making up one's own questions or giving false answers.

Password Longevity

"Password aging" is a feature of some operating systems which forces users to change passwords frequently (e.g., quarterly, monthly or even more often). Such policies usually provoke user protest and foot-dragging at best and hostility at worst. There is often an increase in the people who note down the password and leave it where it can easily be found, as well as helpdesk calls to reset a forgotten password. Users may use simpler passwords or develop variation patterns on a consistent theme to keep their passwords memorable. Because of these issues, there is some debate as to whether password aging is effective. Changing a password will not prevent abuse in most cases, since the abuse would often be immediately noticeable. However, if someone may have had access to the password through some means, such as sharing a computer or breaching a different site, changing the password limits the window for abuse.

Number of users Per Password

Allotting separate passwords to each user of a system is preferable to having a single password shared by legitimate users of the system, certainly from a security viewpoint. This is partly because users are more willing to tell another person (who may not be authorized) a shared password than one exclusively for their use. Single passwords are also much less convenient to change because many people need to be told at the same time, and they make removal of a particular user's access more difficult, as for instance on graduation or resignation.

Password Security Architecture

Common techniques used to improve the security of computer systems protected by a password include:

- Not displaying the password on the display screen as it is being entered or obscuring it as it is typed by using asterisks (*) or bullets (•).

- Allowing passwords of adequate length. (Some legacy operating systems, including early versions of Unix and Windows, limited passwords to an 8 character maximum, reducing security.)

- Requiring users to re-enter their password after a period of inactivity (a semi log-off policy).

- Enforcing a password policy to increase password strength and security.

    o Requiring periodic password changes.

    o Assigning randomly chosen passwords.

    o Requiring minimum password lengths.

    o Some systems require characters from various character classes in a password—for example, "must have at least one uppercase and at least one lowercase letter". However, all-lowercase passwords are more secure per keystroke than mixed capitalization passwords.

    o Employ a password blacklist to block the use of weak, easily guessed passwords

    o Providing an alternative to keyboard entry (e.g., spoken passwords, or biometric passwords).

    o Requiring more than one authentication system, such as 2-factor authentication (something a user has and something the user knows).

- Using encrypted tunnels or password-authenticated key agreement to prevent access to transmitted passwords via network attacks

- Limiting the number of allowed failures within a given time period (to prevent repeated password guessing). After the limit is reached, further attempts will fail (including correct password attempts) until the beginning of the next time period. However, this is vulnerable to a form of denial of service attack.

- Introducing a delay between password submission attempts to slow down automated password guessing programs.

Some of the more stringent policy enforcement measures can pose a risk of alienating users, possibly decreasing security as a result.

Password Reuse

It is common practice amongst computer users to reuse the same password on multiple sites. This presents a substantial security risk, since an attacker need only compromise a single site in order to gain access to other sites the victim uses. This problem is exacerbated by also reusing usernames, and by websites requiring email logins, as it makes it easier for an attacker to track a single user across multiple sites. Password reuse can be avoided or minimused by using mnemonic techniques, writing passwords down on paper, or using a password manager.

It has been argued by Redmond researchers Dinei Florencio and Cormac Herley, together with Paul C. van Oorschot of Carleton University, Canada, that password reuse is inevitable, and that users should reuse passwords for low-security websites (which contain little personal data and no financial information, for example) and instead focus their efforts on remember long, complex passwords for a few important accounts, such as bank accounts. Similar arguments were made by Forbes in not change passwords as often as many "experts" advise, due to the same limitations in human memory.

Writing Down Passwords on Paper

Historically, many security experts asked people to memorize their passwords: "Never write down a password". More recently, many security experts such as Bruce Schneier recommend that people use passwords that are too complicated to memorize, write them down on paper, and keep them in a wallet.

Password manager software can also store passwords relatively safely, in an encrypted file sealed with a single master password.

After Death

According to a survey by the University of London, one in ten people are now leaving their passwords in their wills to pass on this important information when they die. One third of people, according to the poll, agree that their password protected data is important enough to pass on in their will.

Two-factor Authentication

Two factor authentication makes passwords more secure. For example, two-factor authentication will send you a text message, e-mail, or alert via a third-party app whenever a login attempt is made.

Password Cracking

Attempting to crack passwords by trying as many possibilities as time and money permit is a brute force attack. A related method, rather more efficient in most cases, is a dictionary attack. In a dictionary attack, all words in one or more dictionaries are tested. Lists of common passwords are also typically tested.

Password strength is the likelihood that a password cannot be guessed or discovered, and varies with the attack algorithm used. Cryptologists and computer scientists often refer to the strength or 'hardness' in terms of entropy.

Passwords easily discovered are termed *weak* or *vulnerable*; passwords very difficult or impossible to discover are considered *strong*. There are several programs available for password attack (or even auditing and recovery by systems personnel) such as LophtCrack, John the Ripper, and Cain; some of which use password design vulnerabilities (as found in the Microsoft LANManager system) to increase efficiency. These programs are sometimes used by system administrators to detect weak passwords proposed by users.

Studies of production computer systems have consistently shown that a large fraction of all user-chosen passwords are readily guessed automatically. For example, Columbia University found

22% of user passwords could be recovered with little effort. According to Bruce Schneier, examining data from a 2006 phishing attack, 55% of MySpace passwords would be crackable in 8 hours using a commercially available Password Recovery Toolkit capable of testing 200,000 passwords per second in 2006. He also reported that the single most common password was *password1*, confirming yet again the general lack of informed care in choosing passwords among users. (He nevertheless maintained, based on these data, that the general quality of passwords has improved over the years—for example, average length was up to eight characters from under seven in previous surveys, and less than 4% were dictionary words.)

Incidents

- On July 16, 1998, CERT reported an incident where an attacker had found 186,126 encrypted passwords. At the time the attacker was discovered, 47,642 passwords had already been cracked.

- In September, 2001, after the deaths of 960 New York employees in the September 11 attacks, financial services firm Cantor Fitzgerald through Microsoft broke the passwords of deceased employees to gain access to files needed for servicing client accounts. Technicians used brute-force attacks, and interviewers contacted families to gather personalized information that might reduce the search time for weaker passwords.

- In December 2009, a major password breach of the Rockyou.com website occurred that led to the release of 32 million passwords. The hacker then leaked the full list of the 32 million passwords (with no other identifiable information) to the Internet. Passwords were stored in cleartext in the database and were extracted through a SQL injection vulnerability. The Imperva Application Defense Center (ADC) did an analysis on the strength of the passwords.

- In June, 2011, NATO (North Atlantic Treaty Organization) experienced a security breach that led to the public release of first and last names, usernames, and passwords for more than 11,000 registered users of their e-bookshop. The data was leaked as part of Operation AntiSec, a movement that includes Anonymous, LulzSec, as well as other hacking groups and individuals. The aim of AntiSec is to expose personal, sensitive, and restricted information to the world, using any means necessary.

- On July 11, 2011, Booz Allen Hamilton, a consulting firm that does work for the Pentagon, had their servers hacked by Anonymous and leaked the same day. "The leak, dubbed 'Military Meltdown Monday,' includes 90,000 logins of military personnel—including personnel from USCENTCOM, SOCOM, the Marine corps, various Air Force facilities, Homeland Security, State Department staff, and what looks like private sector contractors." These leaked passwords wound up being hashed in SHA1, and were later decrypted and analyzed by the ADC team at Imperva, revealing that even military personnel look for shortcuts and ways around the password requirements.

Alternatives to Passwords for Authentication

The numerous ways in which permanent or semi-permanent passwords can be compromised has prompted the development of other techniques. Unfortunately, some are inadequate in practice, and in any case few have become universally available for users seeking a more secure alternative. A 2012 paper examines why passwords have proved so hard to supplant (despite numerous predictions that they would soon be a thing of the past); in examining thirty representative proposed replacements with respect to security, usability and deployability they conclude "none even retains the full set of benefits that legacy passwords already provide."

- Single-use passwords. Having passwords which are only valid once makes many potential attacks ineffective. Most users find single use passwords extremely inconvenient. They have, however, been widely implemented in personal online banking, where they are known as Transaction Authentication Numbers (TANs). As most home users only perform a small number of transactions each week, the single use issue has not led to intolerable customer dissatisfaction in this case.

- Time-synchronized one-time passwords are similar in some ways to single-use passwords, but the value to be entered is displayed on a small (generally pocketable) item and changes every minute or so.

- PassWindow one-time passwords are used as single-use passwords, but the dynamic characters to be entered are visible only when a user superimposes a unique printed visual key over a server generated challenge image shown on the user's screen.

- Access controls based on public key cryptography e.g. ssh. The necessary keys are usually too large to memorize and must be stored on a local computer, security token or portable memory device, such as a USB flash drive or even floppy disk.

- Biometric methods promise authentication based on unalterable personal characteristics, but currently (2008) have high error rates and require additional hardware to scan, for example, fingerprints, irises, etc. They have proven easy to spoof in some famous incidents testing commercially available systems, for example, the gummie fingerprint spoof demonstration, and, because these characteristics are unalterable, they cannot be changed if compromised; this is a highly important consideration in access control as a compromised access token is necessarily insecure.

- Single sign-on technology is claimed to eliminate the need for having multiple passwords. Such schemes do not relieve user and administrators from choosing reasonable single passwords, nor system designers or administrators from ensuring that private access control information passed among systems enabling single sign-on is secure against attack. As yet, no satisfactory standard has been developed.

- Envaulting technology is a password-free way to secure data on e.g. removable storage devices such as USB flash drives. Instead of user passwords, access control is based on the user's access to a network resource.

- Non-text-based passwords, such as graphical passwords or mouse-movement based passwords. Graphical passwords are an alternative means of authentication for log-in intended to be used in place of conventional password; they use images, graphics or colours instead of letters, digits or special characters. One system requires users to select a series of faces as a password, utilizing the human brain's ability to recall faces easily. In some implementations the user is required to pick from a series of images in the correct sequence in order to gain access. Another graphical password solution creates a one-time password using a randomly generated grid of images. Each time the user is required to authenticate, they look for the images that fit their pre-chosen categories and enter the randomly generated alphanumeric character that appears in the image to form the one-time password. So far, graphical passwords are promising, but are not widely used. Studies on this subject have been made to determine its usability in the real world. While some believe that graphical passwords would be harder to crack, others suggest that people will be just as likely to pick common images or sequences as they are to pick common passwords.

- 2D Key (2-Dimensional Key) is a 2D matrix-like key input method having the key styles of multiline passphrase, crossword, ASCII/Unicode art, with optional textual semantic noises, to create big password/key beyond 128 bits to realize the MePKC (Memorizable Public-Key Cryptography) using fully memorizable private key upon the current private key management technologies like encrypted private key, split private key, and roaming private key.

- Cognitive passwords use question and answer cue/response pairs to verify identity.

"The Password is Dead"

That "the password is dead" is a recurring idea in computer security. It often accompanies arguments that the replacement of passwords by a more secure means of authentication is both necessary and imminent. This claim has been made by numerous people at least since 2004. Notably, Bill Gates, speaking at the 2004 RSA Conference predicted the demise of passwords saying "they just don't meet the challenge for anything you really want to secure." In 2011 IBM predicted that, within five years, "You will never need a password again." Matt Honan, a journalist at Wired, who was the victim of a hacking incident, in 2012 wrote "The age of the password has come to an end." Heather Adkins, manager of Information Security at Google, in 2013 said that "passwords are done at Google." Eric Grosse, VP of security engineering at Google, states that "passwords and simple bearer tokens, such as cookies, are no longer sufficient to keep users safe." Christopher Mims, writing in the Wall Street Journal said the password "is finally dying" and predicted their replacement by device-based authentication. Avivah Litan of Gartner said in 2014 "Passwords were dead a few years ago. Now they are more than dead." The reasons given often include reference to the Usability as well as security problems of passwords.

The claim that "the password is dead" is often used by advocates of alternatives to passwords, such as Biometrics, Two-factor authentication or Single sign-on. Many initiatives have been launched with the explicit goal of eliminating passwords. These include Microsoft's Cardspace, the Higgins project, the Liberty Alliance, NSTIC, the FIDO Alliance and various Identity 2.0 proposals. Jeremy Grant, head of NSTIC initiative (the US Dept. of Commerce National Strategy for Trusted Identities in Cyberspace), declared "Passwords are a disaster from a security perspective, we want to shoot them dead." The FIDO Alliance promises a "passwordless experience" in its 2015 specification document.

In spite of these predictions and efforts to replace them passwords still appear as the dominant form of authentication on the web. In "The Persistence of Passwords," Cormac Herley and Paul van

Oorschot suggest that every effort should be made to end the "spectacularly incorrect assumption" that passwords are dead. They argue that "no other single technology matches their combination of cost, immediacy and convenience" and that "passwords are themselves the best fit for many of the scenarios in which they are currently used."

Website Password Systems

Passwords are used on websites to authenticate users and are usually maintained on the Web server, meaning the browser on a remote system sends a password to the server (by HTTP POST), the server checks the password and sends back the relevant content (or an access denied message). This process eliminates the possibility of local reverse engineering as the code used to authenticate the password does not reside on the local machine.

Transmission of the password, via the browser, in plaintext means it can be intercepted along its journey to the server. Many web authentication systems use SSL to establish an encrypted session between the browser and the server, and is usually the underlying meaning of claims to have a "secure Web site". This is done automatically by the browser and increases integrity of the session, assuming neither end has been compromised and that the SSL/TLS implementations used are high quality ones.

History of Passwords

Passwords or *watchwords* have been used since ancient times. Polybius describes the system for the distribution of watchwords in the Roman military as follows:

> The way in which they secure the passing round of the watchword for the night is as follows: from the tenth maniple of each class of infantry and cavalry, the maniple which is encamped at the lower end of the street, a man is chosen who is relieved from guard duty, and he attends every day at sunset at the tent of the tribune, and receiving from him the watchword — that is a wooden tablet with the word inscribed on it – takes his leave, and on returning to his quarters passes on the watchword and tablet before witnesses to the commander of the next maniple, who in turn passes it to the one next him. All do the same until it reaches the first maniples, those encamped near the tents of the tribunes. These latter are obliged to deliver the tablet to the tribunes before dark. So that if all those issued are returned, the tribune knows that the watchword has been given to all the maniples, and has passed through all on its way back to him. If any one of them is missing, he makes inquiry at once, as he knows by the marks from what quarter the tablet has not returned, and whoever is responsible for the stoppage meets with the punishment he merits.

Passwords in military use evolved to include not just a password, but a password and a counter-password; for example in the opening days of the Battle of Normandy, paratroopers of the U.S. 101st Airborne Division used a password — *flash* — which was presented as a challenge, and answered with the correct response — *thunder*. The challenge and response were changed every three days. American paratroopers also famously used a device known as a "cricket" on D-Day in place of a password system as a temporarily unique method of identification; one metallic click given by the device in lieu of a password was to be met by two clicks in reply.

Passwords have been used with computers since the earliest days of computing. MIT's CTSS, one of the first time sharing systems, was introduced in 1961. It had a LOGIN command that requested a user password. "After typing PASSWORD, the system turns off the printing mechanism, if possible, so that the user may type in his password with privacy." In the early 1970s, Robert Morris developed a system of storing login passwords in a hashed form as part of the Unix operating system. The system was based on a simulated Hagelin rotor crypto machine, and first appeared in 6th Edition Unix in 1974. A later version of his algorithm, known as crypt(3), used a 12-bit salt and invoked a modified form of the DES algorithm 25 times to reduce the risk of pre-computed dictionary attacks.

Password-authenticated Key Agreement

In cryptography, a password-authenticated key agreement method is an interactive method for two or more parties to establish cryptographic keys based on one or more party's knowledge of a password.

An important property is that an eavesdropper or man in the middle cannot obtain enough information to be able to brute force guess a password without further interactions with the parties for each (few) guesses. This means that strong security can be obtained using weak passwords.

Types

Password-authenticated key agreement generally encompasses methods such as:

- Balanced password-authenticated key exchange
- Augmented password-authenticated key exchange
- Password-authenticated key retrieval
- Multi-server methods
- Multi-party methods

In the most stringent password-only security models, there is no requirement for the user of the method to remember any secret or public data other than the password.

Password authenticated key exchange (PAKE) is where two or more parties, based only on their knowledge of a password, establish a cryptographic key using an exchange of messages, such that an unauthorized party (one who controls the communication channel but does not possess the password) cannot participate in the method and is constrained as much as possible from brute force guessing the password. (The optimal case yields exactly one guess per run exchange.) Two forms of PAKE are Balanced and Augmented methods.

Balanced PAKE allows parties that use the same password to negotiate and authenticate a shared key. Examples of these are:

- Encrypted Key Exchange (EKE)

- PAK and PPK

- SPEKE (Simple password exponential key exchange)

- Elliptic Curve based Secure Remote Password protocol (EC-SRP or SRP5) There is a free Java card implementation.

- Dragonfly—IEEE Std 802.11-2012, RFC 5931, RFC 6617

- SPAKE1 and SPAKE2

- J-PAKE (Password Authenticated Key Exchange by Juggling) -- A variant that is probably not encumbered by patents.

- ITU-T Recommendation X.1035

Augmented PAKE is a variation applicable to client/server scenarios, in which the server does not store password-equivalent data. This means that an attacker that stole the server data still cannot masquerade as the client unless they first perform a brute force search for the password. Examples include:

- AMP

- Augmented-EKE

- B-SPEKE

- PAK-Z

- SRP (Secure Remote Password protocol) -- designed to be not encumbered by patents.

- AugPAKE (RFC 6628)

Password-authenticated key retrieval is a process in which a client obtains a static key in a password-based negotiation with a server that knows data associated with the password, such as the Ford and Kaliski methods. In the most stringent setting, one party uses only a password in conjunction with N (two or more) servers to retrieve a static key. This is completed in a way that protects the password (and key) even if N-1 of the servers are completely compromised.

Brief History

The first successful password-authenticated key agreement methods were Encrypted Key Exchange methods described by Steven M. Bellovin and Michael Merritt in 1992. Although several of the first methods were flawed, the surviving and enhanced forms of EKE effectively amplify a shared password into a shared key, which can then be used for encryption and/or message authentication. The first provably-secure PAKE protocols were given in work by M. Bellare, D. Pointcheval, and P. Rogaway (Eurocrypt 2000) and V. Boyko, P. MacKenzie, and S. Patel (Eurocrypt 2000). These protocols were proven secure in the so-called random oracle model (or even stronger variants), and the first protocols proven secure under standard assumptions were those of O. Goldreich and Y. Lindell (Crypto 2001)which serves as a plausibility proof but is not efficient, and J. Katz, R. Ostrovsky, and M. Yung (Eurocrypt 2001) which is practical.

The first password-authenticated key retrieval methods were described by Ford and Kaliski in 2000.

A considerable number of alternative, secure PAKE protocols were given in work by M. Bellare, D. Pointcheval, and P. Rogaway,variations, and security proofs have been proposed in this growing class of password-authenticated key agreement methods. Current standards for these methods include IETF RFC 2945, RFC 5054, RFC 5931, RFC 5998, RFC 6124, RFC 6617, RFC 6628 and RFC 6631, IEEE Std 1363.2-2008, ITU-T X.1035 and ISO-IEC 11770-4:2006.

Trusted Timestamping

Trusted timestamping is the process of securely keeping track of the creation and modification time of a document. Security here means that no one – not even the owner of the document – should be able to change it once it has been recorded provided that the timestamper's integrity is never compromised.

The administrative aspect involves setting up a publicly available, trusted timestamp management infrastructure to collect, process and renew timestamps.

History

The idea of timestamping information is actually centuries old. For example, when Robert Hooke discovered Hooke's law in 1660, he did not want to publish it yet, but wanted to be able to claim priority. So he published the anagram *ceiiinosssttuv* and later published the translation *ut tensio sic vis* (Latin for "as is the extension, so is the force"). Similarly, Galileo first published his discovery of the phases of Venus in the anagram form.

Sir Isaac Newton, in responding to questions from Leibniz in a letter in 1677, concealed the details of his "fluxional technique" with an anagram:

> *The foundations of these operations is evident enough, in fact; but because I cannot proceed with the explanation of it now, I have preferred to conceal it thus: 6accdae13eff7i3l-9n4o4qrr4s8t12ux. On this foundation I have also tried to simplify the theories which concern the squaring of curves, and I have arrived at certain general Theorems.*

Classification

There are many timestamping schemes with different security goals:

- PKI-based – timestamp token is protected using PKI digital signature.

- Linking-based schemes – timestamp is generated such a way that it is related to other timestamps.

- Distributed schemes – timestamp is generated in cooperation of multiple parties.

- Transient key scheme – variant of PKI with short-living signing keys.

- MAC – simple secret key based scheme, found in ANSI ASC X9.95 Standard.

- Database – document hashes are stored in trusted archive; there is online lookup service for verification.

- Hybrid schemes – the linked and signed method is prevailing.

Coverage in standards:

Scheme	RFC 3161	X9.95	ISO/IEC 18014
PKI	Yes	Yes	Yes
Linked		Yes	Yes
MAC		Yes	
Database			Yes
Transient key		Yes	
Linked and signed		Yes	

Trusted (Digital) Timestamping

Trusted timestamping

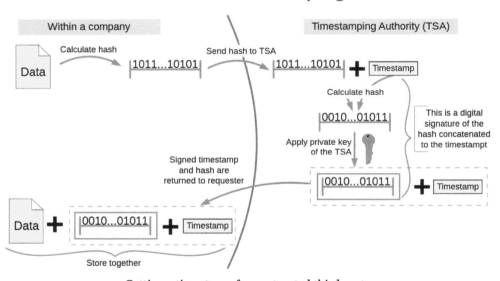

Getting a timestamp from a trusted third party

According to the RFC 3161 standard, a trusted timestamp is a timestamp issued by a trusted third party (TTP) acting as a Time Stamping Authority (TSA). It is used to prove the existence of certain data before a certain point (e.g. contracts, research data, medical records, ...) without the possibility that the owner can backdate the timestamps. Multiple TSAs can be used to increase reliability and reduce vulnerability.

The newer ANSI ASC X9.95 Standard for trusted timestamps augments the RFC 3161 standard with data-level security requirements to ensure data integrity against a reliable time source that is provable to any third party. This standard has been applied to authenticating digitally signed data for regulatory compliance, financial transactions, and legal evidence.

Creating a Timestamp

The technique is based on digital signatures and hash functions. First a hash is calculated from the data. A hash is a sort of digital fingerprint of the original data: a string of bits that is practically impossible to duplicate with any other set of data. If the original data is changed then this will result in a completely different hash. This hash is sent to the TSA. The TSA concatenates a timestamp to the hash and calculates the hash of this concatenation. This hash is in turn digitally signed with the private key of the TSA. This signed hash + the timestamp is sent back to the requester of the timestamp who stores these with the original data.

Since the original data cannot be calculated from the hash (because the hash function is a one way function), the TSA never gets to see the original data, which allows the use of this method for confidential data.

Checking the Timestamp

Checking the trusted timestamp

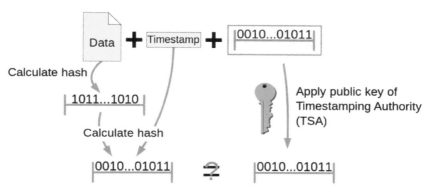

If the calculated hashcode equals the result of the decrypted signature, neither the document or the timestamp was changed and the timestamp was issued by the TTP. If not, either of the previous statements is not true.

Checking correctness of a timestamp generated by a time stamping authority (TSA)

Anyone trusting the timestamper can then verify that the document was *not* created *after* the date that the timestamper vouches. It can also no longer be repudiated that the requester of the timestamp was in possession of the original data at the time given by the timestamp. To prove this (see diagram) the hash of the original data is calculated, the timestamp given by the TSA is appended to it and the hash of the result of this concatenation is calculated, call this hash A.

Then the digital signature of the TSA needs to be validated. This can be done by checking that the signed hash provided by the TSA was indeed signed with their private key by digital signature verification. The hash A is compared with the hash B inside the signed TSA message to confirm they are equal, proving that the timestamp and message is unaltered and was issued by the TSA. If not, then either the timestamp was altered or the timestamp was not issued by the TSA.

Decentralized Timestamping on the Blockchain

With the advent of cryptocurrencies like Bitcoin, it has become possible to securely timestamp information in a decentralized and tamper-proof manner. Digital data can be hashed and the hash can be incorporated into a transaction stored in the blockchain, which serves as a secure proof of the exact time at which that data existed. The proof is due to a tremendous amount of computational effort performed after the hash was submitted to the blockchain. Tampering with the timestamp would also lead to breaking the entire integrity of the digital currency.

Unfortunately, the proof-of-work method using 'mining' requires a huge amount of computational power, making it unfeasible for large scale applications. The energy requirements to run Blockchain are estimated to be around 1GW and may be comparable to the energy usage of Ireland.

Luckily there are alternative methods that do no require a large amount of computational effort. For example, MetroGnomo is an innovative open-source timestamping service based on a mutual distributed ledger or blockchain. Sponsored by the States of Alderney, this globally-available experimental service facilitates commerce through the provision of impartial timing information.

Z/Yen's ChainZy Technology allows Metrognomo to leverage proof-of-validity rather than proof-of-work. Thus Metrognomo is able to take the benefits of mutual distributed ledgers while avoiding the transaction costs, in time and computing resource, associated with convential blockchain proof-of-work validation mechanisms such as 'mining'. Proof-of-validity is possible via a network of independently operated receivers, assuring users that the MetroGnomo mechanism has not been corrupted. MetroGnomo has so far been used for dating financial contracts, proving authorship of books and patents and authenticating information exchange between organizations.

Digital Signature

A digital signature is a mathematical scheme for demonstrating the authenticity of a digital message or documents. A valid digital signature gives a recipient reason to believe that the message was created by a known sender, that the sender cannot deny having sent the message (authentication and non-repudiation), and that the message was not altered in transit (integrity).

Digital signatures are a standard element of most cryptographic protocol suites, and are commonly used for software distribution, financial transactions, contract management software, and in other cases where it is important to detect forgery or tampering.

Explanation

Digital signatures are often used to implement electronic signatures, a broader term that refers to any electronic data that carries the intent of a signature, but not all electronic signatures use digital signatures. In some countries, including the United States, India, Brazil, Indonesia, Saudi Arabia, Switzerland and the countries of the European Union, electronic signatures have legal significance.

Digital signatures employ asymmetric cryptography. In many instances they provide a layer of validation and security to messages sent through a nonsecure channel: Properly implemented, a digital signature gives the receiver reason to believe the message was sent by the claimed sender. Digital seals and signatures are equivalent to handwritten signatures and stamped seals. Digital signatures are equivalent to traditional handwritten signatures in many respects, but properly implemented digital signatures are more difficult to forge than the handwritten type. Digital signature schemes, in the sense used here, are cryptographically based, and must be implemented properly to be effective. Digital signatures can also provide non-repudiation, meaning that the signer cannot successfully claim they did not sign a message, while also claiming their private key remains secret; further, some non-repudiation schemes offer a time stamp for the digital signature, so that even if the private key is exposed, the signature is valid. Digitally signed messages may be anything representable as a bitstring: examples include electronic mail, contracts, or a message sent via some other cryptographic protocol.

Definition

A digital signature scheme typically consists of three algorithms;

- A *key generation* algorithm that selects a *private key* uniformly at random from a set of possible private keys. The algorithm outputs the private key and a corresponding *public key*.

- A *signing* algorithm that, given a message and a private key, produces a signature.

- A *signature verifying* algorithm that, given the message, public key and signature, either accepts or rejects the message's claim to authenticity.

Two main properties are required. First, the authenticity of a signature generated from a fixed message and fixed private key can be verified by using the corresponding public key. Secondly, it should be computationally infeasible to generate a valid signature for a party without knowing that party's private key. A digital signature is an authentication mechanism that enables the creator of the message to attach a code that acts as a signature.

Formally, a digital signature scheme is a triple of probabilistic polynomial time algorithms, (G, S, V), satisfying:

- G (key-generator) generates a public key, pk, and a corresponding private key, sk, on input 1^n, where n is the security parameter.

- S (signing) returns a tag, t, on the inputs: the private key, sk, and a string, x.

- V (verifying) outputs *accepted* or *rejected* on the inputs: the public key, pk, a string, x, and a tag, t.

For correctness, S and V must satisfy

$$\Pr [(pk, sk) \leftarrow G(1^n), V(pk, x, S(sk, x)) = accepted] = 1.$$

A digital signature scheme is secure if for every non-uniform probabilistic polynomial time adversary, A

$$\Pr [(pk, sk) \leftarrow G(1^n), (x, t) \leftarrow A^{S(sk, \cdot)}(pk, 1^n), x \leftarrow Q, V(pk, x, t) = accepted] < negl(n),$$

where $A^{S(sk, \cdot)}$ denotes that A has access to the oracle, $S(sk, \cdot)$, and Q denotes the set of the queries on S made by A, which knows the public key, pk, and the security parameter, n. Note that we require any adversary cannot directly query the string, x, on S.

History

In 1976, Whitfield Diffie and Martin Hellman first described the notion of a digital signature scheme, although they only conjectured that such schemes existed. Soon afterwards, Ronald Rivest, Adi Shamir, and Len Adleman invented the RSA algorithm, which could be used to produce primitive digital signatures (although only as a proof-of-concept – "plain" RSA signatures are not secure). The first widely marketed software package to offer digital signature was Lotus Notes 1.0, released in 1989, which used the RSA algorithm.

Other digital signature schemes were soon developed after RSA, the earliest being Lamport signatures, Merkle signatures (also known as "Merkle trees" or simply "Hash trees"), and Rabin signatures.

In 1988, Shafi Goldwasser, Silvio Micali, and Ronald Rivest became the first to rigorously define the security requirements of digital signature schemes. They described a hierarchy of attack models for signature schemes, and also presented the GMR signature scheme, the first that could be proved to prevent even an existential forgery against a chosen message attack.

How they Work

To create RSA signature keys, generate a RSA key pair containing a modulus, N, that is the product of two large primes, along with integers, e and d, such that $e\,d \equiv 1 \pmod{\varphi(N)}$, where φ is the Euler phi-function. The signer's public key consists of N and e, and the signer's secret key contains d.

To sign a message, m, the signer computes $\sigma \equiv m^d \pmod{N}$. To verify, the receiver checks that $\sigma^e \equiv m \pmod{N}$.

As noted earlier, this basic scheme is not very secure. To prevent attacks, one can first apply a cryptographic hash function to the message, m, and then apply the RSA algorithm described above to the result. This approach is secure assuming the hash function is a random oracle.

Most early signature schemes were of a similar type: they involve the use of a trapdoor permutation, such as the RSA function, or in the case of the Rabin signature scheme, computing square modulo composite, n. A trapdoor permutation family is a family of permutations, specified by a parameter, that is easy to compute in the forward direction, but is difficult to compute in the reverse direction without already knowing the private key ("trapdoor"). Trapdoor permutations can be used for digital signature schemes, where computing the reverse direction with the secret key is required for signing, and computing the forward direction is used to verify signatures.

Used directly, this type of signature scheme is vulnerable to a key-only existential forgery attack. To create a forgery, the attacker picks a random signature σ and uses the verification procedure to determine the message, m, corresponding to that signature. In practice, however, this type of signature is not used directly, but rather, the message to be signed is first hashed to produce a short digest that is then signed. This forgery attack, then, only produces the hash function output that corresponds to σ, but not a message that leads to that value, which does not lead to an attack. In the random oracle model, this hash-then-sign form of signature is existentially unforgeable, even against a chosen-plaintext attack.

There are several reasons to sign such a hash (or message digest) instead of the whole document.

For Efficiency

The signature will be much shorter and thus save time since hashing is generally much faster than signing in practice.

For Compatibility

Messages are typically bit strings, but some signature schemes operate on other domains (such as, in the case of RSA, numbers modulo a composite number N). A hash function can be used to convert an arbitrary input into the proper format.

For Integrity

Without the hash function, the text "to be signed" may have to be split (separated) in blocks small enough for the signature scheme to act on them directly. However, the receiver of the signed blocks is not able to recognize if all the blocks are present and in the appropriate order.

Notions of Security

In their foundational paper, Goldwasser, Micali, and Rivest lay out a hierarchy of attack models against digital signatures:

In a *key-only* attack, the attacker is only given the public verification key.

In a *known message* attack, the attacker is given valid signatures for a variety of messages known by the attacker but not chosen by the attacker.

In an *adaptive chosen message* attack, the attacker first learns signatures on arbitrary messages of the attacker's choice.

They also describe a hierarchy of attack results:

A *total break* results in the recovery of the signing key.

A universal forgery attack results in the ability to forge signatures for any message.

A selective forgery attack results in a signature on a message of the adversary's choice.

An existential forgery merely results in some valid message/signature pair not already known to the adversary.

The strongest notion of security, therefore, is security against existential forgery under an adaptive chosen message attack.

Applications of Digital Signatures

As organizations move away from paper documents with ink signatures or authenticity stamps, digital signatures can provide added assurances of the evidence to provenance, identity, and status of an electronic document as well as acknowledging informed consent and approval by a signatory. The United States Government Printing Office (GPO) publishes electronic versions of the budget, public and private laws, and congressional bills with digital signatures. Universities including

Penn State, University of Chicago, and Stanford are publishing electronic student transcripts with digital signatures.

Below are some common reasons for applying a digital signature to communications:

Authentication

Although messages may often include information about the entity sending a message, that information may not be accurate. Digital signatures can be used to authenticate the source of messages. When ownership of a digital signature secret key is bound to a specific user, a valid signature shows that the message was sent by that user. The importance of high confidence in sender authenticity is especially obvious in a financial context. For example, suppose a bank's branch office sends instructions to the central office requesting a change in the balance of an account. If the central office is not convinced that such a message is truly sent from an authorized source, acting on such a request could be a grave mistake.

Integrity

In many scenarios, the sender and receiver of a message may have a need for confidence that the message has not been altered during transmission. Although encryption hides the contents of a message, it may be possible to *change* an encrypted message without understanding it. (Some encryption algorithms, known as nonmalleable ones, prevent this, but others do not.) However, if a message is digitally signed, any change in the message after signature invalidates the signature. Furthermore, there is no efficient way to modify a message and its signature to produce a new message with a valid signature, because this is still considered to be computationally infeasible by most cryptographic hash functions.

Non-repudiation

Non-repudiation, or more specifically *non-repudiation of origin*, is an important aspect of digital signatures. By this property, an entity that has signed some information cannot at a later time deny having signed it. Similarly, access to the public key only does not enable a fraudulent party to fake a valid signature.

Note that these authentication, non-repudiation etc. properties rely on the secret key *not having been revoked* prior to its usage. Public revocation of a key-pair is a required ability, else leaked secret keys would continue to implicate the claimed owner of the key-pair. Checking revocation status requires an "online" check; e.g., checking a "Certificate Revocation List" or via the "Online Certificate Status Protocol". Very roughly this is analogous to a vendor who receives credit-cards first checking online with the credit-card issuer to find if a given card has been reported lost or stolen. Of course, with stolen key pairs, the theft is often discovered only after the secret key's use, e.g., to sign a bogus certificate for espionage purpose.

Additional Security Precautions

Putting the Private Key on a Smart Card

All public key / private key cryptosystems depend entirely on keeping the private key secret. A private key can be stored on a user's computer, and protected by a local password, but this has two disadvantages:

- the user can only sign documents on that particular computer

- the security of the private key depends entirely on the security of the computer

A more secure alternative is to store the private key on a smart card. Many smart cards are designed to be tamper-resistant (although some designs have been broken, notably by Ross Anderson and his students). In a typical digital signature implementation, the hash calculated from the document is sent to the smart card, whose CPU signs the hash using the stored private key of the user, and then returns the signed hash. Typically, a user must activate his smart card by entering a personal identification number or PIN code (thus providing two-factor authentication). It can be arranged that the private key never leaves the smart card, although this is not always implemented. If the smart card is stolen, the thief will still need the PIN code to generate a digital signature. This reduces the security of the scheme to that of the PIN system, although it still requires an attacker to possess the card. A mitigating factor is that private keys, if generated and stored on smart cards, are usually regarded as difficult to copy, and are assumed to exist in exactly one copy. Thus, the loss of the smart card may be detected by the owner and the corresponding certificate can be immediately revoked. Private keys that are protected by software only may be easier to copy, and such compromises are far more difficult to detect.

Using Smart Card Readers with a Separate Keyboard

Entering a PIN code to activate the smart card commonly requires a numeric keypad. Some card readers have their own numeric keypad. This is safer than using a card reader integrated into a PC, and then entering the PIN using that computer's keyboard. Readers with a numeric keypad are meant to circumvent the eavesdropping threat where the computer might be running a keystroke logger, potentially compromising the PIN code. Specialized card readers are also less vulnerable to tampering with their software or hardware and are often EAL3 certified.

Other Smart Card Designs

Smart card design is an active field, and there are smart card schemes which are intended to avoid these particular problems, though so far with little security proofs.

Using Digital Signatures Only with Trusted Applications

One of the main differences between a digital signature and a written signature is that the user does not "see" what he signs. The user application presents a hash code to be signed by the digital signing algorithm using the private key. An attacker who gains control of the user's PC can possibly replace the user application with a foreign substitute, in effect replacing the user's own communications with those of the attacker. This could allow a malicious application to trick a user into signing any document by displaying the user's original on-screen, but presenting the attacker's own documents to the signing application.

To protect against this scenario, an authentication system can be set up between the user's application (word processor, email client, etc.) and the signing application. The general idea is to provide some means for both the user application and signing application to verify each other's integrity. For example, the signing application may require all requests to come from digitally signed binaries.

Using a Network Attached Hardware Security Module

One of the main differences between a cloud based digital signature service and a locally provided one is risk. Many risk averse companies, including governments, financial and medical institutions, and payment processors require more secure standards, like FIPS 140-2 level 3 and FIPS 201 certification, to ensure the signature is validated and secure.

WYSIWYS

Technically speaking, a digital signature applies to a string of bits, whereas humans and applications "believe" that they sign the semantic interpretation of those bits. In order to be semantically interpreted, the bit string must be transformed into a form that is meaningful for humans and applications, and this is done through a combination of hardware and software based processes on a computer system. The problem is that the semantic interpretation of bits can change as a function of the processes used to transform the bits into semantic content. It is relatively easy to change the interpretation of a digital document by implementing changes on the computer system where the document is being processed. From a semantic perspective this creates uncertainty about what exactly has been signed. WYSIWYS (What You See Is What You Sign) means that the semantic interpretation of a signed message cannot be changed. In particular this also means that a message cannot contain hidden information that the signer is unaware of, and that can be revealed after the signature has been applied. WYSIWYS is a necessary requirement for the validity of digital signatures, but this requirement is difficult to guarantee because of the increasing complexity of modern computer systems. The term WYSIWYS was coined by Peter Landrock and Torben Pedersen to describe some of the principles in delivering secure and legally binding digital signatures for Pan-European projects.

Digital Signatures Versus Ink on Paper Signatures

An ink signature could be replicated from one document to another by copying the image manually or digitally, but to have credible signature copies that can resist some scrutiny is a significant manual or technical skill, and to produce ink signature copies that resist professional scrutiny is very difficult.

Digital signatures cryptographically bind an electronic identity to an electronic document and the digital signature cannot be copied to another document. Paper contracts sometimes have the ink signature block on the last page, and the previous pages may be replaced after a signature is applied. Digital signatures can be applied to an entire document, such that the digital signature on the last page will indicate tampering if any data on any of the pages have been altered, but this can also be achieved by signing with ink and numbering all pages of the contract.

Some Digital Signature Algorithms

- RSA-based signature schemes, such as RSA-PSS

- DSA and its elliptic curve variant ECDSA

- ElGamal signature scheme as the predecessor to DSA, and variants Schnorr signature and Pointcheval–Stern signature algorithm

- Rabin signature algorithm

- Pairing-based schemes such as BLS

- Undeniable signatures

- Aggregate signature - a signature scheme that supports aggregation: Given n signatures on n messages from n users, it is possible to aggregate all these signatures into a single signature whose size is constant in the number of users. This single signature will convince the verifier that the n users did indeed sign the n original messages.

- Signatures with efficient protocols - are signature schemes that facilitate efficient cryptographic protocols such as zero-knowledge proofs or secure computation.

The Current State of use – Legal and Practical

All digital signature schemes share the following basic prerequisites regardless of cryptographic theory or legal provision:

1. Quality algorithms

2. Some public-key algorithms are known to be insecure, as practical attacks against them having been discovered.

3. Quality implementations

4. An implementation of a good algorithm (or protocol) with mistake(s) will not work.

5. Users (and their software) must carry out the signature protocol properly.

6. The private key must remain private

7. If the private key becomes known to any other party, that party can produce *perfect* digital signatures of anything whatsoever.

8. The public key owner must be verifiable

   A public key associated with Bob actually came from Bob. This is commonly done using a public key infrastructure (PKI) and the public key↔user association is attested by the operator of the PKI (called a certificate authority). For 'open' PKIs in which anyone can request such an attestation (universally embodied in a cryptographically protected identity certificate), the possibility of mistaken attestation is non-trivial. Commercial PKI operators have suffered several publicly known problems. Such mistakes could lead to falsely signed, and thus wrongly attributed, documents. 'Closed' PKI systems are more expensive, but less easily subverted in this way.

Only if all of these conditions are met will a digital signature actually be any evidence of who sent the message, and therefore of their assent to its contents. Legal enactment cannot change this reality of the existing engineering possibilities, though some such have not reflected this actuality.

Legislatures, being importuned by businesses expecting to profit from operating a PKI, or by the technological avant-garde advocating new solutions to old problems, have enacted statutes and/or regulations in many jurisdictions authorizing, endorsing, encouraging, or permitting digital signatures and providing for (or limiting) their legal effect. The first appears to have been in Utah in the United States, followed closely by the states Massachusetts and California. Other countries have also passed statutes or issued regulations in this area as well and the UN has had an active model law project for some time. These enactments (or proposed enactments) vary from place to place, have typically embodied expectations at variance (optimistically or pessimistically) with the state of the underlying cryptographic engineering, and have had the net effect of confusing potential users and specifiers, nearly all of whom are not cryptographically knowledgeable. Adoption of technical standards for digital signatures have lagged behind much of the legislation, delaying a more or less unified engineering position on interoperability, algorithm choice, key lengths, and so on what the engineering is attempting to provide.

Industry Standards

Some industries have established common interoperability standards for the use of digital signatures between members of the industry and with regulators. These include the Automotive Network Exchange for the automobile industry and the SAFE-BioPharma Association for the healthcare industry.

Using Separate Key Pairs for Signing and Encryption

In several countries, a digital signature has a status somewhat like that of a traditional pen and paper signature, like in the EU digital signature legislation. Generally, these provisions mean that anything digitally signed legally binds the signer of the document to the terms therein. For that reason, it is often thought best to use separate key pairs for encrypting and signing. Using the encryption key pair, a person can engage in an encrypted conversation (e.g., regarding a real estate transaction), but the encryption does not legally sign every message he sends. Only when both parties come to an agreement do they sign a contract with their signing keys, and only then are they legally bound by the terms of a specific document. After signing, the document can be sent over the encrypted link. If a signing key is lost or compromised, it can be revoked to mitigate any future transactions. If an encryption key is lost, a backup or key escrow should be utilized to continue viewing encrypted content. Signing keys should never be backed up or escrowed unless the backup destination is securely encrypted.

References

- Mark Bando (2007). 101st Airborne: The Screaming Eagles in World War II. Mbi Publishing Company. ISBN 978-0-7603-2984-9. Retrieved 20 May 2012.

- Boyko, V.; P. MacKenzie; S. Patel (2000). "Provably Secure Password-Authenticated Key Exchange Using Diffie-Hellman". Advances in Cryptology -- Eurocrypt 2000, LNCS. Lecture Notes in Computer Science. Springer-Verlag. 1807: 156–171. doi:10.1007/3-540-45539-6_12. ISBN 978-3-540-67517-4.

- Abdalla, M.; D. Pointcheval (2005). "Simple Password-Based Encrypted Key Exchange Protocols" (PDF). Topics in Cryptology – CT-RSA 2005. Lecture Notes in Computer Science. Springer Berlin Heidelberg. 3376: 191–208. doi:10.1007/978-3-540-30574-3_14. ISBN 978-3-540-24399-1.

- "Modern Cryptography: Theory & Practice", Wenbo Mao, Prentice Hall Professional Technical Reference, New Jersey, 2004, pg. 308. ISBN 0-13-066943-1

- "The problems with forcing regular password expiry". IA Matters. CESG: the Information Security Arm of GCHQ. 15 April 2016. Retrieved 5 Aug 2016.

- "You must provide a password between 1 and 8 characters in length". Jira.codehaus.org. Retrieved on 2012-05-20. Archived May 21, 2015, at the Wayback Machine.

- Joseph Steinberg (12 November 2014). "Forbes: Why You Should Ignore Everything You Have Been Told About Choosing Passwords". Forbes. Retrieved 12 November 2014.

- Pauli, Darren (16 July 2014). "Microsoft: You NEED bad passwords and should re-use them a lot". The Register. Retrieved 10 August 2014.

- Techlicious / Fox Van Allen @techlicious (2013-08-08). "Google Reveals the 10 Worst Password Ideas | TIME.com". Techland.time.com. Retrieved 2013-10-16.

- Alexander, Steven. (2012-06-20) The Bug Charmer: How long should passwords be?. Bugcharmer.blogspot.com. Retrieved on 2013-07-30.

- Cracking Story – How I Cracked Over 122 Million SHA1 and MD5 Hashed Passwords « Thireus' Blog. Blog.thireus.com (2012-08-29). Retrieved on 2013-07-30.

- Jaffery, Saman M. (17 October 2011). "Survey: 11% of Brits Include Internet Passwords in Will". Hull & Hull LLP. Retrieved 16 July 2012.

- Managing Network Security at the Wayback Machine (archived March 2, 2008). Fred Cohen and Associates. All.net. Retrieved on 2012-05-20.

- How to prevent Windows from storing a LAN manager hash of your password in Active Directory and local SAM databases. support.microsoft.com (2007-12-03). Retrieved on 2012-05-20.

- Kok-Wah Lee "Methods and Systems to Create Big Memorizable Secrets and Their Applications" Patent US20110055585, WO2010010430. Filing date: December 18, 2008

9

Evolution of Cryptography

Cryptography in earlier times was referred to as encryption; it was an alteration of messages from a comprehensible to a non-comprehensible form. The earliest forms of secret writing needed a little more than writing implements, since literacy was still rare. With more literate opponents came the need for actual cryptography. The evolution of cryptography is of great importance to broaden the existing knowledge on this field.

Cryptography, the use of codes and ciphers to protect secrets, began thousands of years ago. Until recent decades, it has been the story of what might be called classic cryptography — that is, of methods of encryption that use pen and paper, or perhaps simple mechanical aids. In the early 20th century, the invention of complex mechanical and electromechanical machines, such as the Enigma rotor machine, provided more sophisticated and efficient means of encryption; and the subsequent introduction of electronics and computing has allowed elaborate schemes of still greater complexity, most of which are entirely unsuited to pen and paper.

The development of cryptography has been paralleled by the development of cryptanalysis — the "breaking" of codes and ciphers. The discovery and application, early on, of frequency analysis to the reading of encrypted communications has, on occasion, altered the course of history. Thus the Zimmermann Telegram triggered the United States' entry into World War I; and Allied reading of Nazi Germany's ciphers shortened World War II, in some evaluations by as much as two years.

Until the 1970s, secure cryptography was largely the preserve of governments. Two events have since brought it squarely into the public domain: the creation of a public encryption standard (DES), and the invention of public-key cryptography.

Classical Cryptography

A Scytale, an early device for encryption.

The earliest known use of cryptography is found in non-standard hieroglyphs carved into monuments from the Old Kingdom of Egypt circa 1900 BCE. These are not thought to be serious attempts at secret communications, however, but rather to have been attempts at mystery, intrigue, or even amusement for literate onlookers. These are examples of still other uses of cryptography, or of something that looks (impressively if misleadingly) like it. Some clay tablets from Mesopotamia somewhat later are clearly meant to protect information—one dated near 1500 BCE was found to encrypt a craftsman's recipe for pottery glaze, presumably commercially valuable. Later still, Hebrew scholars made use of simple monoalphabetic substitution ciphers (such as the Atbash cipher) beginning perhaps around 500 to 600 BCE.

The ancient Greeks are said to have known of ciphers. The scytale transposition cipher was used by the Spartan military, however it is disputed whether the scytale was for encryption, authentication, or avoiding bad omens in speech. Herodotus tells us of secret messages physically concealed beneath wax on wooden tablets or as a tattoo on a slave's head concealed by regrown hair, though these are not properly examples of cryptography *per se* as the message, once known, is directly readable; this is known as steganography. Another Greek method was developed by Polybius (now called the "Polybius Square"). The Romans knew something of cryptography (e.g., the Caesar cipher and its variations).

Medieval and Renaissance Cryptography

The first page of al-Kindi's manuscript *On Deciphering Cryptographic Messages*, containing the first descriptions of cryptanalysis and frequency analysis.

David Kahn notes in *The Codebreakers* that modern cryptology originated among the Arabs, the first people to systematically document the methods of cryptanalysis. The invention of the frequency-analysis technique for breaking monoalphabetic substitution ciphers, by Al-Kindi, an Arab mathematician, sometime around AD 800 proved to be the most fundamental cryptanalytic advance until WWII. Al-Kindi wrote a book on cryptography entitled *Risalah fi Istikhraj al-Mu'amma* (*Manuscript for the Deciphering Cryptographic Messages*), in which he described the first cryptanalysis techniques, including some for polyalphabetic ciphers, cipher classification, Arabic phonetics and syntax, and, most importantly, gave the first descriptions on frequency analysis. He also covered methods of encipherments, cryptanalysis of certain encipherments, and statistical analysis of letters and letter combinations in Arabic.

Ahmad al-Qalqashandi (AD 1355–1418) wrote the *Subh al-a 'sha*, a 14-volume encyclopedia which included a section on cryptology. This information was attributed to Ibn al-Durayhim who lived from AD 1312 to 1361, but whose writings on cryptography have been lost. The list of ciphers in this work included both substitution and transposition, and for the first time, a cipher with multiple substitutions for each plaintext letter. Also traced to Ibn al-Durayhim is an exposition on and worked example of cryptanalysis, including the use of tables of letter frequencies and sets of letters which cannot occur together in one word.

The earliest example of the homophonic substitution cipher is the one used by Duke of Mantua in the early 1400s. Homophonic cipher replaces each letter with multiple symbols depending on the letter frequency. The cipher is ahead of the time because it combines monoalphabetic and polyalphabetic features.

Essentially all ciphers remained vulnerable to the cryptanalytic technique of frequency analysis until the development of the polyalphabetic cipher, and many remained so thereafter. The polyalphabetic cipher was most clearly explained by Leon Battista Alberti around the year AD 1467, for which he was called the "father of Western cryptology". Johannes Trithemius, in his work *Poligraphia*, invented the tabula recta, a critical component of the Vigenère cipher. The French cryptographer Blaise de Vigenère devised a practical polyalphabetic system which bears his name, the Vigenère cipher.

In Europe, cryptography became (secretly) more important as a consequence of political competition and religious revolution. For instance, in Europe during and after the Renaissance, citizens of the various Italian states—the Papal States and the Roman Catholic Church included—were responsible for rapid proliferation of cryptographic techniques, few of which reflect understanding (or even knowledge) of Alberti's polyalphabetic advance. 'Advanced ciphers', even after Alberti, weren't as advanced as their inventors / developers / users claimed (and probably even themselves believed). They were regularly broken. This over-optimism may be inherent in cryptography, for it was then - and remains today - fundamentally difficult to accurately know how vulnerable one's system actually is. In the absence of knowledge, guesses and hopes, predictably, are common.

Cryptography, cryptanalysis, and secret-agent/courier betrayal featured in the Babington plot during the reign of Queen Elizabeth I which led to the execution of Mary, Queen of Scots.

The chief cryptographer of King Louis XIV of France was Antoine Rossignol and he and his family created what is known as the Great Cipher because it remained unsolved from its initial use until 1890, when French military cryptanalyst, Étienne Bazeries solved it. An encrypted message from the time of the Man in the Iron Mask (decrypted just prior to 1900 by Étienne Bazeries) has shed some, regrettably non-definitive, light on the identity of that real, if legendary and unfortunate, prisoner.

Outside of Europe, after the Mongols brought about the end of the Muslim Golden Age, cryptography remained comparatively undeveloped. Cryptography in Japan seems not to have been used until about 1510, and advanced techniques were not known until after the opening of the country to the West beginning in the 1860s.

Cryptography from 1800 to World War II

Although cryptography has a long and complex history, it wasn't until the 19th century that it developed anything more than ad hoc approaches to either encryption or cryptanalysis (the science of finding weaknesses in crypto systems). Examples of the latter include Charles Babbage's Crimean War era work on mathematical cryptanalysis of polyalphabetic ciphers, redeveloped and published somewhat later by the Prussian Friedrich Kasiski. Understanding of cryptography at this time typically consisted of hard-won rules of thumb; for example, Auguste Kerckhoffs' cryptographic writings in the latter 19th century. Edgar Allan Poe used systematic methods to solve ciphers in the 1840s. In particular he placed a notice of his abilities in the Philadelphia paper *Alexander's Weekly (Express) Messenger*, inviting submissions of ciphers, of which he proceeded to solve almost all. His success created a public stir for some months. He later wrote an essay on methods of cryptography which proved useful as an introduction for novice British cryptanalysts attempting to break German codes and ciphers during World War I, and a famous story, *The Gold-Bug*, in which cryptanalysis was a prominent element.

Cryptography, and its misuse, were involved in the execution of Mata Hari and in the Dreyfus' conviction and imprisonment, both in the early 20th century. Cryptographers were also involved in exposing the machinations which had led to the Dreyfus affair; Mata Hari, in contrast, was shot.

In World War I the Admiralty's Room 40 broke German naval codes and played an important role in several naval engagements during the war, notably in detecting major German sorties into the North Sea that led to the battles of Dogger Bank and Jutland as the British fleet was sent out to intercept them. However its most important contribution was probably in decrypting the Zimmermann Telegram, a cable from the German Foreign Office sent via Washington to its ambassador Heinrich von Eckardt in Mexico which played a major part in bringing the United States into the war.

In 1917, Gilbert Vernam proposed a teleprinter cipher in which a previously prepared key, kept on paper tape, is combined character by character with the plaintext message to produce the cyphertext. This led to the development of electromechanical devices as cipher machines, and to the only unbreakable cipher, the one time pad.

During the 1920s, Polish naval-officers assisted the Japanese military with code and cipher development.

Mathematical methods proliferated in the period prior to World War II (notably in William F. Friedman's application of statistical techniques to cryptanalysis and cipher development and in Marian Rejewski's initial break into the German Army's version of the Enigma system in 1932).

World War II Cryptography

By World War II, mechanical and electromechanical cipher machines were in wide use, although—where such machines were impractical—manual systems continued in use. Great advances were made in both cipher design and cryptanalysis, all in secrecy. Information about this period has begun to be declassified as the official British 50-year secrecy period has come to an end, as US archives have slowly opened, and as assorted memoirs and articles have appeared.

The Germans made heavy use, in several variants, of an electromechanical rotor machine known as Enigma. Mathematician Marian Rejewski, at Poland's Cipher Bureau, in December 1932 deduced the detailed structure of the German Army Enigma, using mathematics and limited documentation supplied by Captain Gustave Bertrand of French military intelligence. This was the greatest breakthrough in cryptanalysis in a thousand years and more, according to historian David Kahn. Rejewski and his mathematical Cipher Bureau colleagues, Jerzy Różycki and Henryk Zygalski, continued reading Enigma and keeping pace with the evolution of the German Army machine's components and encipherment procedures. As the Poles' resources became strained by the changes being introduced by the Germans, and as war loomed, the Cipher Bureau, on the Polish General Staff's instructions, on 25 July 1939, at Warsaw, initiated French and British intelligence representatives into the secrets of Enigma decryption.

The Enigma machine was widely used by Nazi Germany; its cryptanalysis by the Allies provided vital Ultra intelligence.

Soon after the Invasion of Poland by Germany on 1 September 1939, key Cipher Bureau personnel were evacuated southeastward; on 17 September, as the Soviet Union attacked Poland from the East, they crossed into Romania. From there they reached Paris, France; at PC Bruno, near Paris, they continued breaking Enigma, collaborating with British cryptologists at Bletchley Park as the British got up to speed on breaking Enigma. In due course, the British cryptographers - whose ranks included many chess masters and mathematics dons such as Gordon Welchman, Max Newman, and Alan Turing (the conceptual founder of modern computing) - substantially advanced the scale and technology of Enigma decryption.

German code breaking in World War II also had some success, most importantly by breaking the Naval Cipher No. 3. This enabled them to track and sink Atlantic convoys. It was only Ultra intelligence that finally persuaded the admiralty to change their codes in June 1943. This is surprising given the success of the British Room 40 code breakers in the previous world war.

At the end of the War, on 19 April 1945, Britain's top military officers were told that they could never reveal that the German Enigma cipher had been broken because it would give the defeated enemy the chance to say they "were not well and fairly beaten".

US Navy cryptographers (with cooperation from British and Dutch cryptographers after 1940) broke into several Japanese Navy crypto systems. The break into one of them, JN-25, famously led to the US victory in the Battle of Midway; and to the publication of that fact in the Chicago Tribune shortly after the battle, though the Japanese seem not to have noticed for they kept using the JN-25 system. A US Army group, the SIS, managed to break the highest security Japanese diplomatic cipher system (an electromechanical 'stepping switch' machine called Purple by the Americans) even before WWII began. The Americans referred to the intelligence resulting from cryptanalysis, perhaps especially that from the Purple machine, as 'Magic'. The British eventually settled on 'Ultra' for intelligence resulting from cryptanalysis, particularly that from message traffic protected by the various Enigmas. An earlier British term for Ultra had been 'Boniface' in an attempt to suggest, if betrayed, that it might have an individual agent as a source.

The German military also deployed several mechanical attempts at a one-time pad. Bletchley Park called them the Fish ciphers, and Max Newman and colleagues designed and deployed the Heath Robinson, and then the world's first programmable digital electronic computer, the Colossus, to help with their cryptanalysis. The German Foreign Office began to use the one-time pad in 1919; some of this traffic was read in WWII partly as the result of recovery of some key material in South America that was discarded without sufficient care by a German courier.

The Japanese Foreign Office used a locally developed electrical stepping switch based system (called Purple by the US), and also had used several similar machines for attaches in some Japanese embassies. One of the electrical stepping switch based systems referred to earlier as Purple was called the 'M-machine' by the US, another was referred to as 'Red'. All were broken, to one degree or another, by the Allies.

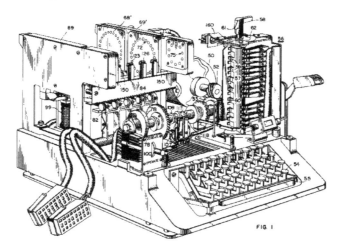

SIGABA is described in U.S. Patent 6,175,625, filed in 1944 but not issued until 2001.

Allied cipher machines used in WWII included the British TypeX and the American SIGABA; both were electromechanical rotor designs similar in spirit to the Enigma, albeit with major improvements. Neither is known to have been broken by anyone during the War. The Poles used the Lacida machine, but its security was found to be less than intended (by Polish Army cryptographers in the UK), and its use was discontinued. US troops in the field used the M-209 and the still less secure M-94 family machines. British SOE agents initially used 'poem ciphers' (memorized poems were the encryption/decryption keys), but later in the War, they began to switch to one-time pads.

The VIC cipher (used at least until 1957 in connection with Rudolf Abel's NY spy ring) was a very complex hand cipher, and is claimed to be the most complicated known to have been used by the

Soviets, according to David Kahn in *Kahn on Codes*. For the decrypting of Soviet ciphers (particularly when *one-time pads* were reused).

Modern Cryptography

Encryption in modern times is achieved by using algorithms that have a key to encrypt and decrypt information. These keys convert the messages and data into "digital gibberish" through encryption and then return them to the original form through decryption. In general, the longer the key is, the more difficult it is to crack the code. This holds true because deciphering an encrypted message by brute force would require the attacker to try every possible key. To put this in context, each binary unit of information, or bit, has a value of 0 or 1. An 8-bit key would then have 256 or 2^8 possible keys. A 56-bit key would have 2^{56}, or 72 quadrillion, possible keys to try and decipher the message. With modern technology, cyphers using keys with these lengths are becoming easier to decipher. DES, an early US Government approved cypher, has an effective key length of 56 bits, and test messages using that cypher have been broken by brute force key search. However, as technology advances, so does the quality of encryption. Since WWII, one of the most notable advances in the study of cryptography is the introduction of the asymmetric key cyphers (sometimes, somewhat loosely, termed) public-key cyphers. These are algorithms which use two (mathematically related) keys; some of them permit publication of one of the keys, the other being extremely difficult to determine from knowledge of the first.

Beginning around 1990, the use of the Internet for commercial purposes and the introduction of commercial transactions over the Internet called for a widespread standard for encryption. Before the introduction of the Advanced Encryption Standard (AES), information sent over the Internet, such as financial data, was encrypted if at all, most commonly using the Data Encryption Standard (DES). This had been approved by NBS (a US Government agency) for its security, after public call for, and a comptetition among, candidates for such a cypher algorithm. DES was approved for a short period, but saw extended use due to complex wrangles over the use by the public of high quality encryption. DES was finally replaced by the AES after another public competition organized by the NBS successor agency, NIST. Around the late 1990s to early 2000s, the use of public-key algorithms became a more common approach for encryption, and soon a hybrid of the two schemes became the most accepted way for e-commerce operations to proceed. Additionally, the creation of a new protocol known as the Secure Socket Layer, or SSL, led the way for online transactions to take place. Transactions ranging from purchasing goods to online bill pay and banking used SSL. Furthermore, as wireless Internet connections became more common among households, the need for encryption grew, as a level of security was needed in these everyday situations.

Claude Shannon

Claude E. Shannon is considered by many to be the father of mathematical cryptography. Shannon worked for several years at Bell Labs, and during his time there, he produced an article entitled "A mathematical theory of cryptography". This article was written in 1945 and eventually was published in the Bell System Technical Journal in 1949. It is commonly accepted that this paper was the starting point for development of modern cryptography. Shannon was inspired during the war to address "[t]he problems of cryptography [because] secrecy systems furnish an interesting application of communication theory". Shannon identified the two main goals of cryptography: secrecy and authenticity. His focus was on exploring secrecy and thirty-five years later, G.J. Simmons would address the issue of authenticity. Shannon wrote a further article entitled "A mathematical theory of communication" which highlights one of the most significant aspects of his work: cryptography's transition from art to science.

In his works, Shannon described the two basic types of systems for secrecy. The first are those designed with the intent to protect against hackers and attackers who have infinite resources with which to decode a message (theoretical secrecy, now unconditional security), and the second are those designed to protect against hackers and attacks with finite resources with which to decode a message (practical secrecy, now computational security). Most of Shannon's work focused around theoretical secrecy; here, Shannon introduced a definition for the "unbreakability" of a cipher. If a cipher was determined "unbreakable", it was considered to have "perfect secrecy". In proving "perfect secrecy", Shannon determined that this could only be obtained with a secret key whose length given in binary digits was greater than or equal to the number of bits contained in the information being encrypted. Furthermore, Shannon developed the "unicity distance", defined as the "amount of plaintext that... determines the secret key."

Shannon's work influenced further cryptography research in the 1970s, as the public-key cryptography developers, M. E. Hellman and W. Diffie cited Shannon's research as a major influence. His work also impacted modern designs of secret-key ciphers. At the end of Shannon's work with cryptography, progress slowed until Hellman and Diffie introduced their paper involving "public-key cryptography".

An Encryption Standard

The mid-1970s saw two major public (i.e., non-secret) advances. First was the publication of the draft Data Encryption Standard in the U.S. *Federal Register* on 17 March 1975. The proposed DES cipher was submitted by a research group at IBM, at the invitation of the National Bureau of Standards (now NIST), in an effort to develop secure electronic communication facilities for businesses such as banks and other large financial organizations. After advice and modification by the NSA, acting behind the scenes, it was adopted and published as a Federal Information Processing Standard Publication in 1977 (currently at FIPS 46-3). DES was the first publicly accessible cipher to be 'blessed' by a national agency such as the NSA. The release of its specification by NBS stimulated an explosion of public and academic interest in cryptography.

The aging DES was officially replaced by the Advanced Encryption Standard (AES) in 2001 when NIST announced FIPS 197. After an open competition, NIST selected Rijndael, submitted by two Belgian cryptographers, to be the AES. DES, and more secure variants of it (such as Triple DES), are still used today, having been incorporated into many national and organizational standards. However, its 56-bit key-size has been shown to be insufficient to guard against brute force attacks (one such attack, undertaken by the cyber civil-rights group Electronic Frontier Foundation in 1997, succeeded in 56 hours.) As a result, use of straight DES encryption is now without doubt insecure for use in new cryptosystem designs, and messages protected by older cryptosystems using DES, and indeed all messages sent since 1976 using DES, are also at risk. Regardless of DES' inherent quality, the DES key size (56-bits) was thought to be too small by some even in 1976, perhaps most publicly by Whitfield Diffie. There was suspicion that government organizations even then had sufficient computing power to break DES messages; clearly others have achieved this capability.

Public Key

The second development, in 1976, was perhaps even more important, for it fundamentally changed the way cryptosystems might work. This was the publication of the paper New Directions in Cryptography by Whitfield Diffie and Martin Hellman. It introduced a radically new method of distributing cryptographic keys, which went far toward solving one of the fundamental problems of cryptography, key distribution, and has become known as Diffie-Hellman key exchange. The article also stimulated the almost immediate public development of a new class of enciphering algorithms, the asymmetric key algorithms.

Prior to that time, all useful modern encryption algorithms had been symmetric key algorithms, in which the same cryptographic key is used with the underlying algorithm by both the sender and the recipient, who must both keep it secret. All of the electromechanical machines used in WWII were of this logical class, as were the Caesar and Atbash ciphers and essentially all cipher systems throughout history. The 'key' for a code is, of course, the codebook, which must likewise be distributed and kept secret, and so shares most of the same problems in practice.

Of necessity, the key in every such system had to be exchanged between the communicating parties in some secure way prior to any use of the system (the term usually used is 'via a secure channel') such as a trustworthy courier with a briefcase handcuffed to a wrist, or face-to-face contact, or a loyal carrier pigeon. This requirement is never trivial and very rapidly becomes unmanageable as the number of participants increases, or when secure channels aren't available for key exchange, or when, as is sensible cryptographic practice, keys are frequently changed. In particular, if messages are meant to be secure from other users, a separate key is required for each possible pair of users. A system of this kind is known as a secret key, or symmetric key cryptosystem. D-H key exchange (and succeeding improvements and variants) made operation of these systems much easier, and more secure, than had ever been possible before in all of history.

In contrast, asymmetric key encryption uses a pair of mathematically related keys, each of which decrypts the encryption performed using the other. Some, but not all, of these algorithms have the additional property that one of the paired keys cannot be deduced from the other by any known method other than trial and error. An algorithm of this kind is known as a public key or asymmetric key system. Using such an algorithm, only one key pair is needed per user. By designating one key of the pair as private (always secret), and the other as public (often widely available), no secure channel is needed for key exchange. So long as the private key stays secret, the public key can be widely known for a very long time without compromising security, making it safe to reuse the same key pair indefinitely.

For two users of an asymmetric key algorithm to communicate securely over an insecure channel, each user will need to know their own public and private keys as well as the other user's public key. Take this basic scenario: Alice and Bob each have a pair of keys they've been using for years with many other users. At the start of their message, they exchange public keys, unencrypted over an insecure line. Alice then encrypts a message using her private key, and then re-encrypts that result using Bob's public key. The double-encrypted message is then sent as digital data over a wire from Alice to Bob. Bob receives the bit stream and decrypts it using his own private key, and then decrypts that bit stream using Alice's public key. If the final result is recognizable as a message, Bob can be confident that the message actually came from someone who knows Alice's private key (presumably actually her if she's been careful with her private key), and that anyone eavesdropping on the channel will need Bob's private key in order to understand the message.

Asymmetric algorithms rely for their effectiveness on a class of problems in mathematics called one-way functions, which require relatively little computational power to execute, but vast amounts of power to reverse, if reversal is possible at all. A classic example of a one-way function is multiplication of very large prime numbers. It's fairly quick to multiply two large primes, but very difficult to find the factors of the product of two large primes. Because of the mathematics of one-way functions, most possible keys are bad choices as cryptographic keys; only a small fraction of the possible keys of a given length are suitable, and so asymmetric algorithms require very long keys to reach the same level of security provided by relatively shorter symmetric keys. The need to both generate the key pairs, and perform the encryption/decryption operations make asymmetric algorithms computationally expensive, compared to most symmetric algorithms. Since symmetric algorithms can often use any sequence of (random, or at least unpredictable) bits as a key, a disposable *session key* can be quickly generated for short-term use. Consequently, it is common practice to use a long asymmetric key to exchange a disposable, much shorter (but just as strong) symmetric key. The slower asymmetric algorithm securely sends a symmetric session key, and the faster symmetric algorithm takes over for the remainder of the message.

Asymmetric key cryptography, Diffie-Hellman key exchange, and the best known of the public key / private key algorithms (i.e., what is usually called the RSA algorithm), all seem to have been independently developed at a UK intelligence agency before the public announcement by Diffie and Hellman in 1976. GCHQ has released documents claiming they had developed public key cryptography before the publication of Diffie and Hellman's paper. Various classified papers were written at GCHQ during the 1960s and 1970s which eventually led to schemes essentially identical to RSA encryption and to Diffie-Hellman key exchange in 1973 and 1974. Some of these have now been published, and the inventors (James H. Ellis, Clifford Cocks, and Malcolm Williamson) have made public (some of) their work.

Hashing

Hashing is a common technique used in cryptography to encode information quickly using typical algorithms. Generally, an algorithm is applied to a string of text, and the resulting string becomes the "hash value". This creates a "digital fingerprint" of the message, as the specific hash value is used to identify a specific message. The output from the algorithm is also referred to as a "message digest" or a "check sum". Hashing is good for determining if information has been changed in transmission. If the hash value is different upon reception than upon sending, there is evidence the message has been altered. Once the algorithm has been applied to the data to be hashed, the hash function produces a fixed-length output. Essentially, anything passed through the hash function should resolve to the same length output as anything else passed through the same hash function. It is important to note that hashing is not the same as encrypting. Hashing is a one-way operation that is used to transform data into the compressed message digest. Additionally, the integrity of the message can be measured with hashing. Conversely, encryption is a two-way operation that is used to transform plaintext into cipher-text and then vice versa. In encryption, the confidentiality of a message is guaranteed.

Hash functions can be used to verify digital signatures, so that when signing documents via the

Internet, the signature is applied to one particular individual. Much like a hand-written signature, these signatures are verified by assigning their exact hash code to a person. Furthermore, hashing is applied to passwords for computer systems. Hashing for passwords began with the UNIX operating system. A user on the system would first create a password. That password would be hashed, using an algorithm or key, and then stored in a password file. This is still prominent today, as web applications that require passwords will often hash user's passwords and store them in a database.

Cryptography Politics

The public developments of the 1970s broke the near monopoly on high quality cryptography held by government organizations. For the first time ever, those outside government organizations had access to cryptography not readily breakable by anyone (including governments). Considerable controversy, and conflict, both public and private, began more or less immediately, sometimes called the crypto wars. It has not yet subsided. In many countries, for example, export of cryptography is subject to restrictions. Until 1996 export from the U.S. of cryptography using keys longer than 40 bits (too small to be very secure against a knowledgeable attacker) was sharply limited. As recently as 2004, former FBI Director Louis Freeh, testifying before the 9/11 Commission, called for new laws against public use of encryption.

One of the most significant people favoring strong encryption for public use was Phil Zimmermann. He wrote and then in 1991 released PGP (Pretty Good Privacy), a very high quality crypto system. He distributed a freeware version of PGP when he felt threatened by legislation then under consideration by the US Government that would require backdoors to be included in all cryptographic products developed within the US. His system was released worldwide shortly after he released it in the US, and that began a long criminal investigation of him by the US Government Justice Department for the alleged violation of export restrictions. The Justice Department eventually dropped its case against Zimmermann, and the freeware distribution of PGP has continued around the world. PGP even eventually became an open Internet standard (RFC 2440 or OpenPGP).

Modern Cryptanalysis

While modern ciphers like AES and the higher quality asymmetric ciphers are widely considered unbreakable, poor designs and implementations are still sometimes adopted and there have been important cryptanalytic breaks of deployed crypto systems in recent years. Notable examples of broken crypto designs include the first Wi-Fi encryption scheme WEP, the Content Scrambling System used for encrypting and controlling DVD use, the A5/1 and A5/2 ciphers used in GSM cell phones, and the CRYPTO1 cipher used in the widely deployed MIFARE Classic smart cards from NXP Semiconductors, a spun off division of Philips Electronics. All of these are symmetric ciphers. Thus far, not one of the mathematical ideas underlying public key cryptography has been proven to be 'unbreakable', and so some future mathematical analysis advance might render systems relying on them insecure. While few informed observers foresee such a breakthrough, the key size recommended for security as best practice keeps increasing as increased computing power required for breaking codes becomes cheaper and more available.

References

- "Combinational analysis, numerical analysis, Diophantine analysis and number theory." Taken from Encyclopedia of the History of Arabic Science, Volume 2: Mathematics and the Physical Sciences, pg. 414. Ed. Roshdi Rasheed. London: Routledge, 1996. ISBN 0415124115

- Lund, Paul (2009). The Book of Codes. Berkeley and Los Angeles, California: University of California Press. pp. 106–107. ISBN 9780520260139.

- Lee, Tom (August 2000). "Cryptography and the New Economy" (pdf). The Industrial Physicist. 6 (4): 31. Retrieved 18 September 2013.

- Berlekamp, Elwyn; Solomon W. Golomb; Thomas M. Cover; Robert G. Gallager; James L. Massey; Andrew J. Viterbi (January 2002). "Claude Elwood Shannon (1916–2001)" (pdf). Notices of the AMS. 49 (1): 8–16. Retrieved 18 September 2013.

Permissions

Index

www.ingramcontent.com/pod-product-compliance
Lightning Source LLC
Jackson TN
JSHW052209130125
77033JS00004B/222